ESSENTIAL HINDUISM

ESSENTIAL HINDUISM

Steven J. Rosen

Foreword by Graham M. Schweig

Westport, Connecticut
London

Library of Congress Cataloging-in-Publication Data

Rosen, Steven, 1955–

    Essential Hinduism / Steven J. Rosen ; foreword by Graham M. Schweig.
      p. cm.
    Includes bibliographical references and index.
    ISBN 0–275–99006–0 (alk. paper)
    1. Hinduism.   2. Vaishnavism.   I. Title.
  BL1202.R55   2006
  294.5–dc22   2006024490

British Library Cataloguing in Publication Data is available.

Copyright © 2006 by Steven J. Rosen

Library of Congress Catalog Card Number: 2006024490
ISBN: 0–275–99006–0

First published in 2006

Praeger Publishers, 88 Post Road West, Westport, CT 06881
An imprint of Greenwood Publishing Group, Inc.
www.praeger.com

Printed in the United States of America

∞™

The paper used in this book complies with the
Permanent Paper Standard issued by the National
Information Standards Organization (Z39.48–1984).

10 9 8 7 6 5 4 3 2 1

Copyright Acknowledgments

The author and publisher gratefully acknowledge permission for use of the following
material:

Permission to reprint the following verses from *Bhagavad-gita—The Song Divine* by Carl
E. Woodham is given by Torchlight Publishing Inc. www.torchlight.com

To Saragrahi Vaishnavas
Throughout the world.
They seek only the essence.

Contents

Foreword

Historian Arnold Toynbee predicted that "India will conquer her conquerors." While addressing The Philosophical Society of Edinburgh University in 1952, he proposed that while the balance of the twentieth century would belong to the West, the twenty-first century would see India become a major world culture. *Essential Hinduism* provides a compelling glimpse into what may have inspired Toynbee's vision.

As the title suggests, Steven Rosen's work reviews the core of Hindu culture, practices, and teachings. It explores this rich tradition through its history, literature, and people. The book focuses, particularly, on the ancient traditions of Vaishnavism (the worship of Vishnu)—the major theistic religion of India—for these traditions collectively constitute the numerically largest portion of the Hindu world. Readers will thus come to see Hinduism from the inside—from the point of view of the majority of its practitioners.

Thus, *Essential Hinduism* will be useful to scholars and the general reader, practitioners, and Indophiles. It is the first book of its kind to use the Vaishnava tradition to reveal overarching truths about the Hindu tradition as a whole. That being said, Rosen does not neglect the other major Hindu religions—Shaivism, Shaktism, and Smartism. Rather, he presents them initially from a Vaishnava point of view, and then with an addendum explaining how these traditions see themselves. The effect is interesting: the reader is thereby invited into the ways in which one Hindu tradition appreciatively views another closely linked tradition, revealing a prominent built-in ecumenism that we are generally lacking in Western traditions.

Rosen also shows how the Vedas, the oldest scriptures in the world, form a foundation for all of Hinduism (even if few Hindus today really know their contents). He provides a thorough treatment of the Vedas, showing how their primary concern is ritual and the cultivation of knowledge. And he goes further, explaining how the Vedic mystery is only resolved with the help of "the fifth Veda" (the Puranas and the Epics). While this is also suggested in other good texts on Hinduism, it is explained here with depth and clarity.

The work is especially important in that it offers Rosen's analysis of Vishnu in the Vedas. The author collects information from primary sources as well as from leading scholars in the field, revealing, perhaps for the first time in a readable, accessible volume, why Vishnu's place is important in Hinduism as a whole, as he connects Vaishnavism with the early Vedic tradition.

In addition, Rosen's summaries of the two Epics share details that will encourage readers to explore the original sacred works themselves. Students of Hinduism, especially, will benefit from these colorful summaries, which accurately convey the essential meaning of the works, giving the teachings and implications of the texts as well as their narratives. This is important. Often, the Epics are quoted or explained in a cursory way, but, overall, remain quite incomprehensible. What are they really trying to say? What is the violence, found in each of the Epics, and war, which is central to both stories, really all about? Rosen explains what the texts are trying to convey in simple and clear language.

A special feature of this book is its readable life cycle of Krishna. To reconstruct this story, Rosen utilizes several sources, such as the *Harivamsa*, the *Vishnu Purana*, and the *Bhagavata*, along with the writings of traditional masters. I have never seen such a succinct retelling, with such attention to detail. The author also explains the implications of the Krishna story and provides metaphorical readings so that students can understand the lessons meant to be gleaned from Krishna's divine descent.

Overall, Steven Rosen is to be commended for this contribution to the study of Hinduism in general and Vaishnavism in particular. It is hoped that this work will stimulate further study into the sophisticated theological systems of thought and the devout life practices of Hinduism— one of the world's greatest religious traditions. And if India—particularly Hinduism—were to be truly appreciated in the twenty-first century, as

Toynbee suggests, then Rosen's book would be a significant step in that direction.

Graham M. Schweig
Associate Professor of Religious Studies
Christopher Newport University
Author, *Dance of Divine Love* (Princeton, 2005) and
Bhagavad-Gita: The Beloved Lord's
Secret Love Song (Harper, 2006)

Introduction

"Truth is one, though the wise refer to it by various names."
— *Rig Veda* 1.164.46

The above verse, found in one of the oldest religious scriptures known to man (which is, incidentally, a "Hindu" scripture), hints at the mystery and diversity that is Hinduism. Since the stanza is central to the Hindu tradition as we know it today, let us look at it more closely, in terms of context and meaning. Just prior to this verse, the *Rig Veda* praises its exotic pantheon of gods, and only then are we told that God, or Truth, is ultimately one, though known by various names. What does this mean? It points to a monotheistic idea of deity, surely, but to what else? And how does it relate to what we today know as Hinduism, with its many gods and goddesses?

On the face of it, Hindus believe in many divinities—Brahma, Vishnu, Shiva, the Goddess, and many others—and because of this, from the outside, the tradition is commonly understood to be polytheistic. Simultaneously, however, Hindus also believe in the existence of one supreme God, whom they call Bhagavan (All-Opulent One), Paramatma (Supreme Self), Parameshwar (Supreme Controller), Parampita (Supreme Father), and so on. Thus, according to Hindu tradition, God is one, but also many. He manifests in innumerable forms and shapes and further expands into lesser divinities, and even into the entire perceivable world, which we will explain later.

This hierarchical series of divine manifestations, of spiritual *separateness* as opposed to oneness, is often neglected in Western scholarship (and even within certain Indic traditions) where it is generally taught that these manifestations are all the same, and that they somehow coalesce in a higher reality.

For now, it should at least be understood that differentiation is as much a part of Hindu spirituality as is oneness. Or, to use the words of a noted Hinduism scholar: "At times, the ordering of the diverse parts of the whole seems best described as hierarchical; yet it is also true that the parts of the whole are knotted together in interrelations that seem more like a web than a ladder. The unity of India, both socially and religiously, is that of a complex whole. In a complex whole, the presupposition upon which oneness is based is not unity or sameness, but interrelatedness and diversity."[1]

As a prime manifestation of that diversity, Purusha (the Universal Male) enters Prakriti (Nature, Matter) and brings forth numerous planets and beings. As Shakti (the Universal Feminine Energy), he, now she, pervades all existence and gives it life. Indeed, the Hindu Godhead goes beyond the common patriarchal dimension of mainstream Western religion. Rather than pandering to sexist perspectives, in India the divine is seen as both male and female, depending on His/Her manifestation. Indic religions expert Graham M. Schweig refers to this as "polymorphic *bi*-monotheism," stating that, in Hinduism, "there are many forms of the one dual-gendered divinity."[2]

And this is just the beginning. Hinduism boasts an inconceivably large number of individual deities—330 million, say the ancient Indic texts. Each of these gods and goddesses, while expressions and manifestations of Brahman, the supreme spirit, is considered an individual, with a distinct story or "history," if transcendental chronology can be referred to in that way. For those who choose to embrace the worship of one of these deities, the scriptures offer a unique set of rituals, tailor-made for that particular form of worship. Some of these deities are male, others are female, while still others are androgynous.

Some resemble humans, some animals, and there are even those who are a combination of the two. Brahman also comes to us in certain trees or stones or other aspects of material nature. But all of these are manifestations of one supreme Truth. In the words of popular author Shashi Tharoor, India is "a singular land of the plural"[3] and, more, a "land of maddening paradoxes."[4]

Westerners should bear in mind their natural difficulty in understanding the paradoxes of the Hindu world: Europeans and Americans, especially, are here confronted with a people of alien history, traditions, climate, and habits, not to mention differing modes of thought, fundamental assumptions, and standards of assessment. Amidst all this, the Indian mind thrives on the idea of unity in diversity, a theme to which we will repeatedly return throughout this book. Unity in diversity, to make a long story short, is at the heart of the Rig Vedic verse.

The multiplicity or diversity of Hindu deities points to the tradition's spiritual hospitality, its willingness to accommodate personal proclivity, and tastes innumerable. Indeed, the "legal definition of Hinduism," established by the Supreme Court of India in 1966, views the Hindu faith as "a spirit of tolerance and willingness to understand and appreciate other points of view based on the realization that truth is many-sided." This principle of tolerance is considered second only to "the acceptance of the Vedic literature—the sacred scriptures of the Hindu East—as the highest authority in spiritual matters," thus establishing the importance of religious tolerance in Hindu doctrine.[5]

To better understand this sense of Hindu catholicity, let us look at two related ideas, both fundamental to the practice of Hinduism: The doctrine of spiritual qualification (*adhikara*), and that of emphasizing one's chosen deity (*ishta devata*). The first of these takes into consideration the spiritual competence of the individual, or the state of his or her spiritual evolution. According to one's *adhikara*, one is inclined or disinclined to worship a particular deity, and to do it (or to not do it) in a particular way. Each person is advised to study, learn, and practice a form of spirituality that is appropriate for his or her needs at any given time.

Accordingly, the divergent forms of religious practice, and the images they serve, are meant to be user-friendly, to assist the masses according to each person's taste, knowledge, and spiritual capacity. It serves little purpose, say the Hindu sages, to teach abstract philosophical concepts to a person whose heart thirsts for interpersonal relationship, and vice versa. Thus, impersonalism and personalism, two forms of Hindu religion, serve different purposes, for different people, and at different times.

The doctrine of one's "chosen deity," which works conjointly with that of one's *adhikara*, allows a person the freedom to choose an aspect of Brahman that speaks to his religious needs, that satisfies his spiritual appetite. Here it is understood that the Hindu deities are the same and yet different as well. They are the same in that they are all aspects of Brahman, but different in how and in what way they actually represent this ultimate spiritual Truth. All this will be explained as the book moves on. For now, it should be understood that despite this diversity in both deity and method of worship, there is a subtle unity that pervades them as well.

This unity extends to concepts of God found in other religious traditions, which Hinduism embraces and supports as alternate aspects of Brahman:

Just as we can say, "the French call a spoon a *cuiller*," the Hindu will say, "the Christians worship a form of Visnu [phonetic: Vishnu] named Christ," because for him Visnu is not an individual god pertaining to a particular religion but a general principle, as inevitably represented in any theology, in any code of symbols, as words representing objects (nouns), actions (verbs), and qualities (adjectives) are inevitably found in any language.[6]

In this way and in many others, Hinduism is unlike any of the world's major religious traditions. To give another example of the religion's uniqueness, in contradistinction to Judaism, Buddhism, Christianity, and Islam, the Hindu tradition cannot be traced to any one historical founder—its origins are shrouded in the mystique of prehistory and, for those who believe, in the actions of supernatural beings.

Historically, Islam goes back 1,300 years and is traced to the Prophet Mohammed; Christianity is 2,000 years old and begins with Jesus; Buddhism was founded by Siddhartha Gautama some 2,500 years ago; and Judaism, as we know it today, began with Abraham 4,500 years ago. The origins of Hinduism, however, are obscure. Some have tried to trace its origins to the Sanskrit literature known as the *Vedas*, but even this is problematic, since the dating of the *Vedas* eludes modern scholarship and the texts themselves claim to be eternal. Modern scholars have for many decades claimed the tradition datable to 1,500 BCE. But this was based on an assumption that is currently being revised—the Aryan Invasion Theory. Details of this theory will be discussed in a later chapter.

Hinduism is also unique in that it is not a monolithic religious tradition, and this hearkens back to the diversity aspect described above. The Hindu tradition is a potpourri of many separate religions, a medley of miscellaneous beliefs and practices. Vaishnavism (the worship of Vishnu), Shaivism (the worship of Shiva), and Shaktism (the worship of the Goddess), are but three—albeit the most prominent—of the many religions placed under the Hindu umbrella. Thus, while the above *Rig Veda* quote certainly embodies a fundamental truth at the core of all Hindu traditions, a diametrically opposed proposition might ring true as well: "Truths are many, though they can all be known by one name—Hinduism." Or can they? This book seeks to explore this question and many others as well.

But before launching into an elaborate explanation and analysis of this ancient Indic tradition, a brief statement is in order about the rather specific methodology chosen for this book. Our focus is squarely on Vaishnavism,

India's largest Hindu tradition, and through this prime example of Hindu spirituality we hope to convey the truth of essential Hinduism. That is to say, unlike other books that tend to merge all existing Hindu traditions or gloss over specifics that define particular religious groups, this work will focus on Hinduism's most elaborate religious enterprise, thus bringing to light the overall flavor of Hinduism in general. Other major Hindu traditions, of course, will be enumerated and explained as well, but only in relation to this central religious tradition.

METHODOLOGY: FOCUS ON VAISHNAVISM

The subject of Hinduism is vast and beyond the scope of any one book. Acknowledging this enormity, our present study, while touching on the many facets of what is today known as Hinduism, will have to choose an area of emphasis, allowing this to serve as an overarching representation of the greater Hindu tradition, as stated previously. For this purpose, again, we choose Vaishnavism, or the traditions surrounding the worship of Vishnu, the "Oversoul" of the universe, and that for the following reasons.

First of all, two-thirds of the known Hindu world identifies themselves as Vaishnavas. Given that India is overrun with numerous religious groups, and specifically with Hindus of all denominations, this statistic might seem unlikely. But the world's leading anthropologists and sociologists attest to its accuracy. Prominent Indic historian, Gerald Larson, is one such person. He is the Rabindranath Tagore Professor of Indian Cultures and Civilizations and Director of Indian Studies at Indiana University. In regard to the high number of Vaishnavas worldwide, he bases his findings on the work of the late anthropologist Agehananda Bharati, whose admission of Vaishnava predominance is particularly significant, for he himself was a Shankarite *sannyasi*, a group whose philosophical position is opposed to that of the Vaishnavas. Klaus Klostermaier, University Distinguished Professor in the Department of Religious Studies at the University of Manitoba, Canada, too, affirms that Vaishnavism constitutes the numerically most significant branch of modern Hinduism.[7]

The implications here are staggering—that the Hindu majority emphasizes Vishnu or one of his incarnations as India's preeminent manifestation of divinity. It should perhaps be pointed out that the high percentage of Vaishnavas in India is likely to include some practitioners from nonexclusivist groups, like the Smartas, who worship numerous gods if also sometimes emphasizing Vishnu. Still, given that there are some 800 million Hindus in India alone, there are more than 600 million people who identify themselves as Vaishnavas of some kind. This being the case, it is not unreasonable to assume that exploring the worship of Vishnu would allow us entrance into the general mysteries of Hinduism.

But there is more: When considering the Hindu trinity of Brahma, Vishnu, and Shiva[8]—who, in pan-Indian consciousness, are the three primary manifestations of divinity, presiding over realms of passion, goodness, and ignorance, respectively—Vishnu is always seen as the cohesive center.

While Brahma (rarely worshipped as a separate divinity in India) represents the passion associated with the act of creation, Vishnu brings equilibrium and a sense of stability—he gives all creation sustenance and meaning. While Shiva (Vishnu's only true contender for primacy in the Hindu pantheon) represents cosmic destruction and the mode of nescience, Vishnu gives us maintenance and the light of goodness. In other words, Vishnu is Shiva's right and Brahma's left. He inhabits central space, both conceptually and theologically, giving a sense of both extremes and what lies in between. As deity in the middle, then, he seems the appropriate candidate for supplying a balanced view of reality in general and of Hinduism in particular.

As an aside, Brahma, Vishnu, and Shiva are yet another example of the One and the Many, of unity in diversity, and this is clear from the *Bhagavata Purana*, considered by many to be India's most important religious text: "The Lord is self-effulgent and supreme. He creates the material world by his personal energy and assumes the names Brahma, Vishnu, and Maheshvara [Shiva] when he performs the acts of creation, maintenance, and annihilation." (8.7.23) And further: "The Supreme Lord accepts the three forms of Brahma, Vishnu and Shiva for the purposes of creation, maintenance, and destruction. Of these three forms, living beings derive ultimate benefit from Vishnu, who is situated in pure goodness." (1.2.23)

To be thorough, we should also mention the Goddess, a study of whom would also tell us much about Hinduism. However, even here we do not find the balance characteristic of Vishnu. Despite the Goddess's more nurturing and loving dimensions, as Earth, or as the Divine Mother, she is more commonly associated with Shiva, the lord of destruction, and her dark side as Durga or Kali is usually emphasized by practitioners. Indeed, the word *kali* means "black" and is usually understood in terms of "time" and "death." Kali and Durga are fierce, even bloodthirsty, manifestations of the divine and, as such, they lean more toward the "terrifying" side of the supreme. Thus, the Goddess does not provide the same balance of forces found in Vishnu.

Moreover, in Indian thought, goodness and truth are interrelated, both conceptually and semantically. The Sanskrit words *sattva* ("goodness") and *satya* ("truth") hearken back to the *Bhagavad-Gita* (14.17), which informs us that, "From the mode of goodness one develops true knowledge." In fact, the two words, *sattva* and *satya*, are cognate, from the verb *as*, "to be," or the neuter present participle, *sat*, "being." From *sat*, comes *sat-tva*, "being-ness," and *satya*, or "truth." In other words, "that which is good and true is that which actually constitutes existence." Thus, implicitly, Vishnu's association with goodness suggests that the acquisition of true knowledge is to be found in him.[9] We will explain this further in our chapter on the *Puranas*.

There are additional reasons for focusing on Vaishnavism: The most valued texts in all of Hinduism—that is, the Epics and the *Puranas*, upon which we will elaborate in upcoming chapters—primarily focus on Vishnu. As Professor Gavin Flood, who teaches in the Department of Theology and Religious Studies at University of Wales, Lampeter, writes in his classic textbook on Hinduism: "The two most important groups of Hindu narrative traditions embodied in oral and written texts are the two Epics, the *Mahabharata* and the *Ramayana*, and the *Puranas*." He elaborates: "Although the Epics contain a wealth of material which cannot be neatly categorized as belonging to any particular tradition, there is nevertheless a case for saying that the Epics are primarily Vaishnava in orientation, as, indeed, are many of the *Puranas*."[10]

In other words, Hinduism's most prominent scriptures basically espouse Vaishnavism, with easily explainable exceptions. Also, the concept of *avatars*, or the idea of God as he descends into the world of three dimensions—so central to Hindu thinking—never became fully established in other Hindu traditions. It is mainly a Vaishnava doctrine, though all Hindus subscribe to it. Here, again, by explaining this fundamental Vaishnava phenomenon, we might more easily understand the greater Hindu tradition.

In Indian courts of law, people swear with their hand on the *Bhagavad Gita* instead of the Bible. Even in America, the Judicial Studies Board has declared that, "Of their many holy scriptures, the *Bhagavad Gita* may be considered suitable for the purposes of swearing oaths." This is not the *Shvetashvatara Upanishad*, which is largely dedicated to Lord Shiva, or the *Devi-Bhagavata*, which sings the praises of the Goddess. It is a Vaishnava scripture. Period.[11]

One of the world's prominent authorities on Hinduism sums up:

The Vishnu tradition is perhaps the most typical of all the forms of Hinduism, and the greatest books of Indian literature reflect it strongly. The *Mahabharata* is mainly a Vaishnava book; the *Ramayana* treats of Rama, the *avatara* of Vishnu. One of the most ancient of the *Puranas* is the *Vishnu Purana* and the numerous Vaishnava *samhitas* have been the models on which the sectarian works of other [Hindu] religions have been based. The most popular book of the entire Hindu literature, the *Bhagavad-Gita*, is a Krishna scripture. Countless inspired devotees of Vishnu have composed throughout the ages an incomparable store of *bhakti* ["devotional"] hymns that live in the literally incessant *bhajans* [devotional recitation] and *kirtans* ["communal religious singing"] throughout India even today.[12]

In other words, Vaishnavism represents a sort of microcosm of the Hindu macrocosm. A microcosm is something that represents the universe, or humanity, in miniature. As it is said, "A single human being is a microcosm of the whole of humanity," or, "Their village was a microcosm of our world." A macrocosm is essentially the converse and is a term either for the universe or for any complete structure that contains smaller structures: "Society is the macrocosm of each of its individual members."

When it comes to Hinduism, Vaishnavism is, in a sense, both microcosm and macrocosm. Since it is, numerically, the largest of the Hindu traditions, it is not a "micro" anything. All of the smaller Hindu traditions can be understood by looking at Vaishnavism's various customs, traits, and practices. But in the present context, it can be seen as a smaller representative of Hinduism as a whole, of the larger Hindu tradition, and in that sense, it is a microcosm of the Hindu universe. Clearly, the outer portions of this universe, including Shaivism, Shaktism, and so on, include galaxies of difference, and Vaishnavism is hardly representative of every nuance of these rich religious perspectives. Still, by looking at Vaishnavism as a sampling of the rest, we can likely get the flavor of all existing Hindu traditions.

The book is conceptually divided into two sections. The first might be called "The Basis." Here we begin with the fundamentals of the Hindu tradition, from antecedents, such as the Indus Valley Civilization and its implications, to the misconceptions surrounding the terms "Hindu" and "Hinduism"; from an explanation of the word *dharma* ("duty") and how, as a concept, it underlies the entire Hindu tradition, to an analysis of India's holy texts, such as the *Vedas*, the Epics, the *Puranas*, the *Bhagavad-Gita,* and the life of Krishna himself. This much background is needed to pursue an understanding of essential Hinduism.

The second section of the book is about "The Practice." In this section, we begin by describing the basic theistic traditions that are today identified as modern Hinduism, always keeping in mind our special focus on the Vaishnava tradition. This will be followed by an exploration of certain philosophical ideas that affect the practice of Hinduism as a whole. We will then highlight specific practices that virtually define the Hindu tradition, including vegetarianism, holy food (*prasadam*), deities (that is, iconic images), temples, religious festivals and holidays, and methods of meditation and worship.

A more thorough examination might have included a look at the six traditional systems of Indian philosophy, as well as Buddhism, Jainism, and Sikhism, which, while not exactly Hindu traditions themselves, impact greatly on the way Hinduism is practiced. We could have also explored the *Manu-Samhita*, Patanjali's *Yoga-Sutras*, or examined the many regional scriptures and traditions that have cropped up over the last several centuries.

Or perhaps we could have looked more into Tantric literature or the seemingly endless writings of the tradition's great teachers, such as Madhva, Ramanuja, Shankara, Vedanta Deshika, Rupa Goswami, Jiva Goswami, and uncountable others. There are certainly numerous practices, too, that didn't work their way into this book. We could have looked at the concept of a personal teacher, or a guru, more closely, or perhaps analyzed the Samskaras, the traditional "rites of passage" experienced by all believing Hindus. The importance of holy places, and descriptions of them, could have filled several chapters as well. Some aspects of these subjects did indeed make their way into the book; a good deal of it did not.

Our task, remember, is to present "essential" Hinduism, and, on that score, our choices should suffice. It would require several volumes to address the above subjects with any modicum of thoroughness, and so they are only peripherally explored in the upcoming chapters, rather than specifically analyzed. If the reader becomes grounded in the facts and procedures outlined in this book, a basic, working understanding of Hinduism's many traditions should unfold, revealing a complex and multifaceted religion indeed.

CHAPTER 1
The Antecedents: Everything Comes from Something

"India's history is shrouded in myth; yet much of Indian mythology, if not all of it, has roots in historic reality."

—Stanley Wolpert, Indian historian,
University of California

Since Hinduism predates recorded history, precious little is known about its foundation. Its own earliest texts, the *Vedas*, refer to its origins as supernatural, not human-made, eternally present, and the whole early part of the tradition is basically viewed in the same way. This makes a search for antecedents particularly discomfiting. In this chapter, therefore, we will look at two options. First, we will see what light, if any, modern scholarship brings to the subject of Hindu beginnings. After a brief analysis, it will quickly become apparent that the scholarly method, at least in this case, offers more heat than light, and so we will also explore the Hindu tradition's own view of the same subject.

A BRIEF LOOK AT INDIAN HISTORY

Conventional wisdom tells us that Hinduism is inextricably linked to the exotic soil of India. And so this seems an appropriate place to begin our inquiry. Historians tell us that India is an ancient land with a continuous civilization that goes back well over 5,000 years. Relatively recent findings reveal an ancient "Indus Valley Civilization" that goes back considerably further, even if its archeological remains tell us precious little about the origins of modern Hinduism.

Buried in the depths of India's prehistory until it was rediscovered in the 1920s, the Indus Valley Civilization shares a unique position with Mesopotamia, China, and Egypt as one of the four earliest civilizations known to man. Scholars say it existed from 3000 BCE to 1800 BCE, but has roots extending into the Neolithic Period, 7000–6000 BCE. They also tell us that the Indus Valley was surprisingly advanced, with planned cities, agriculture, writing, architecture, and so on. Her first excavated sites were on the Indus River, in the northwest of the Indian subcontinent, which explains how the discovery received its name. At its height, in 2200 BCE, say most researchers, the Indus Civilization boasted an area that was larger than Europe.[1]

However one chooses to view this legendary epoch of India's distant past, it eventually gave rise to "the Sanskrit Era." This foundational segment of Indian history is also known as the Vedic Period, usually cited from 1500 BCE to 500 BCE. Here, the Indian world, or so the theory goes, became privy to the *Vedas* and its surrounding culture. Traditionalists will often debate these dates, pushing Vedic compilation back to about 3000 BCE. Indeed, many modern scholars support them in this.[2] Nonetheless, at least officially, the more conservative dates persist.

Parenthetically, traditionalists moved a step forward in 2002, when a new name was given to the Indus Valley Civilization, mentioned above—a gesture indicating that the earlier dates for Vedic compilation were becoming more acceptable. This new name was "Sindhu Sarasvati Civilization," and it can now be found in most Indian schoolbooks. The Sanskritized "Sindhu," rather than the Western "Indus," and the addition of "Saraswati," an ancient river central to Hinduism's sacred geography, suggest that the Indus Valley Civilization was originally part of Vedic culture. This is an attempt by traditionalists to deny the validity of the Aryan Invasion Theory, to be discussed below.

Be that as it may, toward the end of the Vedic Period, or soon thereafter, it is said, the Buddha appeared—this is roughly four or five centuries before the Common Era.[3] The ancient Jain tradition won many adherents during this period, too. But India's initial love affair with these two ascetic traditions was not to last. Before she had time to digest the vegetarian doctrine of these two peace-loving paths, which indeed emphasized noninjury (*ahimsa*), Alexander the Great and his fierce Macedonian troops stormed the homeland about a hundred years later. Alexander's mission in India, of course, was largely unsuccessful, but his assertiveness sparked in Indians a thirst for power and territory that had for some time been dormant on the palate of the subcontinent.

To make a shortened story even shorter, the need to protect interior Indian concerns led to the first of its legendary empires, beginning with the work of Chandragupta Maurya (274–237 BCE), famous for his reign throughout much of India and Pakistan and initiating an entire lineage of conquerors. It was he who forced Alexander to retreat, and his Mauryan Empire became the savior of India, at least temporarily.

Soon after, Emperor Ashoka emerged, along with a second popularization of Buddhism. For many Indians, this was a time of deep questioning and reevaluation. Ancient Vedic rituals and traditions were being replaced by new religious sentiments. Here we find India's first major countercultural milieu—a reordering of priorities and, likely, the rise of Hinduism as we know it today, with its numerous religious systems.

Still, these "new" Hindu religions were based on fragments from much earlier traditions, and so they were not entirely new. The post-Ashoka empires brought ancient Hindu ideas back to the fore: the Gupta, Pratihara, Pala, Chalukya, Chola, Pandya, and Vijayanagara dynasties, among others, were known for supporting traditional Hindu arts and for developing Hindu culture in significant ways.

The Gupta Empire (ca. 320–550 CE), in particular, ushered in a new "Classical Age," if you will, when most of North India became reunited under Hindu rule. Because of considerable royal patronage and pronounced cultural achievements, this period is famous as a type of Hindu renaissance, in which diversity, religious tolerance, and synthesis, for which Hinduism is so well known, came to the fore.

But there were serious challenges during this period, too. Sometime in the eighth century CE, Muslims invaded India and, gradually, established their foreign regime. This gave rise to the Mogul Empire (1526–1757), and with it came an end to much of what might be called "Hindu tolerance." This is when many Hindu temples were destroyed and deities desecrated.

Just prior to this, India was comprised of a vast number of small kingdoms, each with varying degrees of power—but all Hindu. Now things were different. There were alternately Muslim or Hindu sovereigns in the various kingdoms. Without doubt, some Muslim leaders were sympathetic to indigenous Hindu culture and continued to support it, but this spirit of tolerance ebbed and flowed like the tide of the Indian Ocean.

As time went on, the Portuguese, Dutch, Danish, French, and, of course, the British, sometime in the seventeenth century, streamed in. While initially in India for purposes of trade, or so they said, many of these outside forces eventually imposed their religious beliefs (read: Christianity) on the

"Hindoo heathens." Needless to say, these multiple invasions left much of India confused about her own identity, her once impervious walls now eroded by the force of time and by the wear of foreign abuse. India's ceiling, somewhat surprisingly, did not collapse under the pressure. Rather, in the midst of it all, there were those who courageously supported the walls of Hinduism's hallowed traditions.

It is often forgotten, however, that the profound truths at the heart of Hinduism were always the property of the *sadhus*, the saintly people, or those who devoted their lives to the spiritual pursuit. The mass of people inherited abbreviated stories of indecipherable gods, half-truths, or incomplete philosophical notions. That is to say, most of India is comprised of Shudras and Untouchables, the lower classes, who did not study the *Vedas*, Sanskrit, or the higher theological tradition.

Most common folk, then, were ignorant of India's complex spiritual heritage. With the many foreign incursions and their resultant chaos, this situation naturally worsened. But India's highly spiritual culture—as found in her art, music, literature, theology, and so on—would not be lost. It was preserved in the confidential *sampradayas*, or esoteric lineages, that were guardian to these truths from the beginning. This will be described more fully toward the end of this section.

As an addendum, perhaps, it is ironic that Hinduism, as we know it today, appears to arise after Buddhism and Jainism, since these are both considered Hindu heterodoxies. To be clear, Hindu tradition is ancient, with origins in the fertile soil of the *Veda*. But its current traditions and modes of expression are largely traceable to this later period, and, in this sense, it was open to the influence of Buddhism and Jainism. True, Jainism, in particular, has hoary roots in the culture of India's distant past. But both Buddhism and Jainism, as we now perceive them, began about 2,500 years ago, and grew out of dissatisfaction with earlier Hindu religion. Implicitly, Hinduism is the parent faith.

To sum up: Modern Hinduism's rather late genesis on India's historical landscape would account for its divergence from early Vedic practices, as discussed in an upcoming chapter. It would also explain why later traditions, such as Buddhism and Jainism, might appear to be prior, and that the ancient Vedic religion went through transformations causing it to branch off into many individual religions, with one or many gods at their helm. In other words, India's ancient traditions hearken back to the Vedic period, if not to the prior Indus Valley Civilization, where earlier forms of Hinduism are implicit in archaeological finds and in Vedic texts. The tradition took part in a long journey, in which dynasties, conquerors, and foreign invaders came and went. Ultimately, Hinduism emerged as a plethora of sectarian traditions, manifesting, for better or for worse, as we see it today.

THE ARYANS, THE PERSIANS, AND THE INDUS VALLEY

Scholars sometimes trace the Hindu complex of religions to a merger of beliefs, especially those of the Aryans, the Dravidians, and the Harappans, ancient peoples who found their home in the Indian subcontinent. The idea of the Aryans is especially significant in the study of early Hinduism. The word originates from the Sanskrit root *arya*, which means "noble" or "honored." For most of us in the West, an "Aryan" is usually associated with the blond-haired, blue-eyed ideal of Nazi Germany. But it originally referred to a people who looked completely different.

Historically, the word *Aryan* can be traced to the ancient Indo-Iranians—Indo-European peoples who inhabited parts of what are now Iran, Afghanistan, and India. They referred to themselves as *arya* or *riya*, roots from which we get the name "Iran" (the original name for Persia) and even "Ireland." Interestingly, these same linguistic roots are found in early Sanskrit texts, where they refer to the higher echelon of ancient Indian society.

In the nineteenth century, European scholars became aware of the *Aryan* concept, too, and, by the twentieth century, German linguists had maneuvered an Aryan background for anyone with a "Caucasian ancestry," particularly for the Germans themselves. This honorary distinction, of course, soon devolved into the racial theories of the Nazis, popularized by Adolf Hitler in his autobiography, *Mein Kampf* ("My Struggle"). His misuse of the word "Aryan" was rooted in political propaganda meant to feed local vanity.

The idea of "the master race" (German: Herrenrasse, Herrenvolk), as he saw it, was that the Germanic and Nordic people represent an ideal and "pure" human culture. This was not Hitler's original thinking. It can be traced to nineteenth-century racial theory, which proposed a hierarchy of peoples, with African Bushmen and Australian Aborigines at the bottom and white Europeans—the descendents of the Indo-Iranians—at the top.[4]

This concept of an "Aryan race" arose soon after linguists identified Avestan, the ancient language of Persia, and Sanskrit, the honored tongue of Northern India, as oldest among the earliest languages groups. This led to the idea that the major European languages, such as Latin, Greek, and the various Germanic and Celtic languages, all descend from them. The speakers of these languages, it has been argued, must have been the ancestors of all European peoples.

These hypothetical ancestors were given the name "Aryans," and, from this point, the term was associated with "white Europeans"—naturally excluding Jews and Arabs, since their ancestral languages (Hebrew and Arabic) do not belong to the Indo-European family. This, of course, played into the prejudices of the Nazis. For now, let us just say that in the *Vedas* themselves the word *Aryan* is not used in a racial or ethnic sense. Rather, it is used by Hindus, Zoroastrians, Buddhists, and Jains to mean "noble" or "spiritual." It is also used as an epithet of respect.

Still, such ideas about race are not alien to India. One theory posits that the lighter-skinned Aryans and the darker-skinned Dravidians constitute two distinct races. It is further said that the Dravidians were the original inhabitants of India whom the invading Aryans conquered and dominated, sending them to the south. From this came the additional idea that much of what we call Hindu culture was initially Dravidian, later appropriated by the Aryans and never again associated with the people of Dravida. Those with political agendas eventually used such ideas, in a Machiavellian attempt, to turn the people of South India against the people of the north. There are numerous variations on this theme.

But most important in understanding the ancient idea of an Aryan people would be to briefly analyze the Indo-Iranians. It should not be overlooked (though it usually is) that ancient Persia (Iran) might offer certain secrets about the origins of Hinduism. Long before the time of Zarathustra (628–551 BC?),[5] also known as Zoroaster, Persia shared much in common with Vedic culture. Religious reformer that he was, Zoroaster opposed the bloody animal sacrifices of the *Vedas* like his contemporaries Buddha and Mahavira. But unlike those two, his connections with ancient Vedic religion are now lost in historical obscurity.

Still, there is much we do know. Zoroaster addressed the Lord as Ahura Mazda, the supreme God among all others, and was renowned as the founder of a monotheistic religion (known as Zoroastrianism, whose practitioners are called "Parsis" in India), perhaps the first of its kind. In some ways, Ahura Mazda resembled the Vedic sky-god Varuna, though he could just as easily be seen as Vishnu—he was a solar deity, identified with the sun, as is Vishnu in the *Rig Veda*. Ahura Mazda is also represented symbolically by outspread eagle wings—Vishnu's famous eagle carrier is known as Garuda.

Early Persian religion, in fact, does more than merely resonate with the Vedic tradition; the two actually overlap. For example, in addition to Ahura Mazda, Persian texts refer to a host of lesser gods, several of whom are also found in the *Vedas* and are mentioned by the exact same names—Indra, Mithra, Vayu, and so on. Zoroaster often equated these gods with evil spirits, who seduced practitioners from the true worship of the one Supreme Being. A similar phenomenon, again, can be found in Vaishnavism, where worship of the demigods is sometimes considered a pious distraction from the worship of Vishnu.

Ancient Persian religion includes a particular initiation ceremony (*upanayana*) for boys of the three upper classes—a ritual that in both Zoroastrianism and in Hinduism involves a sacred thread. The divine and/or hallucinogenic sacred drink, known as *soma* in Vedic texts, corresponds to the sacred *haoma* of Zoroastrianism. The ideas of *devas* ("gods") and *asuras* ("demons") can be found in both religions, too, though the meanings of the words are reversed in Zoroastrian understanding, and both Vedic and Persian texts tell us about the perennial battle between the forces of darkness and those of light. Finally, the hymns of the *Rig Veda* and the *Gathas*, as some of the Zoroastrians texts are known, exhibit such a similarity in grammar and vocabulary that it is incontestable that they derive from a common parent language and perhaps even a common cultural heritage.

As interesting as all of this is, most scholars do not look to Persian roots for enlightenment about Hindu origins. Rather, they are more concerned with the Indus Valley Civilization, first discovered or defined in 1920, as mentioned earlier, by the British archaeologist Sir John Marshall, whose exploratory work at Mohenjo-Daro is now legendary. Marshall's findings were followed by the contributions of M. S. Vat. The latter's excavations at Harappa, which gives the Indus Valley Civilization its alternate name, the Harappan Civilization, brought Indian archeology to new heights. And with the passage of years came still more significant finds, but not always with answers to the mysteries that came along with them.

Still, the discoveries at these sites reveal impressive town planning and architecture, along with a sense of sophisticated social organization. The remains of cities seem to indicate well-planned roads and houses with efficient drainage systems and ventilation. Tools of stone, copper, and bronze have been found, and these appear technologically advanced, considering the time period in which they were used. The actual origin of the Harappan people, though, is still a matter of dispute. While one group of scholars believes that they were Dravidian (i.e., native to India, or Indo-Aryan), another section believes they were either Sumerians or Cretans.

Most importantly, perhaps, the excavations have given us a rich collection of arts and crafts as well as images of revered deities. Archaeologists have discovered thousands of seals with crude but clear figures of animals, such as unicorn, bull, tiger, elephant, goat, buffalo, and others. The most remarkable seal depicts what appears to be Pashupati, a form of Shiva, one of the Hindu gods, perhaps indicating an early form of his worship. There is another seal of a meditating yogi, and one of a horned goddess, before whom another horned person is kneeling. Thus, both male and female divinities are indicated, as are animal deities, by still other seals.

More, most of these seals are engraved with a pictographic script, a script that is not yet deciphered, even though numerous attempts have been made. One reason for this difficulty is that all the text in question is on small objects like stone seals in terracotta, pottery, faience and stone tokens, copper tablets, and similar objects affording little space.

The script has been described as logographic, a system that uses a number of visual signs, each representing a morpheme, or a minimal unit of language carrying cryptic meaning. A logographic sign might only *represent* a word, or a part of a word, making decipherment especially difficult. Michael Witzel, a prominent Sanskrit scholar and an acknowledged authority on ancient India, recently coauthored an article offering new perceptions about the script, though it must be reiterated that this is merely a theory.[6]

The article asserts that the Indus symbols have been misunderstood as representing letters or syllables, but that they are in fact signs that represent ideas, each of which could be understood in a variety of languages. This is compared to a modern airport with its many signs (no parking here, baggage claim there) that are understood by people in their own languages, suggesting that the Indus society may have been multilingual. The article also addresses the question of why a society would opt for nonliteracy when they were in contact with literate societies in the ancient Near East. The authors suggest that it may be a choice made by the Indus elite for the sake of controlling others.

Despite all such prevailing theories (with the seals being scrutinized for the better part of a century) there have been few conclusive breakthroughs.

This is not to say, of course, that theories do not continue to mount: Some say the writing is a form of early Aryan script (Indo-Iranian or Indo-European). Others propose that it is part of the Munda family of languages, spoken largely in eastern India and related to some Southeast Asian dialects. And, still others—in what is perhaps the most popular of all such theories—say it is from the Dravidian family of languages. But no one really knows. The imagination runs wild over the potential ramifications of an accurate decipherment. It could mean momentous breakthroughs not only in regard to Hindu origins but also for all mankind.[7]

Nonetheless, the Indus script, like Hinduism itself, waits patiently, hoping to one day be understood. It watches without objection, tolerating rubbish and reason in regard to its interpretation. For now, the scholarly world tells us that an Aryan people came to India in its remote past, but we are unable to say with any certainty who they were, nor do we know where they came from. Bits of writing from the indigenous Indus Valley sits before us, but we don't know what it means, and we are no closer to unraveling the mystery than when we first gazed at the newly unearthed seals some seventy-five years ago. All of this leads to the infamous Aryan Invasion theory.

THE ARYAN INVASION THEORY

As stated, academics generally consider the beginnings of Indian/Vedic culture to have originated with Indo-Aryan-speaking tribes invading, or migrating into, the subcontinent near or around the middle of the second millennium BCE. The tracing of these tribes is generally done through language. The tongue of the Indo-Aryans (which is often considered the forerunner of Vedic Sanskrit) is related to a number of languages from Europe and Asia, such as Greek, Latin, German, Slavic, Iranian, and so on.

Just as Hindi, Bengali, Gujarati, Marathi, and others, are all modern Indic languages that evolved historically from Sanskrit (or from other, related Indo-Aryan dialects), so, in turn, the ancient Sanskrit and European languages originally evolved from an even earlier language, or so the theory goes. Although there is no current trace of this language, its existence can be deduced, say modern scholars, by comparing the cognate forms of existing daughter languages. This original language has been called Proto-Indo-European.

Since people speak languages, and people are located in space and time, scholars have postulated that there must have been a point of origin for these Proto-Indo-Europeans prior to their division into the Indo-Aryans, Iranians, and Greeks, among others. The quest for the original homeland of the Proto-Indo-Europeans (borne primarily from a concern for the origins of Western civilization) has obsessed and frustrated Western scholars for the better part of two centuries. Despite hundreds of publications on this topic, in dozens of languages, incorporating a vast array of methods and disciplines (many of which are clearly hampered by nationalistic bias), there is still no consensus as to when or where the original Indo-European homeland existed.

The early nineteenth-century Romantics, for one, assumed that India was the origin. But due to philological and linguistic considerations, Western scholars eventually came to the conclusion that wherever the homeland might have been, it could not have been in South Asia. Some say that the nomadic people who migrated into India were from Central Asia or the Arctic, or perhaps from Russia or northern Europe; others say they were from southeastern Europe, apparently taking a route through Iran and Afghanistan. No one really knows.[8]

The point is this: There are natural suspicions about the original intention of this theory, and just why there was such certainty that the culture of India, along with the *Vedas*, could not come from indigenous peoples. If one explores the history of the Aryan Invasion Theory, it becomes clear that it arose due to colonial-missionary prejudices. It was largely the brainchild of foreign conquerors, who could not imagine the "primitive" Hindoos, as they referred to the indigenous people of India, giving rise to such a complex and noteworthy culture.

The idea of India as "the cradle of civilization" (a theory, by the way, that modern historians are now putting forward with greater frequency) did not sit well with Christians, especially, who sought to replace indigenous religion with their own. Accordingly, all of Indian culture and history was construed as the product of invading Indo-Aryan tribes that originated from some homeland that is necessarily outside the subcontinent and external to the indigenous, pre-Indo-Aryan inhabitants of India.

For nearly a hundred years now, serious doubts have been put forward about this entire Indo-Aryan Invasion theory. Scholar and renowned religious reformer Bhaktivinoda Thakur (1838–1914) is perhaps one of the few orthodox Hindus to give at least nominal credence to the Aryan Invasion Theory, and he is certainly one of the earliest. Citing Western authorities such as Wilson, Pratt, Davis, and Playfair, he acknowledges the possibility of foreigners entering India from the northwest in the subcontinent's distant past—though he pushes the date back to 4463 BCE. He is quick to add, however, that such incursions into India would in no way undermine the sanctity of the *Vedas* or the powerful spirituality in her message.[9]

The questions surrounding the Aryan invasion theory have become particularly piercing over the last decade or so. Indeed, whereas the debate over Indo-Aryan origins was originally the concern of mainly Indian scholars, it has now begun to penetrate mainstream Western academic circles.[10] A significant number of archaeologists, both Indian and Western, have insisted that there is no archaeological evidence to support the theory of external Indo-Aryan origins. And the *Vedas* themselves, written at a time when the invasions would have been fresh in people's memories, do not mention anything resembling an invasion of India.

Moreover, the philological and linguistic evidence that had originally been brought forward to support the theory of invasions has been called into question and reinterpreted. Respected scholars, such as B. B. Lal, of the Archeological Survey of India, and Edwin Bryant from Rutgers University, have shown that the Aryan Invasion Theory is based on rather flimsy evidence. Many who have thoroughly researched the subject are now inclined to believe that the Indo-Aryans might have been indigenous to the subcontinent all along, and that the Indus Civilization itself might have indeed been Vedic. At present, the scholarly world is still divided on the subject, exploring the evidence from various points of view.[11]

HINDU ANTECEDENTS AS EXPLAINED BY HINDUS

Since there is little scholarly consensus on the specifics of Hindu origins, let us look at the well-established "mythological" beginnings of the tradition. That is, let us take recourse in the early accounts of origin put forward by believers themselves, stories that cannot be conventionally proved or disproved but that are part of the longstanding Hindu tradition.

Hindu creation stories abound, but the most popular are found in the *Bhagavata Purana*, especially in its First through Third Books. Our retelling here will be based on these in particular. The reason these stories are significant in the present context is that they include information not only about cosmic creation but also about the creation of the various lineages in which Hindu teaching is passed down—they tell us about the origins of the gods and saints that gave rise to the various Hindu traditions.

The story begins with Brahma, the first created being in the universe. Well, not exactly.

In the beginning, before time and space, there was only Vishnu, the primordial being—God, the source of Lord Brahma. He exists in eternity, fabulously majestic with four arms, crown, regal dress, long black hair, and an exquisitely beautiful dark hue. He alone existed, but with a purpose.

Hindu theologians are aware of the implications of creation, especially in relation to God's unchanging nature, which must remain intact, by definition. In his original form, they say, he remains unchanged, and he engages in unending pastimes (*lila*) with his associates in the spiritual world. However, for the sake of creation he expands into secondary manifestations that are still Supreme. Thus, the creation of the material world does not necessitate a change in God's essential nature because Vishnu, in his original form, never undergoes transformation. Rather, the world manifests through his successive emanations, which result in the unfolding of matter and the material energy in due course. Vishnu does this through His "expanded" forms—and because of this, his original essence remains changeless. This is a form of "emanationism" described in Vaishnava texts.

Why does God create? Hindu texts explain that the material world is an expression of the latent desires of the many souls who eventually populate it. These souls go through the 8,400,000 forms, or species, searching for happiness. These forms begin with single-celled organisms, various insects, plants, aquatics, animals, and culminate in the human species. It is further explained that the human form is like a gateway to transcendence, enabling souls to return to the spiritual realm, but only if they learn their lessons well and sufficiently develop their consciousness.

To continue our creation story: From Vishnu's kingly terrain in the never-ending spiritual world, he created a cloud in the sky. In its shade he actualized a great ocean. The water of that ocean is transcendental—liquid spirituality. It is from here (say Hindu texts) that the material world came into being. It is therefore called "the waters of creation."

In the coolness of these very waters, Vishnu lay down to sleep. While in this restful condition, submerged in the water, he begins to breathe deep, steady breaths, and, with these, time comes into being. Aeons pass. Then, as he continues breathing, bubble-like universes emanate from his divine body, waiting in their turn to become innumerable worlds.

As these transcendent bubbles ease away from him, they are not divorced from his essential being. Rather, he expands into numerous secondary Vishnu forms (almost identical to his original image in cosmic slumber) and enters into each of the "bubbles." Now in each universe, with the basic elements of matter present in preliminary form, he reclines on the coils of a thousand-hooded serpent, Shesha by name, who gently rocks him back and forth, anticipating his primary act of creation. To accomplish this end, Vishnu emits from his navel a magnificent lotus that grows and blossoms into a whorl consisting of a thousand petals. Atop that whorl, Brahma, the first created being, makes his appearance into the world of three dimensions. He is Vishnu's first offspring, chosen to create all the rest.

The similarities between the names Abraham and Brahma have not gone unnoticed.[12] Abraham is said to be the father of the Jews, and Brahma, as the first created being, is often seen as the father of mankind. Abraham's name is derived from the two Semitic words *ab* meaning "father" and *raam/raham* meaning "of the exalted." Some say that the word *Abraham* is derived from the Sanskrit word *brahma*, but the root of *brahma* is *brah*, which means, "to grow or multiply in number." Thus, it is unlikely that there is a legitimate semantic connection between the two names.

Still, we might also note that the name of Brahma's consort Sarasvati seems to resonate with that of Abraham's wife, Sarah. Also, in India, the Sarasvati River includes a tributary known as the Ghaggar. Another tributary of same river is called the Hakra. According to Jewish tradition, Hagar was Sarah's maidservant. There are other connections. Both Brahmins (a word that *is* connected with "Brahma") and Jews see themselves as the "chosen people of God." The Hebrews began their sojourn through history as a "kingdom of priests" (*Exodus* 19.6). Likewise, Brahmins are also a community of priests. Though perhaps coincidental there is enough material here to warrant further investigation.

Again returning to the creation story: Brahma is born as an adult, but he sees only darkness. The sun had not yet been created, nor the moon. There was no one and nothing around him. He looked to his right, to his left, in front and behind—looking in all directions with such intensity, four heads suddenly appeared in place of his one. But even with this increased capacity, he saw nothing and could not understand the rather empty world around him, or his purpose in it.

He decided to climb down the lotus stem, hoping to solve the mystery of his origin. As he cautiously moved down the newly created stalk, he saw a creation in progress—swirling indications of worlds unformed, inchoate planets, and, with all of this, something stirred deep inside of him. He began to intuit his reason for being, his inborn purpose, his service to Vishnu. He was meant to create. This he knew. But he was not sure how to approach it. Then, deeply contemplating the task before him, he prayed for some indication of how to proceed. Frustrated, with little more than a vague sense of what he had to do, he turned and began his long journey back up the lotus stem.

Suddenly, in answer to his prayer, he heard two syllables: "Ta-pa." Listening intently, he heard them again—"Ta-pa"—and his course became a bit clearer. The word refers to "penance and austerity." And he understood by this that the Lord was giving him a message: to serve Vishnu in such a pivotal way—to assist in creation—would require that he qualify himself by deep meditation, the cultivation of which would indeed necessitate a profound sense of austerity. Now fully ensconced in his high lotus cradle, with an ever-widening sense of mission, he sat with legs folded in yogic posture, back erect, meditating on the task ahead.

A brief commentary on the sound that Brahma heard: According to Hindu tradition, early on in creation came sound, the basis of the world. Therefore, Brahma was able to hear the syllables "Ta-pa." From sound came ether and the sense of hearing. The combination of ether and the sense of hearing created texture, which in turn produced air and the sense of touch. The mixing of air and the sense of touch gave rise to material form, from which came fire and the sense of sight. The combination of fire and sight created flavor, which in turn produced water and the sense of taste. By the mixture of water and taste, odor was created, and from this came earth and the sense of smell. Together these elements made up the basic ingredients for creation. The *Bhagavata Purana* (2.10.3) describes how each element was created and how they relate to each other. It shows how the senses of hearing, touching, seeing, tasting, and smelling are each related to a particular element and how all are woven together to form an external world wherein each component is dependent upon the other.

In any case, we return to Brahma. After one thousand celestial years, his meditation broke—he now knew what to do and, more, how to do it. His deep concentration had given him a vision of the spiritual world, where his beloved Vishnu resides. For Brahma, the borders of the material and spiritual worlds melted away, and he could see ultimate reality in all its beauty. Overwhelmed by the Lord's form, nature, and brilliance, and also by his wonderful associates and spectral environment, Brahma composed hundreds of verses, which were later compiled in a book known as the *Brahma-Samhita*.

Then, regaining composure, he turned his attention to the mission at hand. From his mind issued forth progeny, and from them an impressive array of species to fill the planets, the waters, and the skies.

Of all Brahma's initial sons, Narada was most dear, and perhaps most important in our present context. Brahma had explained to him the truth of the spiritual realm, and asked him to share this with the multitudes who now populated the world. Ages elapsed. And Narada's mission knew its greatest success when, in more recent times, say, some 5,000 years ago, he conveyed the message to Vyasa. It was this sage who put these Vedic truths in written form, compiling knowledge that had been passed down orally for millennia.

Vyasa took the one original *Veda* and divided it into four, and these he edited for ease of understanding. He further compiled the *Mahabharata* and the *Puranas*, collectively known as "the fifth *Veda*." Each of these he entrusted to scholars of irreproachable character, and they in turn taught the texts to their disciples and grand-disciples. Thus the respective schools of Vedic thought were established. These, of course, eventually gave rise to Hinduism as we know it today.

It is still in the esoteric lineages that the essential core of Vedic truth is passed down. Brahma to Narada to Vyasa, and it continues on down to contemporary teachers. This initial lineage is known as the Brahma Sampradaya. Shiva, the demigod in charge of universal destruction, is also the founder of an early lineage, known as the Rudra Sampradaya. Lakshmi, the goddess of Fortune, wife of Vishnu, founded another. And the Four Kumaras, saintly personalities from a time in the distant past, began yet another.

These four lines of disciplic descent were systematized by Madhvacharya, Vishnu Swami, Ramanuja, and Nimbarka, respectively, the best of great teacher-saints from Medieval India. There are other traditional lineages, too, but these are not mentioned in the *Bhagavata Purana*.

The other famous lineage is the Shankara Sampradaya, which is also traced to Vishnu. The fact that the Sampradaya originates with Vishnu is significant, since Shankarites and Vaishnavas differ on several important points of theology and practice, and because, in the modern day, most Shankarites are worshippers of Shiva. Be that as it may, Shankara (c. 788–820 CE) acknowledged that the spiritual and philosophical heritage of Advaita Vedanta, which was already present in the *Upanishads*, was preserved through a teaching transmitted through a succession of teachers (*guru-parampara*).

These teachers are recalled in a hymn, the *Parampara-stotra*, recited by Shankarites when they study traditional Vedanta commentaries. The full prayer runs as follows: "To Narayana [Vishnu], to the lotus-born [Brahma], to Vashishtha, to Shakti and to his son Parashara Muni, to Vyasa, to Shukadeva, to the great Gaudapada, to Govinda-Yogindra and to his disciple Sri Shankaracharya, then also to his disciples Padmapada, Hastamalaka, Totraka and Vartikakara [Sureshvara], to these, our masters, we pay our respectful obeisance now and forever."[13] This, then, is the Shankarite disciplic succession.

All such lineages teach that one should live one's life in a spiritual way, following basic principles of religiosity and devotion, so that truth naturally opens up to them, like Brahma's lotus in the beginning of creation.

In fact, commentators on the *Bhagavata Purana* explain that the Brahma story (in addition to telling us something about cosmic creation) is a metaphor for man's spiritual sojourn. Like Brahma, we are connected to our past through an umbilical cord, which is the lotus stem of our genetic background. In addition, we are born in ignorance, the darkness of Brahma's yet uncreated worlds. Like him, we must passionately question our identity and purpose. And when we hear the call of the Lord, we must be willing to meditate and to perform austerities—to be determined in reaching our goal.

The creation story as explained here is typical in India, with countless variations depending upon exactly which scripture one reads. It is perhaps less typical to hear that Brahma not only created the world but also the first lineage of transcendental knowledge, that is, the Brahma Sampradaya, in which he revealed truths that he directly received from God. And yet this is clear from the *Bhagavata Purana*.

Moreover, many of these truths stand at the threshold of modern Hindu thought, with seeds of ideas that eventually blossomed into contemporary Hindu practice, regardless of the specific modern-day tradition. Though this unveiling of Hindu origins is indeed supernatural, it gives Hindus a sense of where their tradition originates. And if we consider the undecipherable script of the Indus Valley and the innumerable questions surrounding the Aryan Invasion Theory, it is likely that this will be the prevailing story of Hindu origins for a long time to come.

CHAPTER 2
Hinduism: The One and the Many

"The word 'Hindu' has nothing to do with Hinduism."
—Srila Bhaktivinoda Thakur, Hindu reformer,
circa, nineteenth century

As commonly understood, Hinduism is one of the world's major religious traditions. But this is only partially true. Though it is indeed counted among the world's major religions, it is actually a medley of religious traditions, all originating in India. As a singular world religion, then, Hinduism requires a footnote—it is not a monolithic entity but rather a conglomerate of religions that share certain traits in common. These religions go by the names Vaishnavism, Shaivism, Shaktism, and many others.

There have been numerous attempts to ascertain exactly what constitutes a Hindu religion. The great Indian nationalist and philosopher, Sri Aurobindo (1872–1950), for example, offered his opinion. The unifying characteristics, he said, were three: (1) One Existence to whom sages give different names. One without a second who is all that is, and beyond all that is, the Permanent of the Buddhists, the Absolute of the Illusionists, the Supreme God or Purusha of the theists—in a word, the Eternal, the Infinite; (2) Man's approach to the Eternal and Infinite is manifold, and God manifests Himself and fulfills Himself in the world in many ways, each itself being Eternal, so that all cosmic powers and all forces are manifestations of the One; and (3) The Supreme or Divine can be approached through a universal consciousness—by piercing through all inner and outer Nature each individual soul can meet That or Him in itself because there is something in the soul that is intimately one with or at least intimately related with the one Divine Existence.[1]

Sri Aurobindo concludes by saying, "These three things put together are the whole of Hindu religion, its essential sense and, if any credo is needed, its credo."[2]

Others have expanded this list to include more specific philosophical doctrines. Thus, by practitioner consensus, a religion may be considered part of the Hindu family of religions if it espouses some variation on the following principles:

(1) Belief in the divinity of the *Vedas*, the world's most ancient scripture, as well as faith in the "fifth Veda," or the Epics and the Puranas, which are the main holy books of the Hindu religion.

(2) Belief in one, all-pervasive Supreme Reality, manifesting as both an impersonal force, which is called Brahman, and as a personal divinity (known variously, according to whichever particular tradition one adheres to).

(3) Belief in the cyclical nature of the time—that there are world ages that repeat themselves like seasons.

(4) Belief in karma, the law of action and reaction, by which each person creates his or her own destiny.

(5) Belief in reincarnation—that the soul evolves through many births until all past deeds have been resolved, leading to ultimate liberation from the material world.

(6) Belief in alternate realities with higher beings—God and His manifold manifestations—who can be accessed through temple worship, rituals, sacraments and prayer.

(7) Belief in enlightened masters, or gurus—exemplary souls who are fully devoted to God and who act as a conduit for others to reach Him.

(8) Belief in non-aggression and non-injury (*ahimsa*) as a way of showing love to all creatures. This includes the idea of the sacredness of all life and its concomitant universal compassion.

(9) Belief that all revealed religions are essentially correct, as aspects of one ultimate reality, and that religious tolerance is the hallmark of true wisdom.

(10) Belief that the living being is first and foremost a spiritual entity, a soul within the body, and that the spiritual pursuit is consequently the essence and real purpose of life.

(11) Belief that an organic social system, traditionally called Varnashrama, is essential in the proper and effective functioning of humankind, and that this system should be based on intrinsic quality and natural aptitude as opposed to birthright.[3]

These principles can be found in most of India's many Hindu religions, even if various groups will embrace them in diverse ways. The Varnashrama social system, to cite one example, is rigidly enforced by some Hindu groups, while others make it a point to reject it and all that it stands for. In either case, however, social status plays a central role in the Hindu mindset, and the Varnashram system underlies even those traditions that rebel against it.

The worshippers of Vishnu, to cite another example, are generally strict supporters of noninjury to sentient beings, taking it to the point of vegetarianism. But Shaktas, or worshippers of the Goddess, tend to deemphasize this principle, and they sometimes go so far as to employ animal sacrifice in their temple rituals. Even here, however, the rationale for such sacrifices is replete with an *ahimsa* sensibility, explaining its related violence in terms of theological necessity and a philosophy of concession to human weakness. While believing that the Goddess requires blood sacrifice, they insist on causing the least amount of pain possible to the sacrificed animals.

Overall, then, the eleven principles outlined above, in one way or another, are found in all religions that call themselves Hindu, and so one *can* speak of an overarching Hindu tradition.

'HINDU': A PRIMEVAL MISNOMER

And yet the words "Hindu" and "Hinduism" themselves are not found in any of the classical writings of India. Nor can they be traced to classical Indian languages, such as Sanskrit or Tamil. In fact, the words have absolutely no origins within India itself—"Hindu," in particular, is a Persian term that was later modified by Muslims and Europeans.[4]

As the story goes, the word Hindu comes to us through the Indo-Iranian root *sindhu*, a word that means "river." In due course of time, as the word evolved, it specifically referred to the "Indus River" and to the culture in and around its long expansive valley. (The river flows from Tibet, through Pakistan, and into the Arabian Sea.)

Historians tell us that, early on, Persian explorers entered the Indian subcontinent from the far northwest, along the Indus River. After returning home, they published details of their journey, and when mentioning the "Sindhu," the phonetic peculiarities of their native language forced the "S" to become an aspirated "H." In this way, the people of the Indus Valley came to be known as "Hindus"—or those who live beside the Sindhu River—first by the Persians and then by others. That is to say, the idiosyncratic pronunciation was inadvertently handed down, most notably to the invading Moguls who had soon conquered much of India. And because these Muslim conquerors referred to the locals as "Hindus," the term was eventually adopted by the Indians themselves. It was by using this term, in fact, that the natives of India distinguished themselves from the outsiders who were forcibly taking over their land.

As an addendum, perhaps, it should also be noted that the word "India" comes to us through the Greek name of the river described above—the Indos (as opposed to the Indus). To make it clear: the same river that is called "Hindu" in Persian is called "Indos" in Greek, thus giving us the words Hindu and India. The plural of this geographical name gave us words for the people who lived there, the Hindus (i.e., the "people of the Indus," or the "people of India,") better known as "the Indians."

All of this is summed up in nearly every good textbook on Hinduism, with added details. To cite but one example by a prominent Western scholar:

The Persian word "Hindu" derives from Sindhu, the Sanskrit name of the river Indus (in modern Pakistan). It originally meant a native of India, the land around and beyond the Indus. When "Hindu" (or "Hindoo") entered the English language in the seventeenth century, it was similarly used to denote any native of Hindustan (India), but gradually came to mean someone who retained the indigenous religion and had not converted to Islam.

"Hinduism," as a term for that indigenous religion, became current in English in the early nineteenth century and was coined to label an "ism" that was itself partly a product of western Orientalist thought, which (mis)constructed Hinduism on the model of Occidental religions, particularly Christianity. Hinduism, in other words, came to be seen as a single system of doctrines, beliefs, and practices properly equivalent to those that make up Christianity, and "Hindu" now clearly specified an Indian's religious affiliation.[5]

For those who might think this a Western construct, these same ideas are clearly articulated by indigenous Indian scholars whose central interest is the Hindu tradition. They often add details and flourishes of historical significance:

The term Hinduism is not only a misnomer but is also misleading because it carries with it the connotation of religion. The terms Indian and Hindu have never been used in India itself to refer to nationality, culture, religion, or philosophy. Indians actually call their subcontinent Bharata, after the ancient king Bharata, whose name means . . . "lover of knowledge," or in this case, "the land that loves knowledge." . . . the current popular usage of the term Hinduism does not correspond to its original meaning.

When Alexander the Great invaded the subcontinent around 325 BC, he crossed the River Sindhu and renamed it Indus, which was easier for the Greek tongue to pronounce. Alexander's Macedonian forces subsequently called the land to the east of this river India. Later, the Moslem invaders called the Sindhu River the Hindu River because in their language, Parsee, the Sanskrit sound *s* converts to *h*. Thus, for the Persians, Sindhu became Hindu, and the land east of that river became known as Hindustan.

More recently, the land was again called India, but during the British regime, politicians frequently used the terms Hindu and Hinduism, emphasizing the religious and political overtones of these words. This was done to differentiate the Hindus from the Moslems, thus aiding the British policy of "divide and rule." Western writers then adopted these terms for the sake of convenience, and Eastern writers conformed to the norms set by those in power.[6]

It should be underscored that the term "Hindu" referred to something geographical, not something cultural, though it was, indeed, also used to distinguish indigenous people from foreigners and their traditions:

As far back as the Old Persian cuneiform inscriptions and in the Avesta, the word "Hindu" appears as a geographic term; and once the Persian King Darius I, in the year 517 BC, had extended his empire to the banks of the Indus, Hindus (inhabitants of the land of the Indus, i.e., the Indians) were incorporated into the multination Persian state and its army. From then on, for more than a thousand years, the Persians and other Persian-speaking peoples lumped all Indians together as "Hindus."

The Arabs, too, later called India "Al Hind." The meaning shift in this word began relatively late, took place quite gradually, and was fully completed only by the Europeans. . . . In the sixteenth century, merchants and missionaries from Europe came to know this expression for the majority of non-Muslims in India; and it was Europeans who for the first time separated the terms "Indian" and "Hindu," applying the first to the secular sphere, the second to religion, and ultimately deriving from it the word "Hinduism."[7]

THE RELIGION THAT NEVER WAS

If the word "Hindu" is problematic, "Hindu*ism*" is more so, for it implies some unified form of Indian religion that comfortably fits under one banner. Considering the varieties of religion that currently exist in India, a single term is simply inadequate—and because the "H" word falls short, Hinduism becomes difficult to define: "It is because we always try to see it as *one* religion. Our problems would vanish if we took 'Hinduism' to denote a socio-cultural unit or civilization which contains a plurality of distinct religions."[8] Thus, the term need not be excised from our vocabulary, but it would be useful to think about it in a different way.

The rectification of our thinking about [this] had to await [the idea] that concepts need not have common attributes and clear-cut boundaries but may be held together by "a complicated network of similarities overlapping and criss-crossing," in other words that a "family resemblance" may exist among their members.[9]

Diverse Hindu religions, indeed, bear a sort of "family resemblance" to each other, tying them together as "Hindu traditions," and yet, at the same time, they are quite distinct. Like the gods themselves, they are one, yet many. But to lump all Hindu traditions together as one religion betrays a narrow understanding of the traditions themselves, or, worse, it constitutes an insult to the practitioners of these traditions.

Compounding this insult is the following: Not only are worshippers of the traditional "Hindu pantheon" often referred to as "Hindus," but so are members of clearly divergent religions:

Even in the 16th century, 500 years after the Muslim conquerors had come, the term Hindu was rarely used—certainly never in Sanskrit or in any even vaguely scriptural document—and when it was, its range was such that it would have embraced Buddhists and Jains as well as the people we today would call Hindus.[10]

True, the phenomenon we call "Hinduism" is pluralistic to a degree rarely seen in sectarian religion, as outlined above, and the contemporary Indian legal system has taken this sensibility further, perhaps too far, by deliberately subsuming Buddhists, Jains, and Sikhs under its banner.[11] But such an ambiguous use of the term makes it practically useless, a lukewarm label that signifies nothing because it includes nearly everything.

The inclusion of religions outside the normative Hindu tradition is even found in a legal document known as the Orissa Religious Endowments Act, 1969 (and Orissa Act 2 of 1970). This Act is still in effect, stating that, "The expression 'Hindu religion' shall include Jain, Buddhist, and Sikh religions, and the expressions 'Hindu' and 'Hindu public religious institutions and endowments' shall be construed accordingly."[12]

Such laws, in tandem with the egalitarian nature of contemporary Hindu pluralism, make the tradition appear excessively accommodating. There is also the "Hindu Marriage Act of 1955," which states that "an Indian is a Hindu if he does not belong to another religion." Tellingly, this evasive definition, and others like it, was not conceived by Indians, but rather by the British.

And, indeed, Hinduism as a "unified" world religion begins with the British, who started describing the religion of India as an "ism" only as far back as the nineteenth century.

Of course, one would have to admit that there is an overarching phenomenon called "Hinduism," and that whether one worships Vishnu, Shiva, the Goddess, or whomever, if his or her worship has a distinctly Indian flavor (i.e., harkening back to that "family resemblance") then, as a matter of common parlance, it *can* be called a form of "Hinduism."

Indeed, in contemporary India, there are even those who use the words "Hindu" and "Hinduism" to establish political identity, distinguishing "Hindus" from Westerners and Muslims, in particular. Such people have a very specific idea of *Hindutva* ("Hindu-ness"), opining that a true Hindu is part of a "Hindu Empire," complete with territorial and nationalist agendas. Radical groups, such as the Rashtriya Svayamsevak Sangha ("National Volunteer Corps," or the RSS, founded in 1925), the Bharatiya Janata Party ("Indian People's Party," also known as the BJP, founded in 1951), the related Shiv Sena ("Army of Shiva," founded in 1966), and the Vishva Hindu Parishad ("World Hindu Council," or the VHP, founded in 1966), hold and promulgate such views.

But, more commonly, Hinduism refers to India's many theistic traditions, and while it may be a convenience to combine all these diverse traditions into one grand category, it is inaccurate as well. We should not, it is argued above, apply the "-ism" category to broad religious traditions that, despite their adherence to a common cultural milieu, have obviously different founders, scriptures, saints, liturgies, and, above all, forms of supreme Godhead.

Such arbitrary homogenization would be tantamount to claiming that Judaism, Christianity, and Islam are merely various sects within the same religion. In fact, these religions are rooted in the same tradition and share much in common, but they now have different saints, scriptures, methods, and names for the highest divinity. In short, they are different religions.

Christian theologian Hans Kung asserts that to speak of these religions as being one would "set up a parallel with 'Hinduism,' but the members of such a Procrustean unit would presumably give a cry of outrage."[13] So, too, would more knowledgeable Hindus. Pandit Rajmani Tigunait, a prominent Hindu theologian, concurs, saying:

The misconceptions surrounding the term Hinduism now make it a virtually useless word. Its usage is roughly analogous to the hypothetical case of invaders occupying the United States and referring to the native way of life as Yankee-ism and then purporting this to be the "American religion." In India, no religion called Hinduism ever existed, and even today the learned and well-informed spiritual and religious leaders of India do not use this term. They use instead the term *sanatana dharma*, which means "eternal law," to refer to their systems of religious belief.[14]

In summary, imagine a young man from India arriving on Western shores. Further imagine that upon seeing our diversity of religious traditions—including Judaism, Christianity, and Islam, among others—he decides to merge them all into one monolithic entity called Jordanism. After all, he might reason, the Jordan River begins in western Asia but flows through the Jordan Rift Valley and into the Dead Sea. More importantly, the Kingdom of Jordan is an ancient land, and it witnessed many of the religious events that form the cornerstone of the West's three great monotheistic faiths—Judaism, Christianity, and Islam. Surely, these three religions, and any others that have arisen in this great area, can go by a name that brings to mind their mighty river.

This is exactly what is now done with Hinduism, for all of the reasons mentioned above.

Some scholars take this even further, claiming that Hinduism, as we know it, is a Western concoction, a vain attempt to understand something so foreign, so alien, that we simply have to explain it in our own way:

Today, without wanting to admit it, we know that Hinduism is nothing but an orchid cultivated by European scholarship. It is much too beautiful to be torn out, but it is a greenhouse plant: It does not exist in nature.[15]

As prominent Indic scholar Wendy Doniger has suggested, "It is Eurocentric to assume that when we made the name we made the game. 'Hinduism'" she continues, "is, like the armadillo, part hedgehog, part tortoise. Yet there are armadillos, and they were there before they had names."[16]

In fact, there are chiefly three circumstances in which the words "Hindu" or "Hinduism" have any real meaning: (1) They are used in ignorance or for accommodation. That is to say, they have meaning in common parlance, when a given individual is unaware of their inappropriateness or, out of convenience, when the words are used to communicate with others; (2) the words have become useful among those with a political agenda, as mentioned above, to rally "Hindus" around a national identity; (3) some use the terms with the understanding that they apply to the overall flavor of Hindu religions, and can thus be used for each of these religions but with the caveat that they are inaccurate and nonspecific.[17]

So Hinduism exists, but what exactly is it?

How should we think about it, both as a modern phenomenon and in terms of what it originally was? In other words, if the terms Hindu and Hinduism took shape with foreign invaders (and are misleading, as we have shown) then what, in terms of religion, do the people of India practice? What have they practiced for millennia? And how does this relate to our subject at hand?

To begin, it should be understood that just as "Hinduism" refers to one particular religion and to many individual religions at the same time, so, too, does the theological reality to which all Hindu traditions adhere partake of a philosophy of the One and the Many, as we shall now explain.

"THE ONE AND THE MANY"

To better understand the Hindu view of divinity, it is helpful to look at several descriptive words conceived by modern Hindu theologians. These words, while accommodating the idea of Hindu polytheism, or the idea that Hindus worship many gods, show the tradition's real leaning toward monotheism: Monolatry, Henotheism, and Polymorphic Monotheism are three prime examples.

Briefly, Monolatry is the worship of one greater god among many lesser gods.[18] Henotheism is the worship of one god at a time. And Polymorphic Monotheism suggests a single unitary deity who takes many forms and manifests at different levels of reality.[19] Hindu theology accommodates all three of these concepts.

According to *Webster's New Universal Unabridged Dictionary*, "henotheism" (or sometimes "kathenotheism") means "(1) a religious doctrine attributing supreme power to one of several divinities in turn; (2) belief in one god, without denying the existence of others." Indologist Axel Michaels elaborates: "The term *henotheism* coined by [the famous German Indologist] Max Muller, the monotheistic worship of a deity in a polytheistic ambiance, or *kathenotheism*, the worship of a god at a certain moment, does not grasp these connections adequately. *Homotheism* or *equitheism* are better terms, because they denote both the idea of god as well as the fundamental identificatory process."[20]

In the West, when contemplating the idea of a personal God, we tend to think of monotheism and polytheism as our only existing options,[21] and we are usually unwilling to explore other categories of divinity. The one well-known exception is the Christian Trinity, in which one God is said to assume three forms. To some, the idea of the Trinity could appear polytheistic, and there are Jewish theologians who aver that it is.[22]

But Christians never think of the Trinity in this way. Along similar lines, most Hindus would never consider the unlimited forms of the supreme, as expressed in the Hindu scriptures, to be disunited—they see harmony between "the One and the Many." The Hindu complex of religions teaches that one God can have unlimited forms (*ananta-rupa*), since, by definition, he is beyond all limitations.

For the Western mind, the idea of "the One and the Many" (or something that is One and Many at the same time) is a paradox, because the two words are often seen as mutually exclusive. In fact, the two words "one" and "many" are themselves perceived as antonyms. That is, something is either "one" or it is "many," a dichotomy that makes sense to us. It comes from our Greek heritage of Aristotelian logic and its system of absolute division. In other words, Aristotle taught that all facets of existence exist in neat, individual categories, and so this is how we, in the West, tend to think.

For example, there is religion, and there is science—and there should be no overlapping between the two. Reality, however, doesn't quite work that way. It is made up of gray areas. And in fact there is a "science of religion," in which components of the scientific method are used to illustrate religious themes—this is the very basis of Sanatana Dharma, which we will explain in the next chapter. Clearly, the harmony of opposites, or the reconciliation of that which appears irreconcilable, is hinted at in the idea of "the One and the Many."

In the West, we can think about the One and the Many by looking at the phrase "E Pluribus Unum," which was a motto that originally meant "out of many colonies, one nation." Eventually, the phrase grew to encompass ethnic and European national dimensions: "out of many peoples, one people." Hinduism, however, goes further, using the principle to expound on religious pluralism, for it recognizes the great variety of human perceptions in relation to God. All of this is implied by the Rig Vedic verse, "Truth is one, though the wise refer to it by various names."

Western mystics have also taken "e pluribus unum" in more metaphysical directions, even to the point of unity among opposites (i.e., among the One and the Many). "The fundamental law of the universe," it is said, "is the law of the unity of opposites."

The idea is usually traced to the Greek philosopher Heraclitus and, later, it is again seen in Plato's *Symposium*. Even in logic, the Greek writers tell us, the unity of opposites is a way of understanding something in its entirety. Instead of just taking one aspect or one part of a given phenomenon, seeing something in terms of a unity of opposites is recognizing the complete dialectical composition of that thing. Because everything has its opposite, to fully understand it one must not only understand its present form and its opposite form, but also the unity of those two forms, or what they mean in relation to each other.

In modern physics, too, we see this same truth at work. In Relativity Theory, for example, the traditional opposites of rest and motion are now recognized as indistinguishable, for each, in a sense, is both. An object that appears to be in motion for one observer is, at the same time, at rest for another. Similarly, the long-standing division between a wave and a particle has now collapsed—the two are understood as "wavicles." These one-time "opposites" are now viewed as two aspects of one and the same reality, and this truth, it is claimed, applies to all that we see, hear, smell, taste, and touch.

In fact, physics states that all opposites (such as mass and energy, subject and object, and life and death) are so integrally related to each other that they are fundamentally inseparable. And yet, they *are* separate, and their separateness is quite real as well. From a practical point of view, then, it is simply incomplete to do away with the kinds of boundaries that define things as "one" or the "other," as some Indic traditions do. But, at the same time, we should be able to see their inherent oneness as well.

This ability to see the harmony of the One and the Many is nowhere more prominent than in Indian theology. The transcending of all pairs of opposites (expressed as *dvandvas*, "dualities," in Sanskrit) is central to Hindu thought. When applied to God, the prime example is his "otherness" and his "accessibility"—he is most exalted, unreachable, and yet, by his grace, certainly attainable. Such polarities define not only God but his creation as well. In Hinduism, the key to understanding such concepts as matter and space, day and night, male and female, left and right, hot and cold, and body and soul—is in their interrelationship as fundamental opposites.

Day and night, for example, both relate to the rotation of one planet. Male and female are each alternate halves of humankind. Left and right are both directions in space. Our material bodies are a reflection of our spiritual life force.

To the Hindu mind, opposites are, in a sense, the same thing. They are different sides of the same coin—inseparable and fundamentally related. Hindu thought posits that opposites are born of unity. And that to understand them properly creates balance. Thus, in Hinduism, the One and the Many might even function as *synonyms*—the One, say ancient Hindu texts, only fully reveals itself when in relation to the Other, as we will see in the interrelationship between Radha and Krishna, the supreme deities of Vaishnavism. This is to say, the Other gives meaning to the One, and vice versa. A fundamental Hindu perception: Opposites attract and inter-penetrate each other. Ultimately, then, the One and the Other coalesce in a higher spiritual reality. This is expressed in various ways in the Hindu tradition.

Therefore, experts in Hindu theology have described the tradition as one that resists the "either/or" approach, portraying it instead as essentially a tradition of "both/and."[23] Of course, the "both/and" motif should not be taken too far, either. Hinduism recognizes detailed dichotomies between forms of Godhead, leading to elaborate "either/or" distinctions. And, in many ways, this hierarchical paradigm of differentiation supercedes the doctrine of perfect oneness.

Still, the harmony of the One and the Many is important in contemporary Hinduism, and it must be understood as far as the human mind allows. That it is a paradox does not sway practitioners from attempting its contempla-tion. To cite one famous example: When the sage Yagyavalkya was asked how many gods actually existed, he answered "thirty-three." When asked a second time, he said, "one." (*Brihadaranyaka Upanishad* 3.9.1) This he said as if there was no contradiction between his two answers.

Similarly, there is a traditional Indian tale about a man who spent much of his life documenting the various deities worshipped along the countryside. From village to village he journeyed, house to house, inquiring about the gods who were worshipped at those places, by those particular people.

Eventually, as the story goes, the weary traveler chronicled 330 million deities, writing the names of each in his multivolume tome, though, at the time, he had not counted them. When he finally returned home, exhausted and in his 93rd year, he was asked to tally how many gods were in his book. He spent 7 years, it is said, counting the gods, and at the end of the book he wrote the grand total: One.

Interestingly, the *Vedas* sometimes refer to the "secret names" of its various deities, names that are meant to convey the Oneness of the Many. For example, in the *Rig Veda* (7.99), we find that Vishnu is referred to by one such name: "Shipivishta." Though the word is difficult to define, it is clear from later exegesis that it indicates Shiva-Rudra-Vishnu, or an amalgam of the gods. A related truth is found in the *Bhagavad-Gita* (10.23), where Krishna identifies himself with Shiva directly. Thus, certain names of the Divine are constructed in such a way as to resolve or harmonize the One and the Many.

Along similar lines, in "Hariharapura," a small town in Karnataka, South India, there is a famous "Sri Vishnu Shiva" temple. Here, the main deity takes the form of half Shiva and half Vishnu—two male bodies existing as one. Generally, it is expected that Shiva would be with Parvati, his female counterpart, or that Vishnu would be associated with Lakshmi. But here it is not so. Why? The same idea of the One and the Many is meant to carry through.

The truth behind the One and the Many is ultimately inexpressible. To assert this fact, Hindu tradition has developed numerous strategies. For example, according to some Hindu philosophers, ultimate truth is usually spoken of indirectly, or apophatically. That is, rather than make precise statements and clear affirmations about the nature of God, some Hindus speak by way of negation. An often quoted version is found in the Upanishads: "*neti, neti*," which means "not this, not that." The expression is meant to communicate the idea that Brahman is beyond words. It is meant to evoke the "mysterium tremendum," or the great mystery of God's nature.

This mystery is also alluded to by the idea of "Arundhati," the Indian name of a dim star in the Great Bear constellation, known in the West as the Big Dipper. Theologically, Arundhati basically means "pointing to the star." The idea is this: Arundhati is nearly impossible to see because it is so dim. Thus, one locates it by first finding a brighter star in its general vicinity. Such bright stars function as "pointers" to the actual star for which one is looking. Here, again, we see an admission of God's inconceivable nature, which can only be hinted at, or "pointed to," with words.[24]

These explanatory devices, and others like them, underscore the harmony of the One and the Many in Indian theology. Bottom line: On the one hand, as stated previously, Hindu traditions clearly teach that there is one ultimate reality. On the other hand, they acknowledge no end to the number of "gods" who exist as expressions of that reality.

The traditional Indian example is that of a singular gem—its full existence must be considered in relation to its colorful array of facets. One cannot speak of the gem apart from its multiple cuts or sides, nor without acknowledging its glistening splendor as a singularity unto itself. Thus, by its very nature, the gem unifies the idea of the stone and its cuts. In addition, even if one favors viewing the gem from a particular perspective, from an angle revealing a nuance of color that becomes one's personal favorite, the gem is still, ultimately, one. Likewise, the One and the Many are inextricably linked as "One" supreme Godhead and his manifestation of "Many" divinities, even if one views a particular form of the divine with personal preference.

A clearer analogy, perhaps, is that of an individual who exhibits various identities according to time and circumstance: as a parent or partner at home, as a worker in the workplace, as a community member, or as an officer in civic or social organizations. Here, the "one" person is perceived as "many" by other individuals. It might be argued that this person's visual appearance is the same in each case, while the Hindu deities actually have different forms. But does a child really see the parent in the same way a lover does? Would a worker view his employer with the loving eyes of a family member?

Appearances defer to the expectations and needs of the viewer. Moreover, one wears appropriate attire and acts in distinct ways based on time and circumstance. Such a change in clothing and disposition can make one appear quite differently in each situation: lounging clothes and informality at home, dressy wear and proper manners when going to work, and so on. Admittedly, the differences here are not as acute as in the diverse visual appearances of the Goddess, Shiva, or Vishnu, or in the many other Hindu divinities. But the principle is the same: One sees through the lens of relationship, through the perception of emotional necessity, and the deity responds accordingly.

The brilliance of Hindu theology consists in its ability to accommodate various psychological orientations toward the Divine. That is, Hindu belief encompasses not only religious and cultural diversity, but emotional and behavioral needs as well. The "One" manifested as the "Many" in Hindu texts speaks as much to the individuality of worshippers as to the pervasive nature of the Worshippable.

The term polytheism, therefore, is inadequate to properly describe the multiplex known as Hinduism. This is so because it denies the importance of Oneness in relation to the Many, as seen in the "poly" part of the word. But let us go further: Indian religion has also been described as presenting radical monism, saying that everything is illusory save and except the one supreme spirit, Brahman. However, this view, too, is counter to Indian religious experience, where the divine in all its (his, her) color and personality plays a role in the daily lives of practitioners.

All this being true, Indian philosophy ultimately emphasizes a doctrine of Achintya Bhedabheda, or "inconceivable and simultaneous oneness and difference."[25] The term Achintya Bhedabheda is technically used to describe the theological system of the Gaudiya Vaishnavas, or those Vaishnavas originating in Bengal who revere the saint Chaitanya Mahaprabhu (1486–1533) as a combined manifestation of Radha and Krishna, to be discussed more fully in an upcoming chapter. But as a general description of Indian metaphysics, especially in relation to the paradox of the One and the Many, the term is equally appropriate.

Hinduism is thus a constant dialogue between One and Zero, form and formlessness, feasting and fasting, yes and no—seeing a harmony in the obvious differences of diametrically opposed phenomena. Hinduism teaches that each is appropriate in its appropriate circumstances. For a Hindu, then, the gods are not at odds! They are various representations of the same person, the same being, but they are also independent at the same time, with various nuances of particularity. This, again, is the unity of opposites, and, like Hinduism itself, it embodies the truth of the One and the Many.

CHAPTER 3
Dharma and the Hindu Social System

"Among all the great religions of the world there is none more catholic, more assimilative, than the mass of beliefs which go to make up what is popularly known as Hinduism."

—W. Crooke, Indian historian

The numerous religions of India—whether Vaishnava, Shaiva, Shakta, or what have you—begin with certain fundamental premises in relation to God and the universe. India also gives us, it is true, "atheistic" traditions, such as Buddhism, Jainism, and Charvaka's system of thought, which do not acknowledge a supreme deity. But these are not viewed as Hinduism proper. Therefore, a brief look at how Hindu traditions view God and reality should shed some light on what Hinduism actually is.

Because the tradition recognizes diverse aspects of God, in multifarious forms, it is sometimes viewed as polytheistic, or believing in many gods. It should be understood, however, that these "many gods" are simply a manifestation of how God descends in an infinity of ways—sometimes manifesting his full power and identity, and, by way of various gradations, manifesting in lesser or incomplete forms as well.

This is not to say that some Hindus wouldn't identify themselves as polytheists. However, the ancient intellectual traditions of India, and most educated Hindus today, explain that the true inner core of their tradition cannot be identified with what is commonly known as polytheism.

Well-informed Hindus, who know their scriptural tradition, say that their conception of God is wholly transcendental, going beyond the normal categories of the One and the Many, as already discussed. And yet there is no end to the varieties of forms with which God reciprocates the love of his devotees.

For example, he exists in his original kingdom, in the spiritual world, and he also has a "Universal Form," which essentially comprises the entire material cosmos. Practitioners who accentuate this latter form favor animism, or seeing God in nature. He also manifests as "the deity," a visible image made of earth, wood, marble, gold, and so on—this is an iconic form that is worshipped according to strict rules and regulations, in one's home or in a temple, as elaborated upon in an upcoming chapter.

The tradition also says that he comes to earth in so many incarnations (*avatars*), the most important of which are all mentioned in the scriptures, and here he interacts with mankind for specific purposes of his own. God manifests as the many demigods, or highly empowered beings, too, and as certain sages, who help humanity in a number of ways.

Chiefly, there are three aspects of the divine that are accentuated in the Hindu scriptures: (1) Brahman, God's all-pervading and formless aspect; (2) the Supersoul, his aspect as the "Lord in the heart" (though here he is not to be confused with the individual living entity, also residing in the region of the heart), who exists within each living entity, and in and between every atom; and (3) Bhagavan, his aspect as the Supreme Person.[1]

These three aspects are seen as equal, in that they refer to the same Absolute Truth. But there is simultaneously a hierarchy, with the personal form of Bhagavan, the Supreme Person, at the top. The hierarchy exists because each successive stage of God realization includes the prior one. That is to say, one who attains Supersoul realization will necessarily have achieved Brahman realization as well. And one who realizes Bhagavan, the Supreme Person, has also perceived the truths found in Brahman and Supersoul.

The impersonal aspect of the Lord, Brahman, is generally approached by the contemplative meditator, the one who renounces the world to pursue spiritual knowledge. The Supersoul aspect is generally the domain of the *yogi*, or the serious practitioner of severe penances and austerities, following the many rules and regulations of *yoga* practice as delineated in the scriptures. Finally, the Personality of Godhead is pursued by the devotee, the loving servant of God who anxiously seeks to reclaim his lost relationship with him.

All forms of Hindu religion accept one or more of these three aspects of divinity, if in diverse ways. The more important principle, for most Hindus, is exactly how one's conception of God plays out in one's day-to-day life. This is the substance of true Hinduism.

IN A WORD: DHARMA

The Hindu complex of religions can perhaps best be summed up by one word: *Dharma*, which comes from the Sanskrit root *dhri*, meaning "to support, hold up, or bear." It is related to the derivative *dhru*, or *dhruva*, meaning "pole"—the balancing of extremes through an axis. It refers to that invariable something at the center of the world's revolutions, holding it in place; the thing that regulates the course of change by not participating in change—by remaining constant.

Dharma is cognate with the Latin *firmus*, the origin of the word "firm," implying that one's *dharma* is something that holds fast. All this being said, it is difficult to provide a single or concise definition for the word, and for this reason most books on Hinduism tend to leave it untranslated. Monier-Williams, whose Sanskrit dictionary is considered standard in the field, offers its numerous definitions: "that which is established or firm, stead-fast decree, statute, ordinance, law; usage, practice, customary observance or prescribed conduct, duty; right, justice; virtue, morality, religion, religious merit, good works"—but none of this conveys the total sense of the word.

In common parlance it means "right way of living," "Divine Law," "path of righteousness," "faith," and "duty." Ultimately, *dharma* is the central organizing principle of the cosmos; it is that which supports and maintains all existence. *Dharma* is the inner reality that makes a thing what it is. It is the *dharma* of the bee to make honey, of the cow to give milk, of the sun to shine, and the river to flow. It is a thing's essence. It is similar to, or resonates with, the Chinese *Tao*, the Egyptian *Maat*, and the Sumerian *Me*. In terms of humankind, as we will see, *dharma* is "service." For whether we serve God or dog, serve we must.

With this brief description of *dharma*, let us now look at the various kinds of *dharma* that are fundamental to Hindu thinking. We begin with Nitya Dharma, or Sanatana Dharma ("eternal law"), mentioned previously. These refer to the eternal function of the soul—it is who we really are and what we really do, in a world beyond our bodies, beyond time and space. It refers to our relationship with God in the spiritual realm. When these terms are used here, in the world of three dimensions, they refer to those activities that free us from illusion, the activities that help us return to our original home beyond the material universe.

Nitya Dharma and Sanatana Dharma are also called Manava Dharma ("the religion of man"), which is meant to convey a sense of universal religion, or religion for Everyone. It transcends sectarian concerns and refers to the "science of religion," a popular phrase among the Hindu elite. These names, Nitya Dharma, Sanatana Dharma, and Manava Dharma, loudly proclaim Hinduism's self-perception, and are used by insiders as the preferred titles for the overarching tradition.

"Hinduism," says a prominent authority on the tradition, "is [believed to be] the remnant of a universal store of knowledge which, at one time, was accessible to the whole of mankind. It claims to represent the sum of all that has come to be known to man through his own effort or through revelation from the earliest age of his existence."[2] Or, to quote Hindu philosopher and politician Sri Aurobindo:

Hinduism . . . gave itself no name, because it set itself no sectarian limits; it claimed no universal adhesion, asserted no sole infallible dogma, set up no single narrow path or gate of salvation; it was less a creed or cult than a continuously enlarging tradition of the Godward endeavor of the human spirit. An immense many-sided and many staged provision for spiritual self-building and self-finding, it had some right to speak of itself by the only name it knew, the eternal religion, Sanatana Dharma . . .[3]

In spite of this lofty self-perception, Hindus are not intolerant of other paths—it is not that they see only their own religion as "Sanatana Dharma," as eternal, universal, and all-encompassing, as opposed to others. Not at all. They say that Sanatana Dharma refers to abiding truths, and that such truths can be found in any religious tradition, if one looks deeply enough. Accordingly, the specific form of Sanatana Dharma found in early Hindu traditions is unique in only two respects: It offers elaborate scriptural information, with details found only in the Vedic tradition, as well as systematic procedure and scientific methodology for achieving one's spiritual goals.

Hinduism, therefore, sees itself as being of universal significance, because it represents an entire range of spiritual possibilities and provides spiritual technologies by which one can practice any religion one chooses. It can accommodate spiritual seekers who see God as personal, and also those who prefer an impersonal Absolute; it speaks to those who call themselves Hindu, and to those who do not. It even includes modes of practice for the gradual elevation of those who disbelieve in spiritual reality and who favor atheistic worldviews.

PHILOSOPHIA PERENNIS

In the West, a similar phenomenon is found in the concept of the *philosophia perennis*, also known as the *religio perennis*, or the *sophia perennis*. The term *philosophia perennis* and its variations go back to the Renaissance, though Sanatana Dharma, which basically refers to the same thing, cannot be traced to a particular point in time. In its Western manifestation, the *philosophia perennis* is associated with such thinkers as Augustine Steuch, Gottfried Leibniz, René Guénon, Frithjof Schuon, T. S. Eliot, H. P. Blavatsky, Mircea Eliade, and Aldous Huxley, among others.

Most of these writers have made the connection between the *philosophia perennis* and Sanatana Dharma. Unfortunately, several of them—Frithjof Schuon, for example—only go so far as the impersonalist school of Vedanta when considering the *philosophia perennis*. Schuon would have done well to further explore *bhakti* ("devotion") and Vaishnavism, which, arguably, more fully embody the essence of Sanatana Dharma.[4]

The basic idea is that certain metaphysical truths always exist (i.e., they are eternal) and, properly understood, make knowledge of the divine particularly accessible. The *philosophia perennis* (and basic Hindu philosophy) states that the essential function of human intelligence is to discern between reality and illusion, or between the permanent and the temporary, and that the essential function of the will is to develop a predilection for the permanent or the real.

It teaches that this sense of discernment and preference are the building blocks of true spirituality, regardless of the religious tradition one uses to cultivate these virtues. It is nurtured by metaphysical axioms whose formulation is not peculiar to any particular religious system. In fact, the *philosophia perennis* points to the essence of every religion—the underlying substance of every form of worship, every technique for prayer, and every system of morality.

As one scholar says, summing up the *philosophia perennis*: "The doctrinal language varies from one religion to another and can embrace concepts as different as those of *sunya* and Yahweh. The method can also vary in numerous ways ranging from Vedic sacrifices to Muslim daily prayers. But the essence and goal of the doctrine and method remain universal within every religion."[5]

Sunya (phonetic spelling: *shunya*), as mentioned above, refers to an impersonal Absolute, or to the voidism of the Buddhist tradition, which is here contrasted with Yahweh, the epitome of a personal Absolute (at least in Western terms). The idea is that the *philosophia perennis* can accommodate completely divergent aspects of ultimate reality, as can Sanatana Dharma.

The *philosophia perennis* teaches that all authentic religious traditions are true, deriving from a transcendent Primordial Tradition, but that the actual teachings of these traditions might not be what they seem. The premise is that we need to dig deep, to unlock the essential mysteries often found buried in our mystical traditions. This is not always easy to do. And it gets more difficult as time elapses. This is so because, as the *philosophia perennis* teaches, our modern idea of "progress" is simply not valid and, as most major world religions inform us, the world is in a state of intellectual and spiritual decline.

We are presently in the Age of Iron, of quarrel and hypocrisy, which Hindus call Kali-yuga. This point is important to the *philosophia perennis*, as it is to Sanatana Dharma, for it implies that we are moving ever further from the undiluted truths of the religious adepts, losing sight of the original principles that make up Eternal Religion. Ultimately, the *philosophia perennis'* most distinguishing qualities are that it consists of universal verities and that it is found at the heart or inner core of all truly spiritual traditions.

This is all Sanatana Dharma. A lotus, as it is said, is a lotus, even if referred to by another name. In using the term Sanatana Dharma, Hindus (and by this we mean people who adhere to any of the multiple religions in the Hindu complex of religions) suggest that they do not view their tradition as partisan or relative. Rather, as stated previously, they see it as a tradition of ultimate reality, not of sectarian dogma. This is their perception even though some of them worship Vishnu, some worship Shiva, and so on, with particularities solely associated with one or another of these spiritual entities.

The system works because Hinduism acknowledges the unique nature of each individual, and this manifests as a social system called Varnashrama Dharma—an extension of *dharma* that applies to each living being according to the body and mind that God has given him.

VARNASHRAMA DHARMA

All Hindu traditions share an underlying respect for Varnashrama Dharma, or the socioreligious system set in place by the sages of India's distant past. While most Hindus adhere to Varnashrama to the best of their ability, others deemphasize it and even rebel against it, as already mentioned. But all acknowledge that it lay at the basis of their theological heritage.

Above and beyond Varnashrama Dharma is the already mentioned Nitya Dharma ("Eternal Duty"),[6] or the essential function of the soul (i.e., service to God). This is the overriding premise upon which Varnashrama is based. In other words, the Hindu social system is only significant if it works in conjunction with deeper spiritual realities, such as the soul's everlasting relationship with God. It is from within the conceptual framework of these two spiritual sensibilities that one might understand essential Hinduism.

While every living being's Nitya Dharma is service to God, such service manifests, or plays out, in a variety of ways, according to each individual's psychophysical makeup. According to all Hindu traditions, this is called *sva-dharma*, or one's personal duty based on idiosyncratic inclination and body type. As the famous philosopher Hegel tells us, "If we say that courage is a virtue, the Hindoo says that courage is a virtue of the Kshatriyas (warriors)."[7] What does this mean? Do Hindus really demarcate virtues according to class? Well, yes and no. Courage, of course, is *always* a virtue, but it may manifest variously according to one's station in life. Varnashrama Dharma explains how this is so.

The most well-known articulation of this Varnashrama system is found in the *Bhagavad-Gita* (4.13), commonly known as the Bible of India. Here, Lord Krishna, accepted by the tradition as the Godhead himself, explains that he created human society with four natural social classes (or *varnas*), as well as four underlying spiritual orders (or *ashramas*). This is where the word Varnashrama comes from. He further explains that these social and spiritual divisions allow for the most effective application of eternal religious principles. How? People practice spirituality in the material world, and, because of this, they need pragmatic engagement according to the minds and bodies that material nature has given them.

The social orders are (1) Brahmins[8]—intellectuals or priestly people; (2) Kshatriyas—politicians, administrators, and warriors; (3) Vaishyas—farmers, merchants, or economists; and (4) Shudras—laborers and artisans. Individuals naturally fit into one or more of these occupational divisions, says the *Gita*, based on their qualifications and work. It should be emphasized that the original system was based on quality and inclination, not on birth.

What we are talking about here are personality types. The Brahmin, for example, is of a sacerdotal nature, contemplative and inclined toward study. He responds to goodness and is gentle and clean. His vision focuses upward, toward higher reality. The Kshatriya, on the other hand, is the chivalrous, knightly type, even if his concerns are generally more "this-worldly" than those of the Brahmin. He leans toward action, and his powers of analysis are keen as well. He is characteristically noble, except when passion gets the better of him. His main focus is on getting things done, but with honor, virtue, and integrity.

Now, the Vaishya, for his part, is necessarily bound to material values; his life revolves around shillings and pence—his motivation is security and prosperity. Embodying a mixture of passion and ignorance, his focus is economic stability, and it is difficult for him to see beyond that. If the Vaishya's vision is somewhat limited, the Shudra's is still more compromised. This is the sort of person who feels good only when he works hard. He is a born assistant, someone who is not usually privy to original ideas. His life revolves around his physical work and immediate bodily pleasures, and he prefers routine to innovative thinking.

As should by now be apparent, such classifications—intellectual, administrator, and so on—can be applied to all human beings, not just to "Hindus." In fact, everyone has a natural proclivity, or an inclination toward a particular kind of endeavor. And all endeavors fit into one of these four broad categories. Thus, the original social system as enunciated in the *Bhagavad-Gita*, say contemporary Hindus, is intended for everyone, or, at the very least, it has some natural bearing in everyone's life. It is thus a component of Nitya Dharma.

But—and this is a "But" with a capital "B"—its current counterpart, the caste system, is *not* an aspect of Nitya Dharma, for by definition caste stratifies people according to birth and family heritage as opposed to aptitude and inclination. Basing one's vocation in life on birth is not only contrary to the *Bhagavad-Gita*, but also impractical and problematic. Can a surgeon's son perform a delicate operation merely because his father is a qualified surgeon? True, one might be predisposed to a certain line of work if handed down by one's parents. But this should stand a long way from making this work mandatory, as we find in India's current social system.

But before exploring the misapplications of Varnashrama, let us briefly address its origin. The idea of *varna*, or the social side of the Varnashrama system, is traceable to the *Rig Veda* (10.90.12), where the mighty Purusha, the Lord, expanded his universal body into the visible universe. By way of metaphor, the *Veda* tells us that his body divided into the four divisions that eventually became known as the *varnas*: "From his mouth came the priestly class, who tell us about the Lord; from his arms, the rulers and administrators; the agriculturists came from his legs and the workers from his feet." So it is in the earliest Vedic texts that the divisions of society are acknowledged for the first time. Since then, *varna* has been an integral part of Indian society, though, as history relates, the system devolved as time wore on.

Much of this devolution can be traced to the *jati* system, a seemingly limitless number of subcastes prevalent throughout the subcontinent. The word *jati* comes from the Sanskrit root *jan* meaning "to beget" or "to produce." It is related to the word *janma*, or "birth." That is to say, *jati* is related to one's birth status, even as *varna* is not. In today's India, it is difficult to overcome the *jati* of one's birth and one must consequently conform to sets of rules governing acceptable occupations, foods, marriage partners, and association. Though there are only four *varnas*, there are thousands of *jatis*, and it is from the latter that India gets its many "castes."

The word "caste" is derived from the Portuguese *casta*, meaning "pure" or "chaste," suggesting a concern about keeping to one's own class, and the harm that might result from the mixing of different peoples. The Sanskrit words *varna* and *jati* are both generally translated as "caste," but this is misleading because it obscures the important differences between them, as outlined here.

There are various theories about how *varnas* were initially conceived. The actual word has two literal meanings—"color" and "veil"—and scholars have made much of both. Suffice it to say, the early commentators never thought of "color," in this case, as meaning "race" or "tribal origin," which was a later idea. Rather, "color" was seen as "proclivity" or "distinctive character"—one is "colored" by personal choices, tastes, and modes of action. As "veil" it was understood that one's *varna* referred to how one worked in this world, not to the nature of one's soul, which remained veiled as long as one was in the conditioned state.

Some would say that the original Varnashrama system has now transformed into a *jati* system, well known for its excesses. The typical example are the "Brahmins"—that is, those born in Brahmin families as opposed to those who are Brahmins by qualification—who exploit the lower classes for power and prestige.

The great Indian epic known as the *Mahabharata* suggests that *varnas* should not be confused with *jatis* (though this latter word is, of course, never used in the Epic), for *jatis* are based on birth, whereas *varnas* are not. Once, the serpent-king Nahusha asked the great King Yudhishthira about the qualifications of a Brahmin.

Without mentioning birth status at all, Yudhishthira answered as follows: "O Lord of serpents! The one who is truthful, generous, patient, and virtuous, who has empathy, is tranquil and has compassion—this is the Brahmin." (*Vana-Parva* 177.15). Indeed, the same section of the *Mahabharata* states it more directly as well: "A person should not be considered a Brahmin just because he was born in a Brahmin family, nor need he be a Shudra just because his parents were Shudras (*Vana-Parva* 180).[9]

Many Hindus believe the original *varnas* are still in place and serve divine justice through reincarnation, often manifesting through the *jati* of one's birth—one is born into the *jati* that one deserves based on previous activities, both good and bad. Unfortunately, those in higher echelon *jatis* generally look down on the large number of less fortunate Indians, or those whose *jatis* are considered outside the *varna* system; this refers to the Untouchables and others born into groups with lower status.[10] Naturally, this leads to exploitation.

Karl Marx defined class distinctions in terms of economics, asserting that in amassing one's own wealth (i.e., power), high-ranking classes generally exploit low-ranking ones, using them for service or labor. This uneven distribution of power, he claimed, naturally leads to conflict between the classes, and, in fact, this has been the case throughout much of human history. His view is especially realized in the *jati* system, for here we see an endogamous, rank-oriented, occupationally defined system of labor. This may well have been one of the systems he had in mind when criticizing class hierarchies.

Marx, in fact, was among the first Western thinkers to emphasize the negative impact of caste on Indian society, specifically because of its causal link with the phenomenon of production. In his famous essay, entitled, *The Future Results of British Rule in India*, he described the Indian castes as "the most decisive impediment to India's progress and power."[11] He correctly argued that the caste system of modern-day India is based on the hereditary division of labor, which, he said, was inevitably linked to an immutable technological background as well as to a grassroots Indian village economy.

Here, again, by emphasizing the "hereditary" nature of class distinctions in India, he is obviously speaking about the *jati* system, and, if so, his words certainly ring true. Its *varna* counterpart is often guilty of promoting qualitative hierarchy as well, with Brahmins on top.

But, as Marx discovered, in the Indian system, high caste does not guarantee higher economic status. Sometimes Shudras are landowners, with considerable wealth, whereas Brahmins can be temple priests who might even be indigent. More, the *varna* system, at least, acknowledges ultimate equality based upon one's inherent spiritual nature. It is therefore called *Daivi-Varnashrama*, or "divine" Varnashrama, which sees each faction of society as being perfectly situated in service to the Lord, thus equalizing the various classes.

Because of the many injustices in the *jati* system, there have been several attempts to reject the idea of caste even from within existing Hindu traditions, as mentioned. In the twelfth century, for example, Basava and the Virashaivas temporarily renounced all notions of class distinction, and in the fifteenth century the poet Kabir, and his disciple Dadu, spoke out loudly against caste as well. But just as water always seeks its own level, the caste system found its way back into these sects, which now constitute castes of their own.

Despite repeated legislation in the Indian Constitution against caste discrimination, it is still very much a part of Indian life. Higher caste Hindus have been known to brutally attack Harijans ("people of God," as Gandhi referred to those beneath caste status) and Untouchables, reacting to the inevitable upward mobility of such lower castes in a postmodern age.

In the cities, class struggles are particularly evident because of interaction with the West, as evidenced in ever-increasing interest in technological progress (i.e., foreign travel, satellite television, and other accoutrements of modern life), which the poor have difficulty acquiring. In the villages, where most of India's people live, modern reaction to caste is more difficult to see, but even here change is taking a slow rickshaw into people's lives.

Still, most Indians, even those who get the shorter end of the staff, will admit that there is something fundamentally true about class distinctions, even if it is equally true that such distinctions are problematic when rigidly enforced. And, when enforced, they should be based on *varna* considerations, not on those of the current *jati* system. They should be acknowledged with some fluidity, and applied by well-wishers, parents, the guru, and others who know a person well.

If it is in this way judiciously applied by those who are wise, and concerned, then, Hindu texts teach, it allows, or facilitates, people to reach their potential. It becomes advantageous rather than restrictive, an asset rather than a hindrance.

The *Bhagavad-Gita*, again, tells us that these class distinctions are natural, and that everyone fits into some social stratification, in one way or another. That there is something natural about the *varnas* is perhaps suggested by the fact that it exists, in one form or another, throughout the world, though it was more prominent in the past, when cultural traditions meant more to people in general.

We find a facsimile of the system, for example, in ancient Babylonia, Egypt, Persia, and China; the Mayan, Aztecs, and Incas had their version of it; and it was a fundamental part Christian Europe in the Middle Ages as well. The most famous Western example, perhaps, is found in Plato's classic work, *The Republic*, where he speaks of "the Ideal State," categorizing society into three classes—Gold, Silver, and Copper. He elaborates by saying that, on top, there are philosopher-kings, who rule; below them are the warriors; and, finally, we have the merchants and the workers, whom Plato combines into one category. This is the *varna* categorization almost to the letter.

Another important thing to know about the *varnas* is that the first three, in other words, the Brahmins, the Kshatriyas, and the Vaishyas (or, in some areas, only the first two), are called the "twice born." This refers to a "spiritual birth" through initiatory rites. Being "twice born" means that you come of age in a religious sense, like Bar Mitzvah or Confirmation in the Judeo-Christian tradition. Being twice born gives you the eligibility to learn Sanskrit, study the *Vedas*, and perform Vedic rituals. Interestingly, the vast majority of people in India are Shudras and beneath class status. Thus, they do not have access to the *Vedas* and to Sanskrit learning.

In any case, according to Hindu texts, when the twice born come of age, they enter into the four *ashramas* or "spiritual stages of life," which brings us to the second part of the Varnashrama system. The first *ashrama* is Brahmacharya, or the stage of the student. For boys, the student is supposed to live with a teacher (guru), who is traditionally a Brahmin by birth, but who at least should be renowned for having spiritual knowledge. Girls are usually trained by the parents, with specific gurus for particular interests. Here the student learns Sanskrit, the *Vedas*, rituals, and so on. The *dharma* of a student includes being learned, gentle, respectful, celibate, and nonviolent.

The second stage is Grihastha, or the stage of the householder, that is, married life, which is taken far more seriously in Hinduism than in Jainism, Buddhism, or in the other ascetic traditions. It is usually regarded as mandatory, and is considered just as important for spiritual development as is being a student. It is usually at this stage that one's *sva-dharma*, or psychophysical leaning, is assessed by the guru, and it is also here that most people perform their most important religious functions (known as *samskaras*, or "rites of passage").

The third stage of spiritual stratification is called Vanaprastha, the forest dweller, now considered the stage of retirement. Husbands and wives leave their secular affairs and possessions with their now grown children, if they have any, and retire to the forest as hermits. This does not involve the complete renunciation of the world, for husbands and wives can still have minimal relations, but the idea here is that they are preparing for renunciation, which, in turn, is meant to prepare them for death. The *Aranyakas* ("Forest Treatises" associated with Vedic texts), to be detailed later, were written by and for people who are at this stage of life, who have largely renounced the world and are starting to seriously consider liberation. For many, this stage is today completely bypassed—people who are serious about spiritual life generally go straight for the Sannyasa *ashrama*, to be discussed next, or they remain Grihasthas and serve the Lord with their spouse.

In old age one traditionally enters the fourth stage of Sannyasa, or that of the wandering ascetic, which is the most respected of all the *ashramas*. The *sannyasi* is considered the spiritual master of society. Ideally, the *sannyasi* is a *sadhu*, or a holy person, who wanders the countryside dedicated to renunciation, to developing his own consciousness, and to instructing others, without worldly distractions.

The *ashramas* described here, then, represent a four-tiered system in which one is first a student, then gets married, and eventually retires and prepares for death. In many ways, these may not sound like spiritual stations as such. Rather, they might appear like ordinary phases of life, playing out according to the passage of time, and indeed they are. Like the social orders enunciated by Krishna, the four spiritual orders can, to one degree or another, be found in diverse human cultures throughout the world. In all civilizations, there are monks, or students of theistic science; married people who want to pursue higher spiritual values; individuals coming to grips with old age and the importance of renunciation; and those recognizing the inevitability of death, vowing to devote the remainder of their days to pursuing God consciousness and sharing it with others.

What is unique about the Hindu scriptures, however, is that here one finds guidance and models of behavior appropriate to each of the four *ashramas*, and these help one to gradually advance in terms of spiritual evolution. One's advancement on the spiritual path can be tested by distinct behavioral patterns that reflect various levels of consciousness, and these too are outlined in the scriptures. Thus, while the basic morphology of Varnashrama exists worldwide, Hindus teach that the system as conveyed in Vedic and post-Vedic texts actually presents a structured methodology for achieving perfection on the path of spirituality.

Therefore, they call it *vaigyanika-varnashrama*, or "scientific" Varnashrama. Indeed, as Bhaktivinoda Thakur, a great nineteenth-century Vaishnava reformer, says: "Truly, all sympathetic and scientific persons will agree that social rules reached their climax at the hands of the *rishis* [sages], who, with scientific understanding, divided the rules of society in a two-fold way: according to *varna* and according to *ashrama*."[12]

To grasp essential Hinduism, then, one must have a working knowledge of certain harmonizing elements of the varying Hindu traditions, such as karma, reincarnation, the nature of the soul, nonviolence, and so on. One would also do well to understand the misconceptions surrounding the terms "Hindu" and "Hinduism." Finally, it is necessary to look at the ancient Varnashrama system and how it impacts on Nitya Dharma, or the eternal function of the soul as a servant of God. Once these basic components of Hindu tradition are understood, it becomes easier to enter into the mysteries of Hinduism proper.

BACK TO SANATANA DHARMA

But before we go too far astray, let us return to Sanatana Dharma as the average Hindu understands it, giving a clearer or more pragmatic definition of what it actually is. First, it should be highlighted that the English world "religion" is a bit different from Sanatana Dharma. Religion conveys the idea of faith, and faith may change. One may have faith in a particular religious path, and then he or she may change this faith to adopt another— a Christian may convert to Judaism, for example, and vice versa.

But Sanatana Dharma refers to that activity or function that cannot be changed. Heat and light, for example, are the *dharma* of fire; without heat and light, fire has no meaning. Similarly, propose the Hindu sages, we must discover the essential part of who we really are, without which we are no longer living beings. We must find those characteristics that constitute our eternal function, and by that search we will find our true *dharma*.

According to most forms of modern Hinduism, the inherent nature of the soul is to serve God. This is our Sanatana Dharma, or our eternal function. India's sacred texts explain that, unfortunately, a transformation often takes place that situates us squarely in the material world. Then, over the course of many lifetimes (for the Hindu view is always set against the backdrop of reincarnation, which will be discussed at length later), we transform further, becoming totally conditioned to material existence. This transformation causes our eternal function to become distorted, and we find ourselves no longer serving God directly. The result is that we lose sight of Sanatana Dharma and become engaged in "unnatural" activity.

Gradually, such activity becomes our common method of engagement, and we forget our original and natural function. Our identity and nature shift into an alien environment, and, in our illusion, this new way of being becomes the only thing that seems real to us.

This distorted nature is necessarily temporary. Still, it gradually takes prominence over our true nature—our real *dharma*—and begins to assert its contrived features in our day-to-day life. The traditional example is water, whose real *dharma* is that of being fluid. When water transforms into ice, its *dharma*, or its original nature, also transforms—its "new" *dharma* becomes solidity, or hardness. This new *dharma* is the distorted nature of water, acting in place of water's true nature.

As time goes on, however, we see that the hardness of water is only temporary. Moreover, when the external forces that made water hard recede into the background, water's true nature manifests yet again, revealing what water truly is.

The truth implied here is that the original spiritual nature of the soul is now dormant, and it is temporarily replaced with a distorted nature—that of identifying with the body and its pains and pleasures. This temporary nature of the soul is called Naimittika Dharma, and the original nature, Sanatana Dharma, is only resumed when the soul is placed in proximity to the spiritual element, either in the form of God himself (through prayer, worship of images, and so on), or in the form of sacred texts, and/or pure devotees of the Lord.

Through such association, the true nature of the soul again becomes established, just as ice once again becomes a pleasing liquid when exposed to the gentle rays of the sun. This is Hindu spirituality, whether one refers to it as Hinduism or by its more correct name of Sanatana Dharma. And it is elaborated upon in the *Vedas* and in supplementary Vedic literature, such as the Epics and the Puranas, which are the subjects of the next few chapters.

CHAPTER 4

What Are the *Vedas*?

"By study of the *Vedas*, the goal is to know only Me; and it is only I who truly know these texts; indeed, I am the creator of its final truth."
—Lord Krishna, the *Bhagavad-Gita* 15.15

The word "Veda" can be traced to the Sanskrit root *vid*, which means "to know," or "knowledge." It is related to the words "wit" and "wisdom" from the German; "idea," (originally *widea*) from the Greek; and "video" from the Latin—one who knows, and sees the truth; hence: video.

In a pragmatic sense, Veda refers to any abiding knowledge. Along these lines, many Indian sages and Vedic scholars refer to all sacred texts as "Vedic," regardless of cultural origin or sectarian affiliation.[1] But these are among the broadest definitions of the term. In a more narrow sense— the one with which most scholars are familiar—Veda refers to the four *samhitas* (holy books) of ancient India. The *Rig Veda* is considered the earliest of the four and it consists of 1,017 hymns, or 1,028, if one includes certain apocryphal verses. It is composed in Sanskrit and is divided into ten books, known as Mandalas.

This long collection of hymns consists of somewhat enigmatic praise of gods and goddesses, divine beings largely identified with aspects of material nature and supernatural powers, such as Varuna, the god of the ocean and the night sky; the heroic Indra, the slayer of demons; Ushas, the goddess of the dawn; Aditi, the goddess of earth and cosmic space; Agni, the god of fire; and there are many others as well. The text tells us that these gods are various manifestations of the same Ultimate Truth, of Brahman, the Supreme Spirit, and yet that they are individuals as well.

Vishnu, who in later tradition is referred to as the "high god" of Hinduism, is also represented here as a solar deity, an assistant to Indra. Though only mentioned in a few verses, Vishnu's presence is not insignificant. The *Rig Veda* refers to his "three cosmic strides"—he takes three steps, and with each he is described as overtaking the earth, the sky, and whatever lies beyond, respectively. In other words, his steps envelop all existence, encompassing the terrestrial, celestial, and atmospheric dimensions of reality. Thus, in a sense, he subsumes the gods and goddesses described above, for they are usually embodiments of these natural phenomena.[2] We will elaborate on this more fully in the section on Vaishnavism.

The *Sama Veda*, or the "Veda of Song," is the second of the four *Vedas*, and here many of the verses of the *Rig* are repeated, though now accompanied by melody and a science of sound. The metrical portion consists mainly of hymns for elaborate sacrifices in which the juice of the Soma plant, a mystical herb known to the ancients, was mixed with other ingredients and offered as a gift to the gods. The most distinguishing characteristic of the *Sama* tradition was the singing, which was comparable to the strophe, antistrophe, and epode of the Greek chorus, though the Greek version was much later, and from a different part of the world.

The *Yajur Veda,* which is the third of the *Vedas*, focuses on liturgy. This is the "Veda of Rituals," or of "Sacrifice" (*yajur* is an alternate form of *yagya*, which literally means "sacrifice"), containing almost 2,000 verses in forty chapters. Many of these verses, too, are repeated from the *Rig Veda,* and they are meant to be used in similar ceremonies for the gods. This text also explains how to construct the altars for new- and full-moon sacrifices and other related ceremonies. The *Yajur Veda* has two divisions called "White" and "Black"—the Black one offering more esoteric explanations of the sacrifices to be performed.

The word *Atharva*, which is the name of the fourth and final of the original *Vedas*, refers to a priest who knows the secret lore of the ancients. This was the Atharvan, the Brahmin priest who lights the sacrificial fire and masters the Vedic chant. The hymns of this Veda were largely composed by two families of fire priests, known as the Bhrigus and the Angirasas, though there were others—all were considered the Atharvans. Thus, this Veda of some 6,000 verses is replete with incantations and invocations from antiquity. It is different than the other three *Vedas* in that it elaborates on material sciences, like Ayurveda (a holistic system of medicine), and also on odd-seeming spells for manipulating material nature. It includes rules for oblations and sacrifices, prayers for averting evil people, and for overcoming diseased conditions. This Veda even has incantations for the destruction of foes, for fulfilling personal desires, and so on—mostly for people's material needs.

It should be clear that opulent sacrifice, to appease the gods and for promotion to higher planets after death, was the religious intent of all four *Vedas*. The ritualistic performance, with its dazzling large altars, priests chanting with prescribed intonation, deep, hollow pits into which the offerings (usually the enigmatic Soma plant, clarified butter, milk, vegetables, and fruits, and often animals) were carefully placed—these were the defining images of ancient India, the food of her people.

The "mouth" was the sacrificial fire, provoking thoughts of mortality and divinity at the same time. It was gleefully fed, and considered an opening to "the other side." The deities of the eight directions were summoned for the intricate ceremonies, and the gods of nature and of natural elements were given their place of honor. Wizened sages, learned priests, extended family members, and, indeed, cosmic forces, were always present, felt if not seen. As the smoke of the holy fire lingered and then floated away, so, too, did one's previous sinful deeds, if any, and believers walked away with a clean slate, ready to start life anew.

The fire was central to the Vedic ritual.[3] The altar and ceremonial arena in which the fire was ignited was usually constructed with bricks, mud, and wood—but most of all with reverence and heartfelt labor. Its building necessitated a sophisticated knowledge of geometry and other mathematical sciences. There were domestic fire sacrifices (*grihya*), held in or near one's home, and more complex ones, held in larger arenas for public consumption (*shrauta*). The domestic ceremonies involved one small fire and a priest, and were usually performed to gain material rewards, such as health, longevity, a qualified spouse, offspring, and wealth. The larger event required several priests and no less than three separate fires—it was a magnificent spectacle—but the rewards were the same.

Interestingly, Vedic rituals often called for animal sacrifices, though these same texts also supported the doctrines of compassion and harmlessness. The *Yajur Veda* (12.32), for example, says: "You should not use your God-given body for killing God's creatures, whether they are human, animal, or whatever." This nonviolent sensibility was often taken to the point of vegetarianism and cow protection, as we will see in an upcoming chapter. The traditional Hindu lawgiver, *Manu* (5.27–56), in fact, disparages humans who eat meat not offered in Vedic rituals, implying that the only exception to vegetarian fare should come from the sacrificial arena. Today, even though later texts clearly state that rituals involving the use of animals are outmoded, there are still blood sacrifices in India, usually associated with the worship of the Goddess. But most practitioners of modern Hindu traditions, and especially Vaishnavas, tend to abjure the use of meat.[4]

The rather mundane spoils of Vedic sacrifices—burnt animal offerings, elevation to higher planets—tell us much about Vedic religion, its limitations, and its goals. To make it clear, Hinduism recognizes three levels of religious endeavor: (1) Karma-kanda, or activity that allows one to live in harmony with nature and the gods; (2) Gyana-kanda, or activity that allows for the above along with the advancement of knowledge; and (3) Upasana-kanda, the essence of worship, which offers adherents the results of Karma-kanda and Gyana-kanda as well as devotion to God.

The *Vedas* proper are said to offer Karma-kanda religion; their appended Upanishads, discussed below, are said to offer Gyana-kanda; while the theistic element cannot be found, at least not fully, in the Vedic scriptures themselves. For this, one must approach "supplementary Vedic texts," discussed in the next few chapters. Only here might one find Upasana-kanda, or the essence of religion.

VEDIC APPENDAGES

In addition to the four *Vedas*, the same body of literature includes many explanatory books as well, known as the Brahmanas and the Aranyakas. The former consists of prose commentaries appended to each of the four *Vedas*; these are primarily liturgical texts concerned with the details of Vedic sacrifice. The latter are known as forest treatises, indicated by the Sanskrit *aranya*, meaning "forest." The original idea was that the *Vedas* were best understood in seclusion, by going off to the forest and immersing oneself in Vedic study. The Aranyaka literature was composed for just such a purpose.

The final portions of these Aranyakas are called the Upanishads. These are 108 separate books, deeply philosophical, which explain the underlying truths of the Vedic hymns. Unlike the actual *Vedas* and their Brahmana and Aranyaka commentaries, these works deal with metaphysics, mystical analyses, and reflective exposition. It is here that one might make sense of the elaborate rituals found in the *Vedas*. The word "Upanishad" is itself telling—it means, "to sit nearby." The basic conception was that to truly understand these texts one must "sit" at the feet of a master—one could imbibe the higher truths of the Upanishads only by submitting to a teacher who has realized the truth.

According to tradition, these works (from the *Vedas* to the Upanishads) and only these works, are considered part of the original Vedic literature. The tradition itself teaches that Vedic knowledge emanated directly from the body of the Lord, or, as the *Bhagavad-Gita* (3.15), a central holy text accepted by all Hindus, puts it, "the *Vedas* are directly manifested from the infallible Personality of Godhead." They were put into written form some 5,000 years ago by Vyasadeva, a sage who is viewed in pan-Hindu consciousness as an incarnation of Vishnu, the Lord of the Universe. There is a contingent of modern scholars, of course, who have an alternate view, with "Vyasa" being a title for a succession of bards who contributed to these texts over the course of millennia. Scholars also suggest a somewhat later date for Vedic texts as a whole.

They trace the date of their compilation to roughly 1500 to 1200 BCE. So, instead of the traditionally accepted 5,000-year-old date, they say the *Vedas* were compiled merely 3,500 years ago, with the last portions of the Vedic corpus, the Upanishads, dating at about 600 BCE. However, the initial instigator of these dates, the German Indologist, Max Muller, revealed his uncertainty: "Whatever may be the date of the Vedic hymns, whether 1500 or 15,000 BC, they have their own unique place and stand by themselves in the literature of the world."[5]

It should also be known that Muller's original thesis was influenced by his belief in Christianity. During his time, many Christians believed that the world was created in 4004 BCE, and using this as a basis, he decided that the *Vedas* could not possibly be as old as most Hindus claimed. Since his time, many other scholars have admitted the motivated and arbitrary nature of his dating system, and themselves posit only tentative dates for Vedic and post-Vedic texts. Both traditionalists and modern academics agree, however, that the Vedic literature has an oral tradition dating back to antiquity.

WHAT DO THE VEDIC TEXTS ACTUALLY MEAN?

In days of old, Brahmin priests handed down Vedic hymns—from teacher to disciple—through a mnemonic technique that enabled them to memorize the sacred texts and to properly pronounce them. These techniques involved distinct accenting procedures and the rigors of a tightly defined poetic method. The end result was a class of priests who knew thousands of traditional hymns and who were able to use these hymns in ritualistic sacrifices of the type described above. However, in due course, the importance of proper pronunciation came to supercede the actual meaning of the *Vedas* themselves:

The Brahminical preoccupation with the phonic over the cognitive dimension of the Vedic words is further illustrated by the fact that there have been so few commentaries dedicated to interpreting the discursive meaning of the *mantras* [hymns]. . . . The preoccupation in the Vedic tradition with sound over meaning, memorization over understanding, and recitation over interpretation has been noted by a number of prominent Indologists . . .[6]

Scholars such as the late A. L. Basham, one of the most renowned academic authorities on Hinduism, were shocked to find that Vedic priests seemed to care little for the meaning behind the words:

The *pandits* [traditional scholars] who transmitted the *Rg-veda* preserved its sound with scrupulous accuracy, but they forgot much of its sense. The standard commentary of Sayana, written in the fourteenth century, shows that much of the original meaning had been forgotten. The earliest gloss of the *Rg-veda*, that of Yaska, generally dated in the sixth century BCE, shows that even then there were doubts about the meanings of many words. Very few traditional *pandits* of older times, though they remembered the *Rg-veda* perfectly, had more than a vague notion of what it meant.[7]

Basham adds, "Most of the Brahmins who had memorized it had only the very vaguest notions of its meaning, because its language is so archaic that it is almost unintelligible to one trained only in classical Sanskrit. It is rather as though modern English speakers had memorized some mediaeval text like the *Vision of Piers the Plowman* without any real training in the grammar and vocabulary of fourteenth-century English."

If the meaning of these archaic texts began to disappear for the priests and sages who actually used them in ancient times, what hope is there to understand their implications today?

The distance in time, space, and cultural environment between the authors of the Veda and modern Indologists, the incompleteness of our sources, the reinterpretation suggested by the Indian traditionalists and the prejudices and limitations of modern scholarship itself have contributed to a deplorable state of affairs. The very plurality of meanings so frequently given in our dictionaries show that a modern language cannot in many cases offer one single equivalent of an ancient Indian term . . .[8]

Thus, the true sounds of the *Vedas* elude us, their meaning disguised by exotic mantras and complicated formulae. Mystical barriers, too, are said to separate man from the confidential knowledge blocked within each verse. The *Rig Veda* (1.164) itself admits that sound is measured in four quarters, and that only the wisest of the Brahmins know them all. Ordinary mortals, say Vedic texts, know only the easiest of the four—we are privy only to one small dimension of sound. That is to say, in the *Vedas* vibrate the tones of transcendence, the inner thoughts of the gods, but only properly trained priests are able to penetrate their mysteries.

THE PRIMEVAL MAN: AN EXAMPLE OF LOST MEANING

The *Rig Veda* contains a hymn known as the *Purusha-sukta* (10.90), which is basically a creation story. It depicts the "Primeval Man" or "Cosmic Person" (*purusha*) as not only God, but also as demigod, the material and efficient cause of the universe, the one who performs the sacrifice, and the one who *is* sacrificed as well. In other words, in this particular hymn, the Cosmic Person embodies several different identities at once. Interestingly, he is both the victim that the gods are herewith sacrificing as well as the divinity to whom the sacrifice is being made—making him the subject and the object of the sacrifice. How can he be both? Was the confusion that naturally bursts forth from this paradox meant to be like a Zen *koan*, a mystical riddle, or is it a product of the *Vedas*' incomprehensibility, the three-quarters of sound to which we, as mortals, have no access? Is it, perhaps, a reminder of the One and the Many?

Among the few things in this hymn that are, indeed, clear, is that the Cosmic Person (whomsoever he might be) took part in a sacrifice, dividing his body into what eventually became the Veda and all of creation. He dismembers himself for the sake of everyone and everything. But is even this part to be taken literally, metaphorically, or as some combination of the two? Does he actually dismember himself, and if so, what does this mean? Vedic exegesis does not explore this, and, consequently, the answers are not forthcoming. The main section of the hymn, brief though it is, appears below:

(1) Thousand-headed is the Cosmic Person, thousand-eyed, thousand-footed. He pervaded the earth on all sides, and stood beyond it by ten fingers.

(2) This is the nature of the Cosmic Person—he is all that had been and all that is to be. He is the lord of eternal life, and grows by virtue of [ritual] food.

(3) Such is his greatness, and yet he is more than even this. One-quarter of him is separated into all beings; three-quarters of him remain in heaven.

(4) Three-quarters of his essence went upward, while one-quarter remained here. From this [smaller portion] he spread in all directions, manifesting as that which eats and as that which does not eat.

(5) From him, the shining one (*viraja*) was born; and from the shining one, he himself also comes. When he was born, he extended beyond the earth, behind it as well as in front of it.

(6) When the gods performed a sacrifice by offering the Cosmic Person himself, spring was used as clarified butter, summer the firewood, autumn the libation.

(7) It was the Cosmic Person, born in the beginning, sacrificed upon the sacred grass. By using him, the gods engaged in sacrifice, as did the perfected beings and the sages of old.

(8) From that sacrifice, once completed, the offered butter was brought together. It created the beasts of the air, and those of the forests and the villages.

(9) From that sacrifice, completely offered, the mantras [*Rig Veda*] and the songs [*Sama Veda*] were born. The associated meters were born from it as well. The sacrificial formulae [*Yajur Veda*] were born from it too.

(10) From it came the horses as well as all that have sharp teeth in both jaws. The cows were born from it, too, as were goats and sheep.

(11) When they divided the Cosmic Person, in how many portions did they do so? By what words did they refer to his mouth? his arms? his thighs? his feet?

(12) His mouth was the Brahmin [priest], his arms were the Rajanaya [Kshatriya, warrior], his thighs the Vaishya [merchant]; his feet the Shudra [worker].

(13) The moon was born from his mind; from his eye, the sun; from his mouth, both Indra and Agni; from his breath, Vayu was born.

(14) From his navel arose the air; from his head the heaven came into being; from his feet, the earth; the [four] directions sprang from his ear. Thus, they built the worlds.

(15) Seven were his altar sticks, twenty-one pieces of kindling, and then the gods, performing the sacrifice, bound the Cosmic Person himself.

(16) The gods sacrificed with the sacrifice to the sacrifice. These were the first holy rites. These powers reached the firmament, where the ancients, perfected beings are, and where the gods are as well.[9]

What does this hymn actually mean? Verse Four states that the Cosmic Person "spread out in all directions," and this could be a reference to Vishnu, the all-pervading one. Indeed, though the hymn itself is unclear as to who the Cosmic Person actually is, the *Yajur Veda* (3.5.2) and the *Taittariya Samhita* (1.7.8) identify Vishnu with "the sacrifice" and thus in-directly with the Cosmic Person. The *Shatapatha Brahmana* (I.2, 5, 1–10) retells the Purusha sacrifice in its own way, and here the Purusha is specif-ically identified as Vishnu. These are all Vedic sources.

The *Bhagavata Purana* and the *Mahabharata*, of course, boldly proclaim Vishnu as the ultimate *purusha* described in the *Purusha-sukta* prayer. And according to prominent Hinduism scholar W. Norman Brown, the above verse is definitely a reference to Vishnu, who, through his three steps, is all-pervading (i.e., "he spreads in all directions.").[10] All is not so clear, though: The *Svetashvatara Upanishad* identifies the Cosmic Person with Shiva, bringing practitioners back to the idea of the One and the Many.

The original hymn talks about "immolation," which is somewhat incomprehensible, especially in relation to the amorphous entity described in the text. Scholars suggest that it is "impossible to establish, on the evidence of the texts of the Vedic tradition, whether this immolation of man was real or imaginary. The *Satapatha Brahmana* and the *Taittariya Samhita* [both Vedic texts] allude more to symbolic offerings [than to literal ones]."[11] This would indicate that the *Purusha-sukta* is perhaps somewhat symbolic, referring to a higher reality.

What we know is this: The Cosmic Person portrayed in this hymn is self-immolated, and his creative act becomes a prototype for all Vedic rituals to come. The *Purusha-sukta* hymn teaches that true creativity demands self-sacrifice. This is a consistent theme in Vedic and post-Vedic texts— the same idea, we may remember, was expressed in Brahma's creation of the universe. Whereas the *purusha* took it to the point of self-immolation, Brahma is told only to perform severe austerities; and by this he achieved his goal of creation. In both cases, sacrifice plays a significant part. Such austerities, as performed by Brahma—and the many later Vedic rituals that embody such austerities—are, in a sense, mere repetitions of the *Purusha-sukta* sacrifice, complete with victim, altar, and even the consequence of a world that functions better once the sacrifice is made.

The macrocosm becomes the microcosm, for the Vedic sacrifice has meaning only in terms of our own interaction with the gods, with nature. It is as if the Veda is telling us that God made a sacrifice at the beginning of creation, and that, in similar fashion, we should do so as well. In emulation of our Creator, we should give all that we have in the service of his creation. One who makes such an ultimate sacrifice is considered a perfected human being.

Christians reading about the Cosmic Person (the Son of Man?), who sacrificed himself for the sake of the world, are likely to think of Jesus. In fact, there have been numerous speculations about this hymn in relation to the Christian Messiah, usually drawing on parallels between the *Purusha-sukta* and the text of *Colossians* (1.15–20), though, of course, the story of Jesus comes much later.[12]

Other aspects of theological interest are as follows: The central player in this hymn is clearly a *Person* from whom everything emanates, not an amorphous void. This will be important in Hinduism's theistic traditions. He divides himself into numerous parts and functions that serve various purposes. This is also adopted by later tradition. We see in this story the earliest reference to India's social system, when the divine being divided himself into priests, warriors, merchants, and workers. But for the purpose of understanding how the Veda is now nearly incomprehensible, we need simply look at this hymn and wonder aloud: Who, ultimately, *is* the Cosmic Person? Is it God, or is it Man? Is it a hybrid deity? Does it matter? What do all of the offerings represent? Is there meaning to his sacrifice and, other than the explanations offered here, is there any way to ascertain what the story is really all about?

In general, the Vedic literature is like a puzzle, with numerous hymns, oblations, gods, and sacrifices. But how does it all fit together? And just who, again, is the ultimate enjoyer of Vedic sacrifice? Vedic seers were fond of such questions. Though the Brahmana, Aranyaka, and Upanishadic literature (and, of course, the Epics and the Puranas) point to Lord Vishnu, as cited above, the earlier sages obviously wanted practitioners to look more closely at fundamental questions. The *Rig Veda* (10.121) itself poses the main one as follows: "Who is the ultimate god to whom we should offer oblations?"

Hinduism eventually immortalized this question by referring to that supreme God as "Ka" (cognate with the Latin *quis*), which means, simply, "Who." This question gradually became a declarative statement: "Indeed, 'Who' is the name of God, and it is to Him that we should offer our oblations." The mystery of "Who" is comparable to the Tetragrammaton— the ineffable name of God—in Jewish mystical traditions. It points to the idea that, when it comes to God, there are no simple answers—his name and identity should be a matter of deep contemplation.

GETTING TO THE BOTTOM OF VEDIC REVELATION

If the words found in the ancient Vedic texts are not altogether lost, which they aren't, it can at least be said that they are, in the ultimate analysis, inscrutable. Why is this so, and what might one do about it? And how is one to understand modern Hinduism, which still claims connection to the original *Vedas*, if one has little true access to the scriptures at its base?

The resolution to this dilemma might be found in the Upanishads, the last stratum of the original *Vedas*. Here we learn that the inner meaning of the Vedic texts was actually more important than the sacrifices at the center of their hymns—the complex rituals of the Veda were meant to bring practitioners to certain realizations about ultimate truth, not to busy them with mere externals. To begin with, if one studies the *Vedas* closely, one sees a tension between its apparent meaning, on the face of it, and something else, something obviously buried just beneath the surface.

For example, when the *Vedas* depict its many gods in terms of nature and atmospheric elements, they are clearly trying to show the connection between the material world, which is the world that we see around us, and the higher domain of the spirit. The text wants people to understand the divine nature of things. This is not to say that the gods do not have substance, or that they do not exist in some higher level of reality, but just that they have particular purpose as presented in Vedic texts. Such a fluid view of the gods is also suggested by certain Vedic hymns that asked practitioners to internalize the gods, to see them in relation to their own bodies.

In other words, those who practiced Vedic religion were expected to see each living being as a manifestation of the larger universe—again, to see the macrocosm in the microcosm. The gods descended, so to speak, to become perceptible in the functions of the human body: Speech was seen as the god known as Agni ("fire"), as was the fire of digestion; the eye was Aditi ("sun"); the vital force, or the soul, was Vayu ("air"); the mind was Chandra ("moon"); and so on. From here, it is easy to see how Hindus developed the conception that everyone is in some sense divine, though there were sages who warned that this idea should not be taken too far.

In India, to this day, there are many who will categorically and unabashedly express their own Godhood, claiming identity with the many Vedic gods and, indeed, with the Supreme Himself. However, Vaishnava sages and the many scriptures identified as the "Fifth Veda," discussed more fully in the next chapter and in the one after that, make clear that the divinity of ordinary souls has its limitations, and that while there is a certain oneness between the soul and God, there is a concomitant separateness as well.

The mystery of how gods and all other living entities are simultaneously one and different is resolved in the Vedic literature, but one must study it in the proper way. Indeed, the Upanishads point to a certain esoteric knowledge found in the heart of the Vedic adept, and there—by studying under a bona fide guru—one learns that there is more to the Vedic deities and their related sacrifices than meets the eye. Indeed, it might be pertinent in this context to remember that the word *upanishad* implies receiving knowledge by sitting at the feet of a master, as mentioned above, and only by so doing can one learn the esoteric truths of the Vedic literature.

"There are two sciences that must be known . . . a higher and a lower," states the *Mundaka Upanishad* (1.1.4–5), "Of these, the lower consists of the *Rig-veda, Yajur-veda, Sama-veda, Atharva-veda*, phonetics, rituals, grammar, etymology, meter, and astronomy. The higher is that by which the imperishable Brahman can be attained." And the *Svetashvatara Upanishad* scorns: "Of what use is the *Rig Veda* to one who does not know the spirit from which the *Rig Veda* comes?"[13] As has often been pointed out:

Vedic sacrifices, the Upanishads assert, were good only for temporal gain, for wealth, power, and progeny, or at best to make for man a sojourn to "the world of the Fathers," from where he will have to return again and again to earth through transmigration, to live and suffer endlessly. For deliverance from *samsara* [the cycle of birth and death], other means are needed.[14]

In other words, as stated previously, the *Vedas* were meant for a specific purpose—to propitiate the gods and to live in harmony with nature, to make this life successful and to attain happiness in the hereafter. But Vedic religion acknowledged a higher goal as well—the Upasana-kanda, mentioned earlier. Though this higher goal was only vaguely stated in the earliest Vedic texts, later tradition evoked its truth with the loudest of trumpets.

Krishna himself, viewed by Vaishnavas as God Almighty, is clear on this subject: "People of meager intelligence are enamored by the flowery words of the *Vedas*, which recommend fruitive activities disguised as religion. These actions may award one heavenly delights, such as good birth, power, and promotion to higher planets. Practitioners who seek such goals miss the true point of religion. But because they are attached to material opulence and sense enjoyment, their intelligence becomes deluded, and they think there is no higher goal." (*Bhagavad-Gita* 2.42–44)

Krishna further tells Arjuna, the great Prince to whom he speaks the *Bhagavad-Gita*, that the *Vedas* deal with higher material conceptions, but material conceptions nonetheless. He advises Arjuna to bid adieu to such mundane ideals and to pursue spirituality in earnest. (2.45) He tells him that when he is actually freed from illusion, he will no longer be attracted to the embellished language of the Vedic texts, and that he will move beyond them. (2.53) And then Krishna delivers the clincher. He tells Arjuna that those involved in the *Vedas* only worship the Supreme indirectly. By doing so, they may become purified and take birth on higher planets. (9.20) But then, after exhausting their accumulated merits, they fall back down to lesser realms, and they take birth once again. (9.21) Only his devotees, who have transcended the four original *Vedas*, become free from material contamination and conditioning. Only by worshipping him, God, can one relinquish all connection to the mundane world and achieve perfection. (9.22)

If the *Vedas* cannot offer its votaries this supreme destination, how does one get there? What does the Vedic literature say for those who want to move beyond the ritualistic sacrifices and enter the esoteric world of truly spiritual religion?

"THE FIFTH VEDA"

All of the Vedic literature discussed thus far is known as "Revelation" (or "that which is heard directly from God"). This literature is considered sacred and beyond reproach. Subsequent literature—and by this we primarily mean the two Epics (the *Mahabharata* and the *Ramayana*) as well as the eighteen Puranas, or sacred histories—might also be considered sacred. Indeed, it might even be deemed "Vedic," but only in a secondary sense. It is sometimes called "the Fifth Veda." Such literature does not enjoy the special status accorded to the original *Vedas*—a status that cannot be overstated. So much are the original *Vedas* revered that most Hindus today refer to their religion as Vaidika Dharma, or "the Vedic Law," even as they also call it Sanatana Dharma,

Brian K. Smith, a prominent scholar of Hindu studies, has eloquently expressed the Hindu dedication to the *Vedas*. "The great paradox of Hinduism," he writes, "... is that although the religion is inextricably tied to the legitimizing authority of the Veda, in post-Vedic times the subject matter of the Veda was and is largely unknown by those who define themselves in relation to it. Its contents (almost entirely concerning the meaning and performance of sacrificial rituals that Hindus do not perform) are at best reworked (being, for example, reconstituted into ritual formulas or mantras for use in Hindu ceremonies), and [in] many cases appear to be totally irrelevant for Hindu doctrine and practice."[15]

The Fifth Veda, considerably more relevant, is called "Tradition" (or "that which is remembered") as opposed to Vedic "Revelation," even if, in common practice, these former works are in some ways more important than the scriptures to which they take a back seat. It is with this literature, in fact, that one finds access to the higher religion described earlier by Krishna.

There are indications throughout the Vedic literature that these secondary works, while not Vedic in its most narrow sense, should also be included within the vast gamut of traditional Vedic knowledge. The *Chandogya Upanisad* (7.1.4), for example, describes the Puranas and the Epics as "the Fifth Veda." And the *Brihad-aranyaka Upanisad* (2.4.10) informs us that, "The *Rig Veda, Yajur Veda, Sama Veda, Atharva Veda*, and Epics, like the *Mahabharata* and the Puranas, all emanate from the Absolute Truth.

Just as one's breath comes easily, these arise from the Supreme Brahman without any effort on His part."

The great Vaishnava teacher, Madhvacharya, too, affirms that much of the traditional literature can be considered as part of the Veda, for in his *Vedanta-Sutra* (2.1.6) commentary, he writes: "The *Rig Veda, Yajur Veda, Sama Veda, Atharva Veda, Mahabharata* (which includes the *Bhagavad-Gita*), Pancharatra, and the original *Ramayana* are all considered Vedic literature . . . The Vaishnava supplements, the Puranas, are also Vedic literature." Thus, functionally, these later writings can also be considered Vedic.

In other words, tradition holds that any literature in pursuance of the Vedic version is just as important as the *Vedas* themselves, at least in principle if not in categorical distinction. In addition to the above, then, the massive writings of the self-realized teachers in disciplic succession, such as Ramanuja, Madhva, Rupa Goswami, and many others—these all bring out the essence of earlier Vedic works and should consequently be counted as part of the Vedic corpus.

It is this "bringing out the essence" that may distinguish the later literature as, in a sense, more important than the original Veda. Take the *Bhagavata Purana*, also known as the *Srimad Bhagavatam*, for example. According to tradition, this profound text was originally revealed to Brahma, the first created being, at the dawn of creation. Brahma conveyed the essence of this knowledge to Narada, and Narada passed it on to Vyasa, who, as previously mentioned, is said to have taken the eternal wisdom of the Veda and divided it into four distinct sections. What was not mentioned, however, is that, after this, he summarized the vast gamut of Vedic knowledge into a huge volume of terse codes known as *Vedanta-Sutra*.

As the story goes, Vyasa became despondent. He felt that in his entire compilation and summarization of the Vedic literature, he had neglected to truly focus on the Absolute Truth. His suspicion was confirmed by his spiritual master, Narada, who told him that, in his writings, he had indeed overlooked the central point of ultimate reality. Narada further told Vyasa that he would be satisfied only if he corrected this indiscretion by directly describing the name, fame, form, and pastimes of Krishna, the Supreme Lord. Heeding the advice of his teacher, Vyasa compiled the *Bhagavata Purana*, the "mature fruit of the Vedic tree of knowledge," the "king of books," the "spotless Purana," as a natural commentary on the *Vedanta-Sutra*. This story will be revisited in our later section on the Puranas.

In this way, for most practitioners, the "later" or "non-Vedic" texts are more "Vedic" than the *Vedas* themselves. Jiva Goswami (ca, sixteenth century), who is a distinguished luminary among Vaishnava philosophers, emphasizes this point in his *Tattva-Sandarbha* (*Anuccheda* 17, text 4).

Here he quotes the earlier *Skanda Purana* (*Prabhasa-Khanda* 2.93): "O Brahmins, one who is fully conversant with the four *Vedas*, the six Vedangas, and the Upanishads, but who has not also studied the Epics or the Puranas, is not actually learned in Vedic knowledge."

Why? Because, according to Jiva Goswami, the Epics and the Puranas are more excellent than the *Vedas*. "The superiority of the Puranas and the Epics is described in the following passage from the *Narada Purana*," says Jiva, "where Lord Shiva, the demigod of destruction, is quoted as saying, 'O beautiful Parvati, I consider that the Puranas and the Epics are superior to the *Vedas*, for whatever truths are present in the *Vedas*—and quite a bit more—are also explained in these ancient works.' Of this there is no doubt." (*Anuccheda* 16, text 11) Clearly, the Vaishnava tradition considers all supplementary Vedic literature indispensable when studying the *Vedas*.

Such ideas are now appreciated by modern scholars as well, who, for many decades, had drawn a hard line between "Revelation" and "Tradition."

According to the above definitions, the term Veda refers strictly speaking only to *sruti* [Revelation] texts and not to *smriti* [Tradition] texts. However, [Indic scholar] Sheldon Pollock has recently brought to light an essential mechanism whereby the domain of the Veda was extended to include not only *sruti* but also *smrti*. He locates this mechanism in the definition of the terms *sruti* and *smrti* themselves, which he argues have been incorrectly construed as representing a dichotomy between "revelation" and "tradition."

He maintains that, according to the etymology . . . *sruti* refers to the extant Vedic texts that can be "heard" in recitation, whereas *smrti* is an open-ended category that encompasses any teachings or practices pertaining to *dharma* that have been "remembered" from lost Vedic texts. Understood in this way, Veda becomes a limitlessly encompassing symbol that includes not only *sruti* but also *smrti*. The meaning of the term Veda is extended beyond the circumscribed boundaries of the *sruti* texts—Samhitas, Brahmanas, Aranyakas, and Upanisads—and through a process of "vedacization" comes to include within its purview not only the Itihasas [Epics] and Puranas but potentially all *sastric* [scriptural] teachings—as enshrined in practices as well as texts—that are promulgated by *brahmanical* [priestly] authorities.[16]

In other words, all the traditional literature of India, and a good deal more, can be considered "Vedic," that is, *shruti*, if it is authorized by priests who know the purpose of Vedic texts. Once authorized, if this literature is "heard" it will serve the same function as the original Veda.

The matter is far from settled, and scholars and practitioners alike tend to define these various texts as belonging to distinct groups, according to traditional categories. Nonetheless, there is much to be said for the secondary literature (*smriti*) accomplishing in this age what the primary texts (*shruti*) did in days of old. This "Fifth Veda" literature is clearly in pursuance of the Vedic version, and so the seers of the tradition, from ancient times to the present, endorse these texts as nondifferent from the Veda, both in sanctity and efficacy.

However one views this, whether one studies *shruti* or *smriti*, Revelation or Tradition, one is looking at the most comprehensive scriptural tradition known to man: the Vedic literature contains information on everything from medicine and farming to a detailed explanation of time sequences on upper and lower planets; from techniques of *yoga* and meditation to household hints and recipes for tasty vegetarian dishes; from detailed explanations of governmental organization to masterful directions on constructing and decorating a temple or residential building. The verses in each of the thousands of Vedic texts conform to strict rules of poetry and meter. The *Vedas* contain drama, history, and complex philosophy, as well as simple lessons of etiquette. Military protocol, use of musical instruments, biographies of great saints and sages of the past—these are but a few of the subjects one will find in the *Vedas*.

CHAPTER 5
Epic Hinduism

"[The Indian Epics are] a mine of information about the science, customs, religion, and arts of India at various stages of its history. . . . [They are] a vast anthology of human knowledge."
—Alain Danielou (1907–1994), Indian historian

The Vedic texts emphasize fire sacrifices, and the Epics arise from their ashes. The connection is more than poetic. Just as Vedic religion focused on the sacrificial arena, with complicated fire rituals and Brahmin priests who were specially trained to perform them, the more soldierly era of the Epics promoted a "sacrifice of battle"—war—as the preferred means of attaining the Supreme. The goal was the same—to preserve cosmic order, *dharma*, by engaging in an all-consuming sacrifice for higher purposes, in pursuit of the spirit.

The Epic battles were reenactments of the wars waged between good and evil as found in Vedic texts, where light was pitted against dark, and the gods fought with demons. And these were not just any gods and demons. Exactly the same personalities who manifest on the pages of the *Vedas* reappear in new incarnations, as the Pandava princes, for example, who were all semidivine beings. But the Epics bring us into a time when Brahminical rituals were obscured by kingly ones, and chivalry seemed more important than fire sacrifices. Not that Brahminical culture is lacking in the Epics, but only that it takes a back seat to the martial world of the Kshatriyas, the warrior class of ancient India.

All of this, of course, is only to make the essential truths of the *Vedas* more accessible, more approachable for the masses. Vyasa, the compiler of the *Vedas* and the author of the *Mahabharata*, specifically chose a martial premise for his latter work. This is because he was writing for the people of Kali-yuga, our current age of quarrel and hypocrisy. This is an age of conflict, and, for this reason, conflict is what people relate to. Therefore, the story of the *Mahabharata* battle, fresh in people's memory at the time, was just suitable for Vyasa's purposes—he would compose a book based on recent historical events that was appropriate for the age.

And the events had all the elements of a good story: love, hatred, jealousy, intrigue, chivalry, moral instruction, and lots of action. He could thus convey the truths of the *Vedas* in the context of an exciting narrative, one that would appeal to his Kali-yuga audience. The *Ramayana* served a similar purpose, though it depicted events that occurred much earlier, and it was the legendary bard Valmiki who wrote it, not Vyasa.

Both the *Mahabharata* and the *Ramayana*—the great Epics of India, essential to Hinduism as we know it today—focus on the supreme deity Vishnu, specifically in terms of his two most beloved manifestations, Krishna and Rama. Such a clearly identified divinity could not be found in Vedic texts, and for this reason certain scholars claim that this theistic side of Hinduism was something new, arising with the Epics themselves. According to the tradition, however, these same essential truths were hidden in the archaic language of the *Vedas*, only to be revealed by studying the texts under a bona fide guru.

Embedded in the stories at the core of these Epic texts is a wealth of philosophy and religion, as well as guidelines for a leading a life of virtue and integrity. Both the *Mahabharata* and the *Ramayana* have thus proven extremely valuable for countless people through the centuries. And they continue to have meaning for millions worldwide. Moreover, familiarity with these Epics is essential in understanding the Hindu mindset. Most of the underpinnings of the modern Hindu's cultural orientation and philosophical conviction come from these two massive works. Therefore, this chapter will summarize, explain, and contextualize them, if in summary form, for those who might have never poured through their pages. It should be understood that these are among the lengthiest works in world literature, and so abbreviation and omission will be necessary in our retelling of them.

To begin with the *Ramayana*, which is the older of the two, we find here a text that has the distinct honor of being called the first poem within the storehouse of Sanskrit literature. Rama walked the earth, it is said, in the world age known as Treta-yuga—not the Treta-yuga of recent memory, thousands of years ago, but a prior one, millions of years before that.

In terms of length, the *Ramayana* is composed of some 24,000 couplets (48,000 lines) eclipsing the well-known Western epics, such as the *Iliad* and the *Odyssey*, which have only 15,693 lines and 12,000 lines respectively. The *Mahabharata*, of course, is well over 100,000 lines.

The *Ramayana* has been compared to the famous Greek Epics in terms of style, and since these works share certain underlying themes, the *Ramayana*, which is the oldest of these texts, is sometimes said to be the original upon which the *Odyssey*, in particular, was based. Rama, for example, defeats the ten-headed villain Ravana and rescues his devoted wife Sita in the same way that Menelaus destroys Troy and brings back Helen.[1] The commentarial tradition of both Greek tragedy and Sanskrit Epic often seeks to resolve problems in similar ways, too.

For example, just as the pure-hearted Sita, according to tradition, could not have really been captured, or even touched, by a demon such as Ravana, so, too, did the poet Stesichorus say that Helen never actually went to Troy with Paris—the Helen in Troy was a substitute apparition and the real Helen faithfully waited for her beloved Menelaus in Egypt. Similarly, the Rama stories tell us of a substitute Sita—a "shadow" or an "illusory" Sita—who was kidnapped by Ravana, while the "real" Sita existed in an unmanifest state, just waiting to be reunited with Rama.[2] Because of such similarities, scholars are currently researching the influence of ancient Indian epics on western culture.

Despite its value as ancient literature, the *Ramayana*'s strongest feature is its sheer beauty—beauty in terms of its sophisticated Sanskrit poetry, and in the provocative discourse that emanates from the mouth of each major character. It is beautiful in terms of its exotic settings in the forest, and in terms of its magnificent cities, depicted in graphic detail—in terms of profoundly philosophical dialogue, and in terms of the morals and ethics it instills in its readers; in terms of its sense of *dharma* and of the importance of doing one's duty, and in terms of the emotions it evokes; and, perhaps most of all, in terms of the characters one meets during a thorough journey through its pages.

Chief among these, of course, is Rama himself. Tall, strong and righteous, he is the embodiment of virtue, a true hero who is not afraid to show his more human side, to love, to feel pain in separation when the woman so close to his heart is taken away from him. He is God in human form. Sita, the woman in question, is not without virtuous qualities herself; she is the very emblem of chastity and all that is good and true. She is strong-willed, intelligent, and the single most important person in the entire story.

Then there are Rama's younger brothers, chief amongst whom is Lakshman. Always at Rama's side, Lakshman is dearer to Rama than life itself—he shares all of Rama's noble qualities, as do Bharata and Shatrughna, his other two brothers. Hanuman, too, is among the most memorable of the *Ramayana*'s characters, and his devotion for Rama is so overwhelming that *bhakti* cults have arisen with this dedicated monkey-god as their central object of worship.

But to worship anyone other than Rama is to miss the point of the *Ramayana*. Indeed, even Hanuman would shun those who worship him (Hanuman) saying, "I, too, am merely a devotee of Ramachandra." Hanuman himself chants Rama's name—a name meaning "the highest pleasure," evoking thoughts of the Supreme Being and how the most intense bliss comes from worshipping Him.

Again, Rama's story was initially retold by a forest-dweller named Valmiki, who, prior to his life as a sage-poet, was a notorious criminal. One day, the great saint Narada had come upon his hermitage and asked him to chant the name of the Lord. But Valmiki replied that he would not. "I am a murderer and a thief," he said, "and so I have nothing to do with the pious acts of religious practitioners." Narada, however, was cunning, and so he asked Valmiki if he would instead meditate on himself as a murderer. He could do so, Narada told him, by merely repeating the word *mara*, which means "death."

Valmiki agreed to do this, and immediately proceeded to embrace *mara* as his own personal mantra. By rapid repetition—"*mara, mara, mara*"—he found that the word became inverted, and that he was in effect saying "Rama, Rama, Rama." Thus, by the power of reciting the name of God, his heart became purified. As a result, he compiled the *Ramayana*, the most in-depth treatment of Rama lore in the massive corpus of Vaishnava literature.

Elaborate though it is, the tale of Rama has been interpreted and retold in various ways, and this is seen in numerous regional variants in local dialects. For our purposes, the essence of the story can be summarized as follows. Millions of years ago, the Supreme Lord appeared on earth as a human prince named Ramachandra. Why does God incarnate as a human? The story begins when a group of demigods approaches Lord Brahma, their leader, with concerns about a demon-king, Ravana, who is plundering the Earth. Because of the demon's intense austerities, Brahma had given him a boon (and Brahma's boons always hold true) saying that he "could never be defeated in battle, not by god nor by any heavenly creature." Accordingly, Ravana had become nearly invincible.

However, Brahma's blessing did not mention humans, leaving open the possibility that a highly qualified human, someone more powerful than any heavenly being or demigod (if such a thing were possible) could perchance conquer him. Of course, Ravana reasoned that this could never be, and that his boon had rendered him undefeatable, for how could a mere human ever supercede a higher being? Still, the concerned demigods began to meditate on just how they could use this loophole in Brahma's blessing to put an end to Ravana's reign of terror. At that moment, Lord Vishnu descended, and He assured them that He Himself would incarnate as a human being named Ramachandra, and by so doing He would destroy the evil Ravana.

By incarnating as a human, Rama not only enabled himself to defeat the demon-king but also set an ideal example for human behavior. He shows that the true hero is not some idealized symbol of perfection, but rather a loving, feeling, individual with high moral character—one that also has "imperfections," making him truly whole. As *Ramayana* scholar Ranchor Prime says of Rama:

Rama is God incarnate, the seventh incarnation of Vishnu. He chose to become human, and for the duration of his human life to forget his divine identity, or so it seemed. He suffered physical hardships, and, when he lost his beloved Sita, a broken heart. On one level, Rama's journey is an allegory for the journey every soul must make. In becoming human Rama shared in our human suffering and enacted the drama of our own lives—each of us endures our own banishment, our own loss, faces our own disillusions, and hopes eventually to learn acceptance of our lot and to find ultimate redemption. Thus to hear or to witness Rama's struggles is to relive our own lives, but in a divine context. Each episode in the story is multi-layered, working through individual karma, or destiny, and the divine lila, or play, of Rama. In the same way, India's present-day Vedic sages point to life itself as being the working out, for each of us, of our own personal web of karma, desires and free will in accordance or in conflict with the will of God.[3]

Though Valmiki often describes Rama as the perfect human, with parents, friends, and so on, Rama's divinity is never far from Valmiki's mind. He mentions Rama's divine birth (1.17.6) early on and consistently shows his identification with Vishnu. But the story is more complex than this.

THE JOURNEY OF RAMA: A SUMMARY[4]

When Lord Rama appears on earth as a man, writes Valmiki, he does so as the son of King Dasharath and Queen Kaushalya, in the line of Ikshvaku, the first ruler of the earth. He is born in the dynasty of the sun, from the most auspicious lineage of the ruling class. As a child, he is the darling of his parents, and he is greatly loved by all of Ayodhya, the capital of what was once a single world kingdom. Dasharath has two other primary Queens, Sumitra, and Kaikeyi, who play a consequential role in Rama's story, as we shall see.

Rama, Valmiki tells us, has all the admirable qualities of a great leader, and has had them since his earliest youth. He possesses exceptional physical strength, beauty, wisdom, fame, and wealth; and yet he is uniquely humble and renounced—so renounced that he is able to easily give up his cherished kingdom and live as a simple forest dweller, a story to which we will soon return. Lakshman is his younger brother, and the two are inseparable. Though born of a different mother, Sumitra—one of the three main wives of King Dasharath—Lakshman is like a reflection of Rama's own self, equal to him in the qualities described above.

Rama's bodily hue is like fresh green grass, and his bearing is deep and natural, like the forest in which he spends a good portion of his earthly sojourn. Lakshman, for his part, is golden-hued. Thus, while appearing as men, their distinct hues, and superhuman feats, are a constant reminder that they are not ordinary. Lakshman is a formidable warrior, like Rama himself. Together, the two brothers appear on Earth to vanquish the nearly invincible warlord King Ravana and his legions of Rakshasa (man-eating) warriors.

The story of Rama's exploits actually begins when he is still a boy of only 16 years. Though not yet formally trained, his reputation as a superior archer precedes him. Hearing of his virtuosity as a marksman, a then famous yogi, Vishvamitra, approaches King Dasharath, asking if his highly qualified boy might travel with him on an important military mission: A band of powerful Rakshasas are attacking the hermitages of saintly persons, interrupting the performance of religious sacrifices. Only the pure and powerful Rama would be able to help, for despite the fact that he is still a youth and green as a warrior (pardon the pun), he is the only person who can set things right. This Vishvamitra knows for certain.

Dasharath is naturally hesitant. He doesn't want his son to be part of a dangerous mission. Nonetheless, after Vishvamitra conveys the severity of the situation, Dasharath agrees to let Rama go—he too is convinced that only Rama can bring the powerful Rakshasas to their knees. And so, possessing little more than a bow and arrow (though far from an ordinary bow and arrow) the divine teenager courageously follows Vishvamitra into the forest. He is accompanied by Lakshman, who is always at his side. The divine brothers believe in the goodness of the sages and want only to battle on the side of justice. Once in the forest, Vishvamitra trains the already capable boys in the art of celestial spells and in the use of miraculous weapons. They excel in their training.

Rama's bow is a gift from the demigod Indra, and, with his arsenal of deadly arrows, enhanced by the power of mantra (mystical incantations with otherworldly potencies), he has the might of a thousand men. Once released, his arrows will not be swayed from their mark, as faithful to his purpose as Hanuman will be when soon they meet. Rama is the divine archer par excellence. Let this be understood by jumping ahead: in the final battle against Ravana, Rama uses an arrow that is the equivalent of a nuclear weapon, the Brahmashtra, whose immense heat is said to frighten the denizens of the uppermost planets in the material universe. "Among weapon wielders," Lord Krishna says in the *Bhagavad-Gita*, "I am Rama." Vaishnava texts assert that God, by definition, is the greatest in all fields. Thus, he is also the greatest warrior, and this is clear from a thorough reading of the *Ramayana*.

To return to our story, Rama's adventure with Vishvamitra proves successful. When brought before the first of these Rakshasas, however, Rama refuses to act, for the demon happens to be a woman—Rama's chivalrous spirit will not allow him to slay a member of the fairer sex. Realizing Rama's hesitancy and seeing that the demoness is relentless in her ravaging of forest hermitages, Lakshman boldly slays her with a single arrow. After this, the dynamic brothers defeat many forest demons—among them is one named Maricha. Rama shoots a "wind arrow" at this particular demon, which carries him several thousand miles and finally lands him in the ocean. Though this act does not kill him, he is sufficiently humiliated, and he goes into hiding. He will emerge later as one of Rama's consequential foes.

Vishvamitra, pleased with young Rama, adopts the role of his guru, narrating many wonderful Vedic stories for him and elaborating upon the valuable lessons they teach. He also tells Rama about a superexcellent bow kept by King Janaka, the father of Sita. As the story goes, Janaka once came to Lord Shiva's aid, and for this he was presented with what is known among demigods as the greatest of all weapons—Shiva's magical bow.

Since Janaka is a warrior-king, the bow seems like an appropriate gift. But it is so large and mighty that no one could even bend it in order to attach its string. Surely, thought Janaka, the bow could only be handled by one who is strong and righteous, like the demigod who offered it to him as a prize. Consequently, he saw it as a sacred object, worthy of veneration. Regularly, he bowed down before it, offering flowers and prayers, praying to one day meet a divine personality who could string it and wield its extraordinary power. In fact, King Janaka offered his daughter Sita in marriage to any man who could properly use the bow.

Sita, of course, was desired by many. But even the most noble and powerful of men failed to win her hand—her dowry was supreme valor and the goodness of God Himself. She was the topmost jewel of Janaka's kingdom, and he treasured her as his most valued object of love.

Aware of Shiva's bow, Vishvamitra brings Rama and Lakshman to Janaka's palace—just to show them this magnificent artifact of the demigods. As the three men enter, a large assembly is gathered to see the weapon. Rama immediately lifts it up in his hands (a feat in itself) and asks Janaka, "What would you have me do with it? Shall I string it for you?"

"Yes," replies Janaka, incredulously.

At once, Rama easily bends the bow and strings it for all to see. So tightly does he affix the string that the bow cracks in two pieces, making a thunderous sound that forces all present to fall unconscious, except for Vishvamitra, Rama, and Lakshman. At that same moment, the gods shower flowers from the sky upon Lord Rama, and there is cheering in the heavens. Like Thor, who is the only living being capable of wielding his hammer, or Arthur, the only man able to pull his magical sword from its stone, Rama's ability to string Shiva's bow has mythical dimensions. We find a parallel, again, in Homer's *Odyssey*, where King Odysseus, returning from the Trojan wars, shows his strength and valor by lifting a miraculous bow as well.

The love of Sita and Rama—the Supreme Love—will soon manifest on Earth, and truth and happiness will reach out to all. As the assembled participants come to their senses, awakening from their slumber, King Janaka proclaims that no one else would be suitable for his daughter: She should be married to the mighty Ramachandra. At this point, Sita herself walks up to Rama and garlands him with fresh flowers, her symbolic acceptance of him as her husband. On the same day that they wed, Lakshman marries Sita's sister, Urmila, and Rama's other two brothers, Bharata and Shutrughna, marry her two cousins.

According to Hindu tradition, Sita is not an ordinary being. It is understood that, as Lord Rama is Vishnu, the Supreme Lord Himself, so Sita is actually Lakshmi, the Goddess of Fortune, the Lord's female counterpart in the spiritual world. Incarnating as the daughter of Janaka, she is sometimes called Janaki. Actually, King Janaka is not her biological father; he found Sita when she was a baby. King Janaka had been plowing a field and he noticed her in a clump of earth.

The *Ramayana* tells us that Sita was actually born directly from the Earth for the specific purpose of putting an end to Ravana's sovereignty, for the demon was degrading the planet with his polluting deeds. It was as if the Earth itself were fighting back, ridding itself of its most decadent impurities. As Rama incarnates as the greatest warrior and expounder of religion and morality, so Sita is the greatest beauty among women, disempowering the evil Ravana with her natural charm.

For some years, Rama and Sita live happily in Ayodhya, as do Lakshman and their other brothers. Reaching retirement age, King Dasharath decides to confer the kingdom on his eldest son, Rama, who is loved by all his subjects. As the news of Rama's imminent coronation spreads, the people of Ayodhya turn to joyous preparation in anticipation of the ceremony.

But fate has other plans: Queen Kaikeyi, Dasharath's wife and mother of the noble Bharata, had raised an orphan girl named Manthara, who now functions as her maidservant. It is Manthara who plants the evil seed that grows into the *Ramayana*'s tree of misfortune. When she hears the news of Rama's coronation, she is overcome with a feeling of rage. Charging into Queen Kaikeyi's room with a heart full of jealousy, she insists that the coronation of Rama is the worst of all possible actions, a slap in the Queen's face.

Manthara shrewdly outlines how Dasharath had recently sent Bharata away to visit his uncle. He did this, she says, to crown Rama as the King without anyone getting in the way. And, after the coronation, Rama would surely see that Bharata was killed, for he would never tolerate his younger brother seizing the throne. With such misbegotten logic, Manthara predicts all the grief that lay ahead for Kaikeyi, and in this way she implants envy and wrath in the Queen's heart.

Queen Kaikeyi is now convinced that Rama must be eliminated, for the sake of her own son. As Dasharath's wife, she is naturally dear to him and, because of a promise he had once made to her, she will be able to achieve her ends. Dasharath, it seems, had once fallen on a battlefield, badly wounded. At that time, Queen Kaikeyi had lovingly nursed him back to health. Seeing her affection, he promised her two boons—anything she wanted. But she had said she would ask for them at a later time. Now influenced by Manthara, the time had come.

Kaikeyi awaits Dasharath's arrival in her private chamber. When he enters and finds her there, her venom infects the coronation day like a snake biting an innocent child. "According to your promise," she says, "I desire the following two boons—first, let Ramachandra be banished to the forest for 14 years, and, second, let my son Bharata be crowned as king in his stead." Unable to bear the implications of her words, Dasharath falls unconscious.

As he revives, he exclaims: "Oh, how sad! How painful! I suffer intensely by hearing what you say, and yet I am oath-bound to accommodate you!

My current suffering must be a result of misdeeds committed in a previous birth!"

One might wonder why Dasharath does not simply reject the Queen's request. The answer: He is not able to. Warrior-kings in the days of the *Ramayana* stood by their word as if life itself depended upon it. He had made a promise, and as a Kshatriya (a noble administrator) he must abide by it. His religion was integrity. Because he had vowed to offer Kaikeyi any two boons when she saved his life, he must now grant her wishes, whatever they might be.

Dasharath summons Rama to his court on the very day of the latter's coronation. As Rama arrives in his chariot to answer his father's call, he appears to be shining with an effulgence of glory, just as the moon emerges from behind dark blue clouds. Lakshman stands by his side, cooling him with a special fan. Elephants and horses follow his chariot; and music, glorification, and cheers permeate the atmosphere. As he passes the windows of stately kings and beautiful women, they throw colorful flowers that rain down all around him. Some onlookers praise Kaushalya, the mother of Rama, and others say that Sita is a gem amongst women, and that she must have practiced great penances in former births to have such a husband as this king-to-be.

But when he finally reaches his father, Rama finds that the old King appears inconsolable, seated on a sofa with Queen Kaikeyi. Anxiously, the Queen personally tells Rama of his unfortunate destiny. Dasharath wants to deny it, but he cannot. Rama looks to his father, hoping that there might be some misunderstanding. If only there were.

Magnanimous and detached, Rama assesses the situation. He responds with maturity. "Very well," he replies. "I shall leave everything I hold dear and proceed to the Dandaka Forest for 14 years. Moreover, I shall go with an unwavering mind. My father has made a vow, and, as his eldest son, it is my duty to help him keep it." Rama proceeds to inform all those faithfully preparing for his coronation that he is changing his plans—that he is leaving at once to embrace the forest life of a mendicant. He fears, however, telling his mother—as he thinks she might die at the thought of being separated from him. At first, it is true, she was not able to accommodate the news; she simply will not hear it. As he continues to tell her the story, she insists on accompanying him to the forest. He tells her that she cannot go, and that her place is at her husband's side, to help him through this difficult time. She reluctantly agrees.

The dreaded news soon spreads. People throughout the kingdom, men and women alike, begin to cry bitterly. Unfortunately, they could not join Rama in exile, though they wanted to. Indeed, thousands proposed that they accompany him, but Kaikeyi would not allow it: If everyone went into the forest, it would defeat the purpose of the exile. So much did the people of Ayodhya love Rama that only one chant was heard in every home: "No! Dasharath should have never agreed to this!" Rama assures them, however, that there was no other way.

Lakshman argues that Rama must not submit; he suspects, in fact, that the whole story of promised boons is just an excuse to crown Bharata as the King—a plan instigated by Queen Kaikeyi. Accordingly, Lakshman is prepared to engage in warfare with his own family to reinstate Lord Rama. But Rama replies that the best course of action is to obey his father's orders.

The hardest part, Rama thought, would be telling Sita of his fate—that he would now have to leave her behind while fulfilling his vows in the forest. Not surprisingly, however, Sita, like so many others in the kingdom, was unattached to her lavish lifestyle: "If you repair to the forest," said Sita, "I shall go in front of you and make smooth the path by crushing the thorns under my feet. I shall not leave your company, nor will you be able to dissuade me. I shall feel no sorrow in passing 14 years with you in the difficult conditions of the forest."

But Ramachandra, aware of the hardships that accompany life outside Ayodhya, tells her about Dandaka's many prowling animals, crocodiles, and sharks in muddy rivers; how it is sometimes difficult to even get good drinking water—no bed, hunger appeased merely by fruits that fall to the ground, matted locks, bark for clothes, inclement weather, reptiles roaming free, pythons, scorpions, and mosquitoes. Rama says it is too dangerous, but Sita insists that, as a devoted wife, she must stay with him no matter what, *especially* when times are difficult. This, Rama remembers, is the same advice he had recently given his own mother, telling her that she must stay with King Dasharath. Sita, he now knows, is correct. She tells him that only by staying at his side will she find life's hardships heavenly; but if they are separated, even pleasures would seem painful. It is clear that she cannot be swayed. Rama realizes that he too feels as Sita says, and that he could not bear her separation for the same reasons.

Lakshman, who is present when Rama speaks with Sita, falls at his brother's feet, the thought of being separated unbearable for him, too. Rama tries to dissuade both Sita and Lakshman one last time, but to no avail. Rama even tries asking Lakshman to stay in the kingdom as a special service to him, to carefully watch the activities of the court. But Lakshman will not hear it. He replies that Bharata can maintain the kingdom; for his part, he must be given permission to come along to the forest. He would go before Sita and Rama as their guide and procure their food; the divine couple could enjoy forest life while he does all menial tasks. The divine archer is pleased, and asks Sita and Lakshman to prepare for departure at once.

Shortly after the resplendent threesome begin their journey, Dasharath dies of grief. Young Bharata is called back to Ayodhya to assume his position as heir. Bharata arrives before his mother, Queen Kaikeyi, and learns first that his father is dead, and then that his brother is exiled on the wish of his mother. Bharata is shaken with remorse, and calls Kaikeyi, his own mother, a murderess. To Bharata, there is no question of assuming the throne without Rama and Lakshman. In other words, as Rama's brother, he is righteous and virtuous and wants no part in the plan.

After performing the funeral rites for his father, Bharata sets out without delay, with an army behind him. He intends to bring Rama back and to place himself in exile in his elder brother's place. He feels that only by doing this could he hope to remove the stain of his mother's depraved deed.

After some time, Bharata and his army arrive in the vicinity of Rama's forest hermitage. One of his soldiers climbs a tree and sees smoke issuing from a cottage. Bharata and a few others then move forward on foot, and they soon behold Rama's dwelling place. Upon entering, they find Rama's formidable bow plated with gold. The quiver is full of sharp arrows flaming like the sun. There are swords in golden sheaths, and gloves laden with gold. In the midst of it all, Bharata sees lotus-eyed Rama, seated on black deerskin, with matted locks on his head.

The brothers embrace. Bharata tells him of Dasharath's death and pleads for Rama to return and take his kingdom. Rama is visibly shaken by his father's unexpected demise. But he replies philosophically, sharing with his younger brother his realizations of the body's temporary nature, and of the eternality of the soul. Rama asks him to note how people are generally pleased to see the seasons change, though this very change means that one's duration of life is coming to an end. He tells Bharata that when a person takes a simple walk, death is with him, waiting to claim his pound of flesh. Knowing this, Rama says, intelligent people subdue grief. They go on with their lives, knowing that their loved ones had accomplished all that they were meant to, and that they have now moved on according to God's plan. Rama tells Bharata to return to Ayodhya and to take charge, because this was the wish of their father. He concludes, "Let me pursue my duties here. There is much that is yet to be done."

Bharata insists that he is only a boy, and that Rama must guide his rule. But Rama is firm in keeping his father's pledge. Seeing the determination of his brother, Bharata agrees to do as he asks, but takes back with him a pair of Rama's sandals. Upon returning, he places the sandals on an altar and daily bows before them, letting Rama rule by his symbolic presence.

Bharata waits in ascetic observance for the expiration of the 14-year exile.

THE BATTLE WITH RAVANA

As Rama and Sita, along with Lakshman, become accustomed to life in the forest, they come across a plethora of personalities, both good and evil, and find themselves in the midst of many interesting adventures. In such exotic places as the Dandaka Forest, the Panchavati Glade, and the Krauncha Jungle, the famous trio spends their entire exile in either pleasure or peril. One of the perilous encounters has larger meaning in terms of their destiny: the battle with Ravana begins through an incident involving the demon's sister, Shurpanakha.

Shurpanakha is a hideous witch-like monster who happens upon the cottage of Rama, and, upon seeing the handsome prince, is struck with lust. She begins to malign Sita, eventually threatening to kill her. By this, she hopes to show her determination for Rama and to win him over. Instead, she merely wins the wrath of Lakshman, who cuts off her ears and her nose. Running back to the camp of Ravana, she begs for revenge. Ravana, however, is more interested in his sister's description of the beautiful Sita than in her own disfigurement. Still, here is the seed from where the War of Wars starts.

Ravana is a power-mad villain who has nearly everything he wants. Through yogic discipline and the performance of austere penances, he has gained great power, including the specific boons of Lord Brahma, as already noted. He reigns in a vast island kingdom called Lanka, and possesses nearly infinite amounts of material opulence. He and his Rakshasa allies enjoy roaming through the forest, killing and eating the flesh of solitary hermits engaged in spiritual practices. In Ravana's early life, he was known for violating beautiful women wherever he found them, mercilessly raping them without a second thought. But he had long ago been cursed by a powerful yogi that if ever again he attempted to enjoy a woman by physical force, or, in other words, against her will, his head would literally split into pieces.

Because of this, he now merely brings stray women back to his large harem of exploited slaves, hoping to one day overcome the curse.

Thinking that no one would dare challenge him in any way, he is incensed when he hears of Shurpanakha's torment. Immediately, he dispatches 14,000 Rakshasa warriors to slay Rama and Lakshman, the perpetrators of this serious crime against his sister. En route, Nature tries to warn Ravana's troops that they are treading on divine territory: they experience a downpour of evil omens. The handsome horses pulling their chariots suddenly stumble; huge vultures attack their royal flags; birds, beasts, and jackals howl in eerie tones; and blood showers from the skies as dark clouds show their ghostly forms.

Despite these omens, the Rakshasas thirst for blood. Rama is informed of their imminent arrival but is peaceful and calm. While doom had presaged the Rakshasas by dark clouds and raining blood, the arrows of Rama are flaming with brilliant colors, and his gold-plated bow seems to vibrate with unlimited energy. He is surrounded by happy people, including his lovely wife and the noble Lakshman, as well as by the many friends he has met during his sojourn in the forest.

In a battle that stands above all others in terms of ferocity, Rama destroys the 14,000 warriors single-handedly and on foot (though many of his opponents are on chariots). His arrows, resembling inflamed trees, cover the entire sky. The Rakshasas had never encountered such a warrior, and it becomes clear to them that their evil master is doomed. One of them survives the conflict, and runs back to Ravana with the news that Ramachandra had virtually devoured them with his might. Wherever they fled, he reported, they found Rama standing before them.

Ravana is outraged and tells the lone survivor that even Vishnu had better run and hide—the entire universe will now feel his wrath. But the Rakshasa pleads with Ravana, for he had just seen what Rama is capable of. He tells him to beware of Rama's valor, and humbly submits that Rama can bring down the stars and planets and raise the submerged Earth by his arrows, and that he can destroy all creatures and create them anew. Ramachandra, he tells Ravana, cannot be defeated.

The surviving Rakshasa also mentions that he had seen the beautiful Sita. He says that no woman is her equal in beauty and character. She is in the bloom of youth, he tells Ravana, and the most graceful being that he has ever seen. She is Rama's chief prize, the Rakshasa concluded, and if Ravana could somehow distract Rama long enough to take her away, he would then be able to vanquish him, for surely Rama could not bear separation from his radiant wife. Ravana likes his servant's idea, and proceeds accordingly.

To implement the abduction of Sita, Ravana calls on his warlord, Maricha. This particular warlord had a score to settle with Rama: he is the same Rakshasa who was carried for miles by Rama's wind arrow, when, years earlier, the divine 16-year-old had assisted Vishvamitra. The plan was now as follows: Maricha will take the form of a golden deer (Rakshasas can change their form at will) and run playfully in front of Sita. Since the divine princess loves deer, she will want the deer for her own.

At that time, Rama and Lakshman could be induced to try and capture it and, while they are tending to the deer, Sita would be carried off by Ravana.

The plan is carried out immediately. Maricha appears in the forest as a wonderful deer with silver spots and the glow of jewels. As it gallops before Sita, she becomes totally entranced, begging Rama to go off and capture it for her. Rama, of course, suspects that this is Rakshasa magic, and even that it might be Maricha himself. He decides to go after the deer as Sita asks, but, if he is correct about its identity, to kill it. Meanwhile, Rama firmly orders Lakshman to stay behind with Sita, to protect her in his absence.

He pursues the deer, chasing it through the forest. After a while, it becomes elusive, even invisible. He is now certain that this is a Rakshasa in the form of a beautiful deer and resolves to destroy it. With bow and arrow in hand, he releases a deadly shaft that enters Maricha's heart like a flaming snake. The Rakshasa's illusory guise fades away, and he appears in his original hideous form, bathed in blood and about to die.

With his last breath, Maricha cries out in imitation of Rama's voice, "Sita! Lakshman! Help me!" When Rama hears this, his heart drops; he realizes what is going on. Sure enough, Sita, from her cottage, hears the call of the demon and is certain that it is her beloved husband. She believes her dear one is in danger. She tells Lakshman to go at once and help him. Lakshman, however, dismisses the idea that any calamity could befall someone as great as Rama. Besides, he knows his duty is to remain, to protect Sita. But the princess, in great anxiety over Rama, insists that Lakshman go, and he complies.

Before leaving, however, he draws a magical circle (composed of Rama's name) around their hut—this would protect her if she would only stay within its boundaries. As Lakshman runs off, Ravana adopts the guise of an ascetic, approaching the hermitage to beg alms from Sita. As a monk, he cannot enter a woman's home without another male present, and so he beckons Sita to please come outside. Luring her beyond the circle drawn by Lakshman, he resumes his fearful form as Ravana and carries her off by force.

On a large, ornate chariot (one whose size and power surpasses that of a modern aircraft) Ravana, the demon with ten heads and twenty arms, flies into the night, holding on to Sita as a spider engulfs a fly. The man-bird Jatayu, a pious devotee, sworn to protect the princess, flies to her rescue. But Ravana, with his ruthless sword, cuts off the giant bird's wings, leaving him to die. After this, the evil Ravana brings Sita to Lanka, his magnificent home, full of sensuality and pleasures innumerable. Sita, it is said, is protected from gross sexual violation by her power of chastity. And by Ravana's curse.

Thus unable to satisfy his lust, Ravana hopes to win Sita's heart. He gives her a tour of his opulent city, showing her swans and ponds, and his harem of beautiful women—indicating that his sex mates live comfortably, with magnificent resources. He shows her how thousands of mighty Rakshasas wait to serve him, and how they hang on to his every word. He assures her that all of this can be hers. He speaks harshly of Rama, calling him a weak outcaste who would never be able to penetrate the fortress of Lanka.

Ravana invites Sita to rule over his opulent land, telling her that he would become her slave. Though emotionally distraught, she manages to convey a truth he did not want to hear: for his reckless and outrageous behavior he would be destroyed by Rama and Lakshman in due course. In the face of his intimidating ferocity, she further tells him, "How can the consort of a swan, one who sports with her mate amidst lotuses, favor a water crow, who is straying amongst weeds and bushes? This body is now useless to me. You may chain it or destroy it. I shall not care for it anymore, nor will I ever bear the stigma of an unchaste woman. I am the devoted wife of Rama, and you will never be able to touch me."

Thus provoked, Ravana threatens her: "Woman, if after one year you do not change your mind, I will cut you into pieces and have my cooks serve you for dinner." She looks away in disgust, while Ravana has several servants show her to her chambers.

In Sita's absence, Rama is plunged into deep grief. He walks through the forest moaning like a madman, asking the bowers and trees if they have seen his love. He fears that his wife has been eaten by Rakshasas. He and Lakshman search everywhere. Their beautiful sylvan retreat no longer has color or life. Rama questions the sun: "Where has my darling gone?" He asks the wind if she is dead or alive, or if he has seen her in his travels.

Lakshman attempts to assuage Rama's despair by various arguments, but he is ignored. Finally, the brothers find signs of Sita—pieces of clothing torn while resisting Ravana, and ornaments that had fallen off as she was carried away in his magical chariot. They also found the bloodied, dying body of Jatayu, who, it should be remembered, had made a valiant attempt to stop Ravana as he made off with Sita. With his last words, Jatayu informs Rama that Ravana, King of the Rakshasas, had taken Sita, and that he had seen this with his own eyes. He also tells them that they could obtain help in finding Ravana's kingdom by joining forces with Sugriva, the King of the Vanaras (who are a race of monkeys with humanlike characteristics).

The Vanaras, Jatayu further informs them, live in Pampa, a nearby region dominated by rivers and lakes. As Jatayu dies in Rama's arms, they mourn the passing away of this dedicated soul. After performing the death rituals for the King of Birds, the two brothers immediately set out in search of Sugriva.

As they approach Pampa, Sugriva's surveillance notices them coming in at a distance. He is fearful, for he and the Vanaras are hiding from Vali, his brother, and Rama and Lakshman look like formidable foes, perhaps coming to battle on Vali's behalf. The monkeys range from peak to peak, and quickly confer with their leader on what to do about the two mighty young men in their midst. The chief counselor to the King, named Hanuman, assures Sugriva that Vali and his men could not be in Pampa— for a complex series of reasons, they would be denied access to the general area. Why, then, should Sugriva fear these two godlike warriors?

Certain that their fears are illfounded, Hanuman approaches Rama and Lakshman on behalf of the king. With humility and eloquent words, he invites them to meet the monkey chieftain. Rama is at once taken with Hanuman, and feels great affection for him. In due course, they arrange a meeting with Sugriva. The two brothers sit with him and work out a pact of honorable friendship. The monkey chief tells Rama how he came to be confined to Pampa, and how he now fears for his life. Originally, he was the great king of Kishkindha, but his forceful brother Vali overthrew his king-dom and stole his wife. Hearing this, Rama feels that Sugriva is a kindred spirit, one who has suffered through similar hardships. Accordingly, he agrees to help him seek vengeance on Vali. In exchange, the monkey chief promises to aid Rama in rescuing Sita by employing his vast, worldwide army of Vanaras.

Sugriva, however, expresses doubt that Rama can actually subdue his evil brother. After all, Vali is among the most powerful warriors on the planet, and he has highly trained armies at his disposal. Sugriva thus asks Rama to prove his merit as an archer. To assure Sugriva of his powers, Rama shoots one arrow that forcefully pierces through seven palm trees, continuing on through a huge boulder and even through the innermost region of the Earth—and then, in one sudden moment, it returns to Rama's quiver, like a boomerang! Little more needed to be said. Rama and Sugriva set out to find Vali, and, when they do, Sugriva and his brother battle. At the height of this momentous duel, Rama shoots an arrow into Vali's back, ambushing him in an unexpected way. This, Rama believes, is the only way to rid the world of this evil culprit. Finally, Vali is no more, and the kingdom of Kishkindha is returned to Sugriva.

The great monkey chief begins to mobilize his forces, keeping his word to Lord Ramachandra. He sends thousands of Vanaras in search of Lanka, where Sita is imprisoned. But after months of futile searching, the armies begin to lose hope. Some return, and some disappear. Finally, Hanuman, along with his friend Jambavan, a leader among Vanara bears, acquires information that the kingdom of Lanka is an island as far south as one can possibly go—far across the Indian Ocean.

This is a great distance, but Hanuman resolves to go there on Rama's behalf; he will do reconnaissance work to see if Sita is indeed being kept captive in Lanka. He is the son of the wind god, Vayu, and is thus able to fly. He can also change shape at will, like the Rakshasas.

Both powers prove useful, as we will see. Passage across the ocean is arduous, even for one who can move like the wind. Hanuman's monkey brothers gather to see him off. As he jumps, he speaks these words to them: "I shall reach Lanka with the velocity of the wind, just like an arrow shot by Rama, and if I do not find Sita there, I shall at the same speed go to the region of the gods. And if I do not meet with success even there, then I shall uproot Lanka itself and bring Ravana here in bondage." With this, he springs up and disappears into the distance. Like Garuda, the Eagle of Vishnu, Hanuman flies over the ocean, raising great waves by his speed; the aquatics look up in reverence as Hanuman passes by.

Arriving in the beautiful city of Lanka, which is ornate and sensually alluring, he reduces himself to the size of a cat, so that he can walk through the city undetected. "If I lose my life," thought Hanuman, while walking the densely populated streets amid the nightlife of Lanka, "great obstacles will arise in the fulfillment of my master's mission. I must be successful." He decides that walking across roofs would be safer, and so, in his cat-like form, he does so.

A short distance away, he sees the palace of Ravana, surrounded by a glittering, massive wall. Gently treading past noisy drinking parties, big mansions and colorful parks, Hanuman finally comes closer to Ravana's home. The palace looks like a city unto itself. It exists in the heart of Lanka, hovering in the sky like a colossal spaceship. Defying gravity, its beauty surpasses nearly anything Hanuman has ever seen. The main gate is guarded by armed Rakshasas. It was now past midnight, and the monkey warrior observes a virtual sea of beautiful women, all waiting for a few moments with the lord of Lanka.

Though surrounded by such a radiant harem, Hanuman is single-minded in his determination to find Sita. His mission is difficult, however, for he has never seen her face-to-face. Just then, in the center of Ravana's central chamber, on a crystal dais, he sees an elaborately decorated bedstead. Upon the bed lay Lord Ravana himself. He is obviously intoxicated, spread out across his silken sheets with saliva dripping from his lips. His body is smeared with red sandal and his eyes half closed. He is the paradigm of a sensualist in royal power.

But where is Sita?

Thankfully, she is not in Ravana's bedroom. Hanuman continues his search. Finally, the noble man-monkey finds her in the heart of the dense Ashoka forest, appended to Ravana's estate, seated under a tree. It is clearly Sita, for she fits Rama's description to a tee. Her beauty is unmistakable, even amongst the finest women of Ravana's court. Wracked with grief, but still radiant, tears flow down her face. She is described as "Lakshmi without the Lotus"—seated on the ground like an ascetic, crying for the absence of Rama. Her days are filled with the taunting of hideous misshapen Rakshasa monsters, who dance in a ring around her, telling her rumors of Rama's weakness and death. At night, she has regular nightmares of separation from her beloved.

While Hanuman watches from afar, Ravana comes to visit her: "For 10 months you have evaded me, denying my advances. You have 2 months left," says the demon-king. "After that I will turn you into a pie and consume you without a second thought." Hanuman cannot believe his ears. Sita, for her part, is brave while Ravana speaks. But as soon as he leaves, she breaks down and starts crying again.

Hanuman's first step is to communicate with her, to assure her of Rama's safety. He has to gradually gain her confidence, to prove that he is not another Rakshasa. He also wants to convey that Rama and the Vanaras will soon be on their way to rescue her. He begins to speak while concealed within the branches of a tree. "I am sent by Rama." Sita is delighted to hear his sweet voice. She has some reservations, but Hanuman is clearly no demon. He recites for her the history of King Dasharath and Ramachandra. Hearing these words, her heart opens.

With great reverence, Hanuman approaches and gives her a ring that belongs to Rama, a ring with which she is familiar. Rama had specifically given the ring to Hanuman for this purpose. Now, seeing Rama's ornament, she is certain. In blissful exchange, she pulls a jewel that adorns her raven black hair: "Give this to Rama," she says. "And tell him to come quickly, or I will surely die."

Before going back with Sita's message, Hanuman decides to gauge the enemy's power. He creates a disturbance in such a way that he will be captured, hoping that Ravana's soldiers will bring him before the demon-king himself. In a miraculous display of prowess, Hanuman breaks down all the trees in the Ashoka forest except the one under which Sita sits. Frightened Rakshasas rush out to see him expanding himself to gigantic size, ranging the sky, determined to fight. They attack, and Hanuman single-handedly destroys thousands of Rakshasa warriors, including many of Ravana's top military personalities. Finally, he allows himself to be captured and is indeed brought before Ravana.

They briefly speak. Ravana has him bound from head to toe. He seeks to further humiliate the great monkey warrior by setting his tail on fire. Hanuman, however, uses this humiliation to create havoc throughout the city: He grows to an even greater size, flying from house to house and setting them on fire with his tail. As he does so, he declares again and again: "None of you will survive when you make an enemy of Ramachandra!" Then he flies back across the ocean, and lands in the midst of the Vanaras. He tells them the good news, and they rejoice.

Without delay, the Vanaras mobilize under Sugriva, building a miraculous bridge of stones across the ocean. Literally millions, with military equipment, march across that bridge and into Lanka. Soon Vanaras engulf the city, battling Rakshasas and searching for Sita. In hand-to-hand combat, great heroes from both sides fight to the death day after day, with thousands of fatalities. Finally, one by one, great Rakshasa chieftains, such as Kumbhakarna, Narantaka, and Indrajit, Ravana's son, fall before the unlimited powers of heroes like Hanuman, Lakshman, Sugriva, and Ramachandra. Ravana's own brother, Vibhishana, had already joined Rama before their invasion of Lanka. He could not tolerate his brother's evil ways and resolved to battle for all that was proper and just. Now he fights heroically on the side of righteousness, much to Ravana's dismay.

During the course of one of the blood-drenched battles against the Rakshasa army, Lakshman is rendered unconscious by Ravana's magical spear, and Rama responds emotionally: "If I lose the kingdom—this I can bear. But I cannot bear the loss of Lakshman! I cannot go on if Lakshman dies!" Horrified by the sight of Lakshman lying on the battlefield, Hanuman determines that only certain herbs growing in the Himalayas can cure him. Thus, in the midst of battle, like the wind itself, the noble monkey flies to the famous mountainous region in search of the herbs. He has only moments to accomplish his task. And the herbs are nowhere to be found. Realizing that he must act quickly, he lifts up the entire mountain area, and, in flight, carries it back to the site of the battle, saving Lakshman just in time.

As the battle comes to a close, Rama slays Ravana with a Brahmashtra released from his bow. Valmiki tells the origin of this weapon: it was handed down by Lord Brahma, and passed from sage to sage. Thus, the same Brahma who gave Ravana his boon also supplied the weapon that caused his demise. The Brahmashtra is sophisticated, utilizing immense power and emitting smoke like doomsday fire. When shot by Ramachandra it splits Ravana's heart in two, depriving him of life. Their leader dead and the vast majority of Rakshasas defeated, the war is won.

Immediately after the victory, Rama gives control of Lanka to Vibhishana, Ravana's pious brother. And Rama returns to Ayodhya. All seems well and everything right—until Sita is brought before him. The divine couple had been separated for some time, and under the most vexing of circumstances. Everyone expected this to be a joyful reunion. But before the thousands of people gathered, Rama announces that he cannot take Sita back because she has lived with Ravana in his house.

In the West, this might seem like extreme behavior, but in the East such principles are observed with the strictest tenacity. Rama, it must be remembered, is Vishnu as a human, wanting to set the example of what a perfect human king must do. According to the mores and social customs of his day, he rejects Sita, even though he has faith that she is perfectly chaste during her stay with the demon-king Ravana. A king's wife must be beyond suspicion, and because, in this case, she might be doubted by some of his constituents, he decides to put her to an ultimate test.

Hearing Lord Rama make such an accusation before the multitude, Sita speaks in defense of her chastity. But the test is already determined: Sita must walk into a pure sacrificial fire. If she survives, she, too, is pure, having never been touched by Ravana. As the flames leap up to a great height, she approaches the pyre and bows down, praying to the fire god, Agni, for protection. She then courageously walks into the blaze. At once, Lord Brahma himself, foremost of all the demigods, descends from the sky and humbly asks Rama, "Why have you done this to Sita?" As the question lingers in the air, Agni appears from the fire itself, carrying Sita, who was completely unharmed due to her purity. All present could thus be satisfied that Sita had retained her sanctity even though she had spent long months with Ravana.

Years later, however, when Sita and Rama are ruling over a joyous Ayodhya, Rama chooses to banish his wife yet again. His subjects resume their talk against her, of the time she had spent with Ravana. Rama decides to use their doubt to relish "love in separation"—he asks her to undergo another fire ordeal, knowing that his request goes too far. Incensed, Sita retreats back to the earth from whence she came. Gradually, the people of Ayodhya come to venerate her and do not doubt her again. But she has already returned to the earth. Rama never takes another wife, and keeps a golden statue of her always at his side. No Hollywood ending here. However, years later, after the duration of his earthly existence (when he returns to the Ayodhya in the spiritual kingdom), he is reunited with her in full glory.

THE MAHABHARATA[5]

The *Mahabharata* is the world's longest poem, and it is said that all existential truths are contained in its pages. The word *maha* means "great" and Bharata refers to an important patriarchal king of ancient India and his descendents, the people who shaped the destiny not only of Bharata's land but also, in some ways, of the rest of the world.

As far as the text itself, Vyasa, its legendary author, claims that he composed the epic in two distinct ways: one elaborate and one more concise. Actually, tradition asserts that he composed a version consisting of 6 million stanzas, of which 3 million are known to those of the heavenly sphere, 1 1/2 million to the forefathers, 1 million and 400 thousand to the angels, and only 100 thousand to the human world. This last figure is justified by the extant version available today, although the critical edition is naturally somewhat shorter.

In its voluminous pages, the *Mahabharata* deals with just about everything, with countless digressions and subplots. But its central narration focuses on the furious quarrel between the Pandavas and the Kauravas, two groups of related cousins who were monarchs some 5,000 years ago. The quarrel escalates into a full-scale civil war—involving gods and men, Brahmins and royalty, and even Krishna, the Supreme Being. According to scholars who have pored through the massive archeological, astronomical, and literary evidence, the war depicted in the *Mahabharata* took place around 3102 BCE. Its main battlefield was in the modern state of Haryana, India, but it had numerous outposts in other areas as well. While some scholars question whether the war actually took place, most acknowledge that it did, if in some abbreviated form. Traditionalists and countless practitioners, of course, attest to its veracity, claiming that its supernatural dimensions are a natural part of God's earthly pastimes.

The story begins with King Dhritarashtra, the father of the Kauravas, who is congenitally blind. Though normally, as the elder brother of the royal family, the throne should have been his, his blindness precludes him from his rightful position. Instead, in accordance with Vedic law, it is given to his younger brother Pandu, father of the Pandavas (Yudhishthira, Arjuna, Bhima, Nakula, and Sahadeva—all born in miraculous ways). Dhritarashtra resents Pandu for gaining the throne and never forgives him.

After Pandu's early death, Dhritarashtra receives at his court Pandu's five sons, the Pandavas, and raises them with his own boys, the Kauravas, the eldest of whom was Duryodhana. Yudhishthira, as Pandu's eldest son, was now the rightful heir to the throne. This infuriated Dhritarashtra: it was difficult enough to relinquish the throne to Pandu. But now, as if to add insult to injury, Dhritarashtra's son, Duryodhana, would have to abdicate the throne to Yudhishthira and the Pandavas. All the boys are trained as warriors (Kshatriya) according to ancient standards of military excellence and chivalry that are today all but lost.

Even when the Kauravas and the Pandavas were still children, rivalry developed between them. True, it began with Duryodhana's envy of the Pandavas and their rightful place as leaders of the kingdom. But it eventually went further. The Kauravas became devious; the Pandavas, virtuous.

As they grow older, the Kauravas use their military might for selfish reasons, while the Pandavas are spiritual-minded political leaders, and thus greatly loved. Still, Dhritarashtra naturally favors his own boys, even though it is becoming more and more clear that the Pandavas are better suited to rule the kingdom; and he successfully plots to enthrone his eldest son, Duryodhana.

The sons of Pandu are eventually given territory of their own, where they erect a great city. However, Duryodhana is jealous, and he develops a plan to take the Pandavas' land by dubious means: He rigs a game of dice in which the eldest son of Pandu, Yudhishthira, is sure to lose. The plot succeeds, Yudhishthira loses his kingdom, and the Pandavas are sent into exile for 13 years.

Just as Rama, many centuries earlier, had embodied the essence of Kshatriya spirit, the Pandavas, too, were perfect Kshatriyas. And because of their Kshatriya character, they honor their defeat, even though they are cheated, and enter the forest, believing they will regain their kingdom upon their return. But after the 13 years (with forest adventures that, again, resemble those in the *Ramayana*), Duryodhana denies them the kingdom that is rightfully theirs. They then ask for five small villages, because, as Kshatriyas, it is their inclination and duty to rule. Their livelihood depends on it as well.

Nonetheless, Duryodhana is cruel. "If they want as much land as fits under a pin," he sneers, "they will have to fight for it." Thus, by his humiliating response and his refusal to grant them even small villages, he instigates what was to become a devastating battle. Though there is, at this time, still hope that the war can be averted, the Kauravas cement their fate by attempting to disrobe Draupadi, wife of the Pandavas, in a public arena. Krishna comes to her rescue by supplying unlimited cloth to cover her body. As much as Duhshasana, a leading Kaurava tyrant, pulls at her garment, to that same degree newly appearing cloth mystically manifests.

But it is too late for the Kauravas—no amount of cloth could cover the Pandavas' eyes to this humiliation, to this call for certain war.

By this time, the Kauravas become infamous as exploitative kings. In contrast to the five sons of Pandu, whom, as stated previously, the *Mahabharata* describes as incarnations of godly personalities (*Adi-parvan* 109.3), Duryodhana is seen as the Kali Purusha—the demon Kali in human form (*Adi* 61.80). In other words, he was the embodiment of quarrel and hypocrisy, of everything evil in society. His mistreatment of the Pandavas and of everyone else in the kingdom is symptomatic of who he is.

He and the Kauravas are "evil-doers" by any standard. From the Vedic point of view, they are guilty of six acts for which lethal retaliation is justified: (1) administering poison; (2) setting fire to another's home; (3) stealing; (4) occupying another's land; (5) kidnapping another's wife; and (6) attacking with a deadly weapon. Duryodhana had fed Bhima, the strongest of the Pandava boys, a poisoned cake in one of several attempts to kill him; he had arranged for a house made of lacquer to be built for the Pandavas and then had it set ablaze while they and their mother were still inside; the Kauravas stole the Pandavas' land on several occasions; they had kidnapped Draupadi (when they attempted to disrobe her); and now, with war pending, they are about to attack them with the most lethal of weapons.

Such aggressors, or criminals (*atatayi*), say Vedic texts, should be killed by protectors of the righteous. *Manu-Samhita* 8.350–1 says: "Whether he be a teacher . . . an old man, or a much learned Brahmin, if he comes as a criminal (*atatayi*) in any of the above six ways, a Kshatriya should kill him. . . . There is no sin in killing one so heartless." In fact, Hindu tradition asserts that "such a criminal is in reality killing himself by his own outrageous behavior."

Again, the Pandavas were not the exclusive target of the Kauravas' hatred. As the Kauravas' unjust reign grew, they wreaked havoc throughout the country, causing hardship for all their subjects. So the Pandavas' retaliation was not a vendetta but an attempt to save their fellowmen. Professor Pandit Rajmani Tigunait paraphrases the *Mahabharata* when he summarizes the reign of the Kauravas during the Pandava exile:

During this period of exile, the false king and his sons gathered an enormous military force, stockpiled weapons, and formed alliances with neighboring countries. Their subjects were miserable—taxes were heavy, with every penny used to increase the strength of the army; corruption was rampant, and women and children were not protected. People were praying for the rightful king and his four brothers to return from exile. When they did, the rightful king sent an emissary to the court with a proposal for getting his kingdom back. The emissary was mistreated and the proposal spurned.[6]

It should be underlined that the Pandavas prefer peace—a fact carefully recorded in the *Mahabharata*. Indeed, the *Udyoga-Parvan*—interestingly, "the *Book of Effort*," highlighting the intense endeavor made by the Pandavas to avoid the war—cites several instances in which both Krishna and the Pandavas plead for an end to the senselessness that lay before them. But all such requests, heartfelt though they are, fall on deaf ears. Without any other recourse, then, battle ensues.

Lord Krishna, known by the cousins as God incarnate, was acting as the leader of the Yadavas from Dvaraka, a magnificent city on India's western coast. He offers himself and his entire army to the cause of the upcoming battle. But each party has to choose either one or the other—they cannot have both. Krishna stipulates that he would not engage in battle; the side that chooses him will have to be content with his moral support. He will also act as a charioteer. The opposing side could have his nearly countless legions of warriors, all highly trained.

Materialistic Duryodhana quickly chooses the armed battalions. The righteous Pandavas, on the other hand, ask for Krishna alone, confident that God's grace is more significant than all material facility. Krishna, the *Mahabharata* tells us, in letting the two sides choose him or his army, shows that God is unbiased—if one turns to Him, He reciprocates accordingly; if one prefers material amenities, He grants them whatever they desire, in accordance with their karma.

The respective choices made here by the Pandavas and by Duryodhana reveal the actual reason for the *Mahabharata* war: It was ultimately not about the land denied to the Pandavas but rather about establishing a God-conscious kingdom. As we have seen, God-consciousness was the furthest thing from Duryodhana's mind. While the Pandavas wanted to rule on Krishna's behalf, the Kauravas did not. Indologist Angelika Malinar explains the situation:

As to the immediate context of the *Bhagavad-gita*, the *Udyoga-parvan* presents in a sequence of debates the pros and cons of war, of Yudhishthira's entitlement for kingship and Duryodhana's claim to establish himself as an absolute monarch. He and his allies furnish sophisticated arguments in order to legitimize their claims for an "absolute" government, centered on the interests of the king. Duryodhana intends to establish his supremacy over the three worlds, inclusive of gods and demons, and does not hesitate, against the warnings of those in authority . . . to sacrifice the traditional family ties and the code of kinship for his own self-interest.

In his programmatic speech in the *Mahabharata* (5.60) he presents himself as a god-king and rejects all obligations with regard to the traditional gods as well as to ascetic, i.e., self-restrictive, values.[7]

To defend the righteous and to establish a God-conscious kingdom, then, the Pandavas have no alternative but to engage in battle. Thus, with Krishna as Arjuna's charioteer, the *Bhagavad-Gita*, which is in the Sixth Book of the *Mahabharata*, begins. The actual events precipitating the *Gita*'s recitation may be summarized as follows.

Both armies are arrayed and ready for combat. But before the fighting commences, Krishna pulls Arjuna's chariot into the middle of the battlefield. There, the fabled bowman sees friends, relatives, and countrymen on both sides. He becomes paralyzed with fear, with second thoughts about committing to the massive war that lies ahead—in which no one can really be the victor. And Krishna begins to speak, or, rather, to sing. This is the *Bhagavad-Gita*.

The *Gita*'s song appears in the form of a dialogue—Arjuna hopes to resolve his existential crisis by placing his questions before Krishna. The complex philosophical ideas that come out of their deeply moving exchange range from details on the soul and life after death to material nature and the way it interacts with the psychology of man, culminating in an explanation of the nature of God. A subsequent chapter will treat the *Bhagavad-Gita* in detail.

For now, let it be said that, by the *Gita*'s end, Arjuna feels relieved, even enlightened, and is ready to fight.

As Arjuna makes up his mind, powerful forces can be seen on both sides of the battleground. In addition to the major armies, there are seemingly numberless smaller troops from various parts of the world. The Pandavas manage to amass a military force that is traditionally broken down into seven broad divisions. Though somewhat formidable, the Kauravas have mobilized a much larger force consisting of eleven such divisions. Modern *Mahabharata* scholars have determined that each of these divisions comprised 21,870 chariots, an equal number of elephants, three times as many horsemen, and five times as many foot soldiers.

The Pandavas, then, have an army of 153,090 chariots and equal number of elephants; they have 459,270 horsemen and 765,450 foot soldiers. The Kauravas, for their part, boast an army of 240,570 chariots and elephants, 721,710 horsemen, and over 1 million foot soldiers.[8] Tradition holds this to be a conservative estimate, suggesting that many millions were actually killed in the war. In whatever way one chooses to calculate the numbers, inconceivably large armies find themselves on this battlefield preparing to fight. In fact, it is often described as a world war. In the words of Hinduism expert Linda Johnsen:

The conflict described in the *Mahabharata* may be called the true first world war. . . . Soldiers from as far away as Greece and Java participated. This is not so surprising when one considers that for most of history, India represented one of the wealthiest and most erudite cultures in the world. Until as recently as four hundred years ago, sailors from European countries were desperately seeking routes to India. The struggle between Duryodhana and Arjuna's brother involved control over some of the most important trade routes in the world. Archaeological discoveries like those at Mohenjo-Daro reveal that even thousands of years before the birth of Christ, northern India was a sophisticated and cosmopolitan area visited and inhabited by people of many races. The text claims that many hundreds of thousands were killed during the war.[9]

The battle is initially fought according to the standards of Kshatriya etiquette: actual combat takes place only in daylight. In the evening, all warriors mix in friendship. One-on-one combat takes place only among equals. Horsemen do not attack soldiers who are only on foot. Warriors in chariots only fight with others in chariots. Those retreating for any reason are not attacked, nor are those sitting in a yoga posture. If someone drops their weapon, they are left alone, and musicians, conch blowers, and civilians—all are immune to the surrounding warfare. Animals, too, are never killed deliberately, though if, in the course of battle, they happen to fall, it is overlooked.[10] As in all wars, however, these rules fall to the wayside as passions mount, and during the last days of the battle, they become altogether compromised.

Critics have wondered how the ideals of *dharma*, of proper duty, could be so abused on the battlefield when Krishna himself was personally present. It should be understood, however, that this abuse of *dharma* was according to Krishna's plan. It was a necessary evil, one that allowed *dharma*'s true virtue to emerge with full force. Exactly how this manifests is interesting. The *Mahabharata* battle goes through three phases, showing first the surfacing of *dharma*, when Arjuna sees the virtue in fighting for a noble cause; then its inevitable compromise, as when the principles of Kshatriya ethics disintegrate on the battlefield; finally, the reestablishing of *dharma* manifests in the end, when Krishna, as the story goes, saves the Pandava clan from extinction, reestablishing cosmic order yet again.

Let us flesh this out a bit. The battle was initiated for noble reasons. But then, as stated, senseless destruction takes over. This is attributable, in large measure, to Shiva's presence on the battlefield. That is to say, the lord of destruction brings his distinct brand of *dharma* to the battlefield, as per Krishna's plan, of course. How does this happen? On the 13th day of a war that will last for 18 (each bloody day is discussed below), Shiva himself appears and wreaks havoc. He appears, too, as a partial incarnation in the person of Ashvatthama, who is at the center of much chicanery in the battle's latter days, as we shall see. He is also at the helm of a nighttime massacre, in which he kills most of the Pandavas' as yet unborn descendents. In these ways, Shiva assists Krishna's purposes—the death of numerous combatants—enacting, as Krishna calls it, fated events.

Thus, *dharma* comes to the fore and then is nearly destroyed. But Krishna ultimately intervenes by rescuing one of the Pandava grandchildren, Pariksit, protecting the child from Ashvatthama while it is still in its mother's womb. Pariksit will figure prominently in the Puranas, the culmination of India's spiritual literature, to be discussed in the chapter after next.

But we get ahead of ourselves. As the fighting begins, the blind King Dhritarashtra stands behind Kaurava boundary lines, listening to his minister Sanjaya, who describes the battle to him.

THE BATTLE OF BATTLES

On Day 1 of the 18-day conflict,[11] it looks as though the Pandavas might lose. The valiant Bhishma, a saintly general, grandsire of the clan, finds himself on the side of the Kauravas. He fights with Abhimanyu, Arjuna's son, and, due to age and experience, naturally gains the upper hand. Uttara, who is also related to Arjuna, fights on the side of the Pandavas, attacking the Kaurava prince Shalya, brother of Madri and uncle of Nakula and Sahadeva. In the midst of this battle, Uttara accidentally kills Shalya's horse, enraging him and enabling him to fight with additional ferocity. Consequently, he kills Uttara, who is the first casualty of the war—a great blow to the Pandava princes.

Soon after this, Shveta, a Pandava warrior, retaliates against Shalya, and, single-handedly, manages to challenge the entire Kaurava army with his skills as a marksman. When he comes up against Bhishma, however, he is finally killed. And so the Pandavas are less than hopeful as the first day draws to a close.

As the sun rises on the 2nd day, Dhrishtadyumna, the Pandava commander-in-chief, sets up his men in strategic formation. Though this garners good results for the Pandavas, allowing them to fare better than they did on the first day, Grandsire Bhishma thwarts most of their plans. Arjuna confides in Krishna, "The grandsire must be slain." This is difficult for him to admit, for Bhishma is a greatly respected warrior, a senior family member and teacher, from whom Arjuna and the others have learned much of what they know. Nonetheless, Arjuna attacks the noble grandsire with determination and skill. The Kauravas try to protect him, recognizing that he is one of their most prizefighters. Arjuna finds himself fending them off, which distracts him from his central concern of killing Bhishma. In the heat of battle, Bhishma hits Krishna (now acting as Arjuna's charioteer) with an arrow. Though this greatly angers Arjuna, he is unable to get Bhishma at this time.

The fact that Drona (an important spiritual master—the main teacher of both the Pandavas and the Kauravas, as well as the father of Ashvathama) is fighting on the side of Kauravas also angers Arjuna. But a complex series of events made this unavoidable. Thus, on this second day, we find Drona attacking Dhrishtadyumna, the Pandava general, who almost dies as a result of Drona's efforts. Bhima, however, comes to Dhrishtadyumna's aid, rescuing him in his chariot. Duryodhana then sends massive troops after Bhima, who kills them one by one. The war escalates immensely, and it is only Day 2 of the assault. The Kauravas are forced to back off, relieved that the day is finally coming to an end.

Day 3 finds several Kaurava warriors attacking Arjuna at once. He manages to fend them off with dazzling skill. Duryodhana's main counselor, Shakuni, lunges for Satyaki, an important Pandava warrior. Abhimanyu manages to save him, even though the latter's chariot is destroyed while doing so. Drona and Bhishma both go after Yudhishthira, thinking that if they could down this senior-most Pandava brother, they could quickly win the war. But they are unsuccessful. Duryodhana rebukes Bhishma, telling him that he is not fighting up to par. Incensed, Bhishma fiercely attacks the Pandavas, and they are forced to run for their lives. Bhishma, even while fighting the Pandavas and their assistant warriors, continually praises them. And is ashamed to find himself battling those so virtuous. As he lightens his attack, the Pandavas again win the upper hand. By the end of the day, the Kauravas are on the run.

On the 4th day, however, the Kauravas advance their cause once again— Bhishma, Drona, and Duryodhana fight like men possessed. Several Kaurava warriors surround Abhimanyu, and are about to kill him. But his father, Arjuna, comes to his rescue. Just then, Dhrishtadyumna arrives with reinforcements, including the powerful Bhima. Seeing this unstoppable powerhouse, who had almost single-handedly crushed them on a prior day, the Kauravas unleash a large force of elephants to trample him.

Bhima, however, manages to scatter the elephants in all directions, causing fear and panic among the Kaurava troops. Using the confusion, he also attacks Duryodhana, nearly killing him. Amazingly, the evil Kaurava is able to hold his own against this superbly skilled Pandava, and eventually gets the better of him. But Bhima's son Ghatotkacha is able to rescue him before Duryodhana delivers a decisive blow. Rejuvenated, Bhima kills eight of Duryodhana's brothers. By nightfall, the Pandavas have won a temporary victory, and the Kauravas are severely depressed.

The 5th day sees the Pandavas nearly win the entire battle. Though it begins with Bhishma leading a well-planned attack on the Pandavas, causing much carnage and nearly decimating many of their important troops, Arjuna leads a retaliation that nearly equals the damage done by Bhishma. Duryodhana cannot tolerate the incompetence of his men and complains to Drona about their weakness.

Drona then assaults Satyaki, thinking that the death of such a capable general might serve as an equalizer. But Bhima comes to his defense, saving him from Drona's attack. At this point, Satyaki's valorous sons are slain. Responding emotionally, Arjuna himself slaughters thousands of Kaurava warriors. The day ends as a great victory for the Pandavas.

The 6th day is a day of massive genocide. Warrior kills warrior and thousands die. The air was dense with arrows and the ground saturated with blood. In an interesting side scene, Bhima defiantly fights with eleven of Duryodhana's primary warriors, single-handedly. During this encounter, he finds himself behind Kaurava lines, and Dhrishtadyumna bravely goes to rescue him. While the two Pandava heroes are on enemy grounds, the Kauravas attack them both.

Surrounded, Dhrishtadyumna uses a mystical weapon that he had received when he was very young—Drona had given it to him when he was a student. The weapon affects the mind, causing stupefaction. As a result, the Kauravas are wandering here and there, as if intoxicated. Duryodhana, however, arrives on the scene and employs a similar weapon, making the Pandavas fall to the ground. All troops work their way out of the infected area, and the effect of the weapons soon wears off. The day is declared a victory for the Kauravas.

On the 7th day, there are again many one-on-one battles. Well-trained soldiers fall, more on the Kaurava side than on the Pandavas.' Much of Duryodhana's army is shattered. Bhishma battles all five Pandava princes by himself, and each man is honored to have such a noble opponent. Other warriors fight gallantly, but bodies just pile on top of bodies. The carnage is unprecedented. At sunset, the nursing of wounds takes the place of evening meals.

Bhima kills eight of Duryodhana's brothers on the 8th day of the battle. Iravat, one of Arjuna's sons, is killed on the same day. Arjuna is emotionally crushed but battles on. Ghatokacha charges the Kauravas with great success. In a touching scene, Duryodhana lashes out with great skill but almost loses his life; he is rescued just in time by Drona. Sixteen of Dhritarashtra's boys are executed that day.

On the 9th day, thousands of Pandava warriors are killed by Grand-sire Bhishma. Krishna suggests that Arjuna make an extra effort to take Bhishma out, saying that this is the only way that the war can be won. But, Arjuna, once again, could not bring himself to kill his old teacher. Annoyed, Krishna dismounts the chariot and sets out to personally attack Bhishma on foot. Arjuna, however, pulls him back. Krishna was not to engage in direct battle, and Arjuna would, when the time comes, do the needful. As the day wears on, Satyaki duels with Ashvatthama, Drona with Arjuna. Overall, these 24 hours favor the Kauravas.

The next day, however, tells a different story: Bhishma falls. Arjuna attacks him with a plethora of arrows and is ultimately successful; he is mortally wounded. The Grandsire dies a slow death, lying on a cushion of arrowheads. He claims it an honor to be killed by Arjuna. The demigods come from beyond the cosmos to offer salutations to the most famous of noble warriors. The battle, in fact, comes to a temporary halt while both sides pay homage to this senior-most personage who had trained them all. Bhishma asks for water, and Arjuna shoots an arrow into the ground, causing water to spring up into the sky, and into his teacher's mouth.

Lying on his battlefield deathbed, Bhishma preaches the need for peace. He survives for 58 days—through his yogic powers, he keeps himself alive so that he can die during the northern phase of the sun, and by so doing attain perfection in death. During this time, he speaks philosophically, and his discourse is preserved not only in the *Mahabharata* but also in the *Bhagavata* and in other Puranas. The Grandsire, lecturing for the remainder of his 58 days, lives well beyond the close of the 18-day battle.

As the war rages on, the Kauravas decide to capture Yudhishthira alive. No sooner does Duryodhana devise the plan, than does Drona accept it with full enthusiasm, mainly because he does not want to see Yudhishthira killed. Duryodhana's fundamental purpose in capturing the leading Pandava is to trick him into another game of dice. The other Pandavas soon find out about the plan, however, and make arrangements to counter it.

On the next day, Drona attempts to carry out the plan to capture Yud-hishthira. The great Pandava prince, however, flees on horseback; though a true Kshatriya would never run from another Kshatriya, Yudhishthira reasons that Drona is in fact a Brahmana, and thus it is not disgraceful to escape his attack. Meanwhile, there is vicious one-on-one combat be-tween Sahadeva and Shakuni, the Kauravas' maternal uncle. Many great warriors fight their best on this day: Shalya against Nakula; Dhrishtaketu against Kripa; Satyaki against Kritavarman; Virata against Karna. Abhimanyu fights like a madman—dueling with four well-trained Kauravas at once. Drona sees Yudhishthira in the distance and again tries to capture him. But Arjuna gets in the way, forcing Drona to retreat. This 11th day is difficult for the Kauravas, and many of their troops begin to lose morale.

By the 12th day, the Kauravas realize that they will never capture Yudhishthira as long as Arjuna is there to counter them. And so they devise a plan to kill him. They send Susharman and his four brothers to attack our unsuspecting Pandava hero. But his flawless Kshatriya instinct allows him to slay them instead. After the plan to kill Arjuna fails, Drona again tries to capture Yudhishthira. Once again, however, he is not able to—Dhrishtadyumna and his comrades are waiting nearby to protect him. The Kauravas repeatedly try to kidnap the leading Pandava, and they repeatedly fail.

Other magnificent battles are taking place just a few yards away. For example, Arjuna's son, Abhimanyu, finds himself surrounded by Kaurava forces. In a colossal exhibition of courage, he holds his own against the entire Kaurava army, including Duryodhana. The other Pandavas try to come to his aid, but they cannot even get close. The Kauravas concentrate their efforts on him alone. At one point, he has only a chariot wheel as his weapon, and he swings it madly, holding them off. Finally, Lakshman, son of Duhshasana, strikes him down, finishing him with one strong blow. One of Dhritarashtra's sons, Yuyutsu, is so taken aback by the foul play that he drops his weapon and leaves the field. Many on both sides feel anguish over the way Abhimanyu is killed.

Still, the battle continues. On the 13th day, Arjuna destroys many Kaurava soldiers, finally confronting Duhshasana, an important Kaurava prince who, in many ways, was a central perpetrator of the war. Arjuna gets the better of him, and he flees. At this point, Arjuna blows his conch, signaling a minor victory. The Pandavas fight as they never did before. Bhima, especially, is battling Kauravas as if they are toy soldiers, their bodies flying in all four directions. But there is an extra presence on this day: Shiva is here, and the mood and tone of the entire war turns.

On the 14th day, many of the main warriors are weary. Bhurishravas, the prince of a minor kingdom, raises his sword against Satyaki, king of the Vrishnis (important Pandava allies), and defeats him, letting him live, if also toying with him. Observing Satyaki's difficulty, Arjuna, though battling another opponent several yards away, manages to send an estuary of arrows in Bhurishravas' direction, cutting off his right arm. Realizing his defeat, Bhurishravas decides to give up the battle and immediately proceeds to practice yoga, sitting in a lotus posture while still on the battlefield. Seeing this, Satyaki, in a fit of anger, beheads Bhurishravas on the spot, which is clearly foul play. The rules of proper warfare are now being ignored on both sides, as the thirst for blood causes all involved to do whatever is deemed necessary to win.

Arjuna battles with all his might against Jayadratha, an important Kaurava ally, and eventually resorts to trickery. Jayadratha's father had made a prediction, or, rather, a curse: "Whoever causes my son's head to fall to the ground will find that his own will burst into a hundred pieces." Krishna informs Arjuna of this curse, and Arjuna beheads Jayadratha with a stream of arrows that carry the head into the lap of his father, who is meditating nearby. When the father is thus roused from meditation, he immediately stands up and inadvertently lets his son's head fall to the ground. Since it is he who is the direct cause of the boy's head dropping to the ground, it is his head that bursts into pieces, as his own curse had demanded. After this, the battle continues into the night with the help of torchlight, a direct abrogation of the rules of war.

By the evening of the 15th day, most standards of Kshatriya ethics are set aside. Even Krishna compromises knightly etiquette in favor of helping the Pandavas. He suggests naming one of the Pandava elephants Ashvatthama, which is also the name of Drona's son, and then killing the animal. The idea is to tell Drona that "Ashvatthama" is dead, and by this he would think that he had lost his son, which would, in turn, make him give up on life itself. He could then be easily defeated.

The plan is put into effect, but Drona decides to ask Yudhishthira for confirmation, knowing that Yudhisthira never lies. Yudhishthira shouts the confirming words across the battlefield, that Ashvatthama was in fact dead. As a side note, popular Hindu tradition asserts that King Yudhishthira had to go to hell for telling a lie on Krishna's behalf—for saying "Ashvatthama is dead." But the Vaishnava tradition teaches instead that his visit to hell was instigated by his *hesitation* to tell that lie. God's will, says the tradition, supercedes all mundane morality, even if such morality is considered binding in all other circumstances. In other words, only if God is personally present, ordering the suspension of worldly ethics—as He did with Yudhishthira—should one do so. Otherwise, it is a sin.

In fact, Yudhishthira actually said that, "Ashvatthama 'the elephant' was dead," which was true. But Krishna blew his conch at that moment, conveniently drowning out the words "the elephant" so that Drona would think that his son was dead.[12]

Crying piteously for the death of his son, Drona lays down his weapons and is instantaneously decapitated by Dhrishtadyumna. And so the plan worked. The remaining Pandavas and Kauravas could now see the horror of war, that it can turn even the noblest of Kshatriyas into opportunistic automata, with little vision beyond the desire to win, at any cost. After Drona's death, Karna takes charge of the Kaurava army. But few have any will to fight.

On the 16th day, Karna challenges Yudhishthira to one-on-one combat, and they fight for some time. At the height of the skirmish, however, Yudhishthira flees, unable to continue the senseless fighting with people he holds dear. Bhima, however, has no such reservations and, remembering Draupadi's humiliation as the Kauravas attempted to disrobe her, he attacks Duhshasana.

Tearing his body apart with his bare hands, Bhima's defeat of this horrible Kaurava thug is perhaps one of the most memorable if also disturbing episodes in the entire *Mahabharata* battle. The warriors on both sides are appalled by Bhima's uncompromising act, but all agree that Duhshasana, scoundrel that he was, could not but die a horrible death.

The 17th day sees an intense and drawn-out duel between Arjuna and Karna. Though both fight valiantly, Arjuna ultimately wins, if in a questionable way. Yudhishthira, in fact, reprimands him for the way in which the battle is won. Arjuna, however, is not about to listen to his elder brother, who had run off in shame on a previous day. He is enraged that his brother would question him, and, in his anger, intends to thrust Yudhishthira with his sword. Krishna, however, intervenes, and the brothers come to their senses. After the death of Karna, Shalya assumes command of the Kaurava forces, and all know that the war is soon to come to an end.

Though the Pandavas had been quarreling among themselves, on the 18th and last day of the war, they manage to rally together and win for the cause of righteousness. Duryodhana, toward the end, is practically alone. Sensing his ultimate defeat, he absconds, concealing himself in a nearby lake—he has the mystical ability to remain under water for inordinate lengths of time. As he disappears, Sahadeva defeats Shakuni and Yudhishthira slays Shalya, two major setbacks for the Kaurava army.

Next, Bhima kills the remaining sons of Dhritarashtrà, except Duryodhana, who is still underwater. He searches the remaining Kaurava leader out, however, finding his hiding place in the lake. Taunting him, he forces Duryodhana into the light of day. As the demon-king comes up from the lake, they proceed to battle with huge clubs. Finally, Bhima hits him below the belt, breaking both his legs, and then he tramples across his body.

Yudhishthira is angered by this unfair and brutal act, and he slaps Bhima across the face. Balarama, Krishna's brother, who is not present for most of the war but who arrives just in time to witness Bhima's underhanded behavior, is so disgusted that he attacks Bhima with his plow (Balarama's weapon of favor). He is halted by Krishna, who feels compassion for the Pandavas, and he and his brother both leave for their capital city Dvaraka. Duryodhana, still alive, criticizes Krishna as he goes, but no one listens, as the now crippled demon's voice gets lower and lower—the others walk away, and Duryodhana dies.

The battle is over. Among the Pandavas, the original five survive, along with Satyaki, their general, and, of course, Krishna. Only three Kaurava warriors—Kripa, Ashvatthama, and Kritavarma—live to tell the story. The children of the Pandavas have all been killed, with the exception of Arjuna's grandchild Pariksit, who will one day be king. The bodies of the main warriors are gathered, wrapped in perfumed linen, laid upon a great funeral pyre, and cremated. Yudhishthira is proclaimed King of Hastinapura, but all wonder about the price of the war.

Dhritarashtra, at least, is certain that it is not worth the loss of his many sons. He embraces Yudhishthira as a sign of peace and reconciliation. But when Bhima is announced to the blind king, Krishna puts a metal statue in his place, and Dhritarashtra crushes it in anger. Dhritarashtra and his wife cannot forgive the Pandavas, but nonetheless bless them, knowing their cause to be just. Yudhishthira reigns over Hastinapura, but he has ill feelings about the war and the many lives it took. He and his brothers, he knows, must pay by literally going to hell for some time, and the *Mahabharata* indeed describes their journey there. Afterwards, however, they emerge godlike, and go to Krishna's supreme abode.

TEACHINGS

What do Hindus glean from these mammoth texts? The plots and subplots of the *Ramayana* and the *Mahabharata* include numerous morals and codes of conduct that have guided people for centuries and, over the course of time, filled volumes. In addition, smaller books have been extracted from the Epics, such as the *Bhagavad-Gita*, the *Vishnu-Sahasranam*, the teachings of Bhishma, the love story of Nala and Damayanti, the tale of Shakuntala, Sita's story, the adventures of Hanuman—each with elaborate philosophical instructions, leading to virtuous behavior and a religious way of life. This being the case, it might seem a bit strange that both Epics center on war and have martial underpinnings, apparently endorsing violence as an appropriate response to injustice.

And yet, few Hindus would claim that this is what the Epics are really all about. Instead, they see *dharma*, duty, as the main teaching that comes to the fore. When properly executed, they say, *dharma* brings peace and happiness. And when practiced in the highest possible way, under the direction of a spiritual master, it leads to liberation and love of God. This, according to most Hindus, is the overriding teaching of both the *Ramayana* and the *Mahabharata*.

Interestingly, the Epics talk about *dharma* as the ultimate virtue, existing for the common good of everyone. More, they promote nonviolence to God's creatures as among the highest aspects of *dharma*. In fact, the *Mahabharata* states it directly: "Nonviolence is the highest duty and the highest teaching." (13.116.37–41) But all is not so simple. If the Epics extol the virtues of nonviolent interaction, which they do, why do they wave their peace flag from a violent battlefield?

The answer, again, can be found in that distinctly Indian word, *dharma*, which, we may remember, comes in many forms. The Varnashrama system specifically addresses the kind of *dharma* that is peculiar to each individual. So whereas nonviolence is certainly a virtue for most, it is actually considered misconduct for others, particularly for Kshatriyas, or military officers sworn to protect the masses. Or, to put it another way, total nonviolence might be appropriate for a Brahmin, but not for one whose duty it is to see that people abide by the law—nonviolence, for such a person, reverberates in more aggressive tones, as protection, or as the tendency to defend others.

For example, Arjuna, in the *Mahabharata*, was a Kshatriya, and Krishna indeed gave him the mandate to fight. If Arjuna had simply sat back and propounded a doctrine of nonviolence, millions would have lost their lives and havoc would have engulfed the kingdom. So there are times when violence becomes a greater form of nonviolence, albeit in very particular circumstances. The Epics hope to make this point by illustrating extreme situations in which violence might serve nonviolent ends—situations, that is, in which only violence would do.[13]

This tension between violence and nonviolence is one of the Epics' main themes. As an example, one need look no further than Yudhishthira, the eldest of the Pandava Princes. It is he who, although a powerful Kshatriya, repeatedly begs for peace, so much so that his brothers begin to see him as a coward. And yet he makes good arguments for a passive way of life, the likes of which cannot be debated. In fact, the agonizing conclusion of the *Mahabharata* war bears him out, showing that while the principles of peace might be temporarily suspended for a higher good, such suspension always comes with a price. In this case, both sides lost loved ones and otherwise suffered the ravages of war.

The Epics thus teach that even when war is justified, it never awards the peace and harmony that comes from nonviolence, the preferred ideal. In this sense, then, it might be said that the Epics approve of war only as a last resort. Rama, for his part, merely wanted Sita back, and would have given anything to avoid conflict. But it was not to be. As in the *Mahabharata*, where every attempt was made for reconciliation, the hero shows disdain for battle, but also the courage to pursue truth and justice. The Epics, then, teach compassion, even if this teaching is tempered by the duty to do the necessary.

Many seek to address the martial nature of the *Mahabharata*, and that of the *Ramayana*, too, for that matter, by viewing the entire story as a metaphor. They see Arjuna as Everyman and the five Pandavas as the five senses, with the battlefield as an external representation of humankind's internal struggle. Along similar lines, the name of Rama's father, Dasharath, means "a chariot of ten," implying the human body, with its five working organs and five sensory organs. He is said to have attracted the three modalities of nature—goodness, passion, and ignorance—embodied in Kaushalya, Sumitra, and Kaikeyi, his three wives. He further gives birth to four sons, who are, in reality, the four goals of human life—duty, economic development, pleasure, and liberation. Sita is wisdom and Ravana is selfishness and ego. The teaching is straightforward: if one wants wisdom to disappear, one need simply engage Ravana's lesser characteristics.

From this point of view, it might be said that the battles of both Epics never took place. In fact, the traditional commentator Madhvacharya acknowledges that the Epics can be understood in three distinct ways—the literal, the ethical, and the metaphorical—and that all are considered legitimate.[14] But he is clear that literal interpretation conveys the most accurate reading of the text, and that the others provide ancillary teachings by which one might glean additional, esoteric information. In fact, Hindus in general understand their scriptures as nonfiction, historical records of a time when beings from higher planets walked the earth, and when God himself descended to call his children back to him. The most instructive teachings, to be sure, are only applicable if one interprets the text literally.

For example, the suffering associated with the lives of the Pandavas and the Kauravas, the humiliation undergone by Draupadi, the heart-rending kidnapping of Sita, the cruel death of Jatayu, the countless other tragedies found in the Epics—all lose meaning if they did not occur to real people, with emotions and feelings. Interpreted literally, such human devastation softens the readers' hearts. By depicting the hardships of life in a very real way, the texts seek to underline the harsh realities of material existence. Concomitantly, they show the virtue of bravery and fortitude, whether exhibited by a queen or by a vulture, and that worthwhile goals remain worthwhile, even if one must undergo severe austerities and penance to attain them.

The Epics teach us that pain, both our own and when observed in others, can be a blessing in disguise. It can turn the mind toward spirituality and instill mercy in the heart—it can strengthen the will and foster the development of patience and endurance. These qualities, as exhibited by the Epics' heroes, are essential for those trying to develop love of God. And by seeing how they manifest in the lives of the Epics' central characters, ordinary souls can bring them into their own lives. In this way, readers are expected to imbibe the qualities prerequisite to God realization.

Truth and Righteousness, with capital letters, are the Epics' main messages. Both texts urge their readers—not with barefaced instruction but with compelling story—to walk the path of Hanuman, serving Rama, and to avoid the selfishness of Ravana; to follow Yudhishthira's example, who wanted peace and would never lie, and to shun Duryodhana's, who wanted only power, whatever the cost. The Epics show how to distinguish reality from illusion, good from bad, particularly when it comes to human behavior.

This is one of the real contributions of the Epics: They clearly express the psychology of human relationships, showing how to interact with others in ways that ultimately lead to God consciousness. A close reading reveals that the discovery or establishment of common ground between individuals is a fundamental component for enduring interpersonal relationships. The camaraderie between the Pandava brothers, for example, shows how this is so, and eggs us on to develop such relationships in our own lives.

But instruction in relationships does not end there. For each relationship type, essential skills are needed, and without these skills more advanced relationships are not possible. The Epics, through their virtuous characters, show how this is so. They also reveal a hierarchy, from simple servitude to friendship, from familial responsibility to conjugal love—from one's relationship with one's country to relationship with God. Expertise in each relationship type (in this hierarchy) requires the skills of all previous relationship types. In the ultimate analysis, then, one who loves God, loves everyone.

Vyasa specifically compiled these texts for the common people, not for the elite Brahmins who study the *Vedas* or devote countless hours to rituals. The same Vedic teaching, it is said, is presented here in story form, so that anyone can appreciate it, or learn from it. Thus, what we find in the Epics is pragmatic wisdom and perceptive insights into human nature and human relationships, which allow us, ultimately, to develop love for God.

Of course, the Epics are complex, with countless philosophical nuances. Therefore, without assistance, it is difficult to eek out their inner message, or to understand how all their many stories and teachings interconnect. Coming from the Upanishadic tradition, it is expected that one study these texts at the feet of a master. In fact, say the Epics, the entire Hindu tradition becomes incomprehensible, at least in terms of its originally intended meaning, without the virtue of a spiritual teacher. Still, one can derive immense benefit from a simple study of the scriptures, even if their underlying meaning and overall message will likely remain a mystery. For this reason, it is highly recommended throughout these texts that one search out a bona fide guru.

The Epic orientation is that of pragmatic idealism, with a deep understanding of human weakness, selfishness, and aggressiveness. Shoot for higher understanding, say the holy texts, but take the help of spiritual adepts. The world of the Epic hero is not unlike our own. It is one in which people work, raise families, and contend with an all too often corrupt society; life pushes them toward renunciation and a religious way of life, and ultimately, of course, they succumb to death.

Epic characters do their best to make the world a better place to live and they work diligently to do the right thing. True, their world is replete with supernatural beings and uncanny powers beyond ordinary human reckoning. But in terms of desires, wants, and goals they are very much like us, and their lives can thus be used as models for our own. First and foremost, we should note that they all accept spiritual preceptors. But beyond any one specific teaching, such as the importance of accepting a spiritual master, it is this kind of bridge between their world and ours that the Epics hope to give their readers. And they do this, chiefly, through human relationships.

The *Ramayana*, specifically, shows how to interact with others, in any walk of life, in any kind of relationship. It begins with the personality of Rama, the perfection of duty, honesty, and harmony—*dharma* personified. He is the ideal son, the consummate king, and a loving husband. Sita is the perfect wife, beautiful, chaste, and dedicated, if also strong-willed and intelligent. Lakshman and his brothers are determined companions and assistants to Rama, their elder brother, for whom they would do anything. Hanuman is the ideal servant, unquestioningly obeying his master and tending to his needs with single-minded love. Conversely, the dangers of submitting to lust and ego are seen in Ravana and in the evil beings that associate with him.

We are taught to consider well before making a promise. This is exemplified in the suffering of King Dasharath, which was a result of his promise to Kaikeyi. And yet his example also shows the importance of keeping promises no matter how difficult the results. His integrity is equaled only by that of Rama, who agrees to retreat to the forest—giving up an entire kingdom—just to keep his father's word. The Epic also shows (through the life of Sita and Rama in their forest hermitage) the importance of living peacefully wherever we might find ourselves, and to be grateful for what we have, however humble. They could have lived there forever, until a horrible villain disturbed their private paradise. But even then, they were willing to forgive.

Ultimately, the conflict between Rama and Ravana, or between the Pandavas and the Kauravas, is really about cosmic harmony and the forces that would disrupt it. This disruption works on three levels—in the realm of the gods, in that of humans, and in regard to nature itself. Ravana, for example, undermined the powers of the gods by using his yogic abilities and unwavering skills to develop supernatural powers, and by using those powers for materialistic ends. Similarly, he gained control of other self-interested souls and, together, they created an army that caused pain to humankind, with exploitation and fear as his main calling cards. Finally, he polluted nature by sensuous living and by abusing his surroundings; by battling with Hanuman and Jatayu, too, the text further shows his animosity toward the natural world. And if Duryodhana's life is studied, a similar scenario unfolds.

Thus, the Epics teach that until we recognize the importance of liberation, of freedom from disharmony and disruption—from aversion to *dharma*—we are destined to suffer or enjoy life in a world of duality, a world that is inferior to the spiritual realms of existence promised by both the *Ramayana* and the *Mahabharata*. To achieve these latter realms, we must reverse the process, as it were, learning to fully respect nature, to properly interact with humankind, and, in the final analysis, to achieve transcendence. The Epics methodically take us through each realm.

Until we are free from worldly concerns, we must learn the etiquette of the material world. Knowledge of the *Vedas*, charity, compassion, and nonviolence—all allow life to flourish in this world, with respect to nature and to our fellow humans, and they are necessary stepping stones to a life of spiritual accomplishment. But eventually we must go beyond the dualities of material existence, beyond happiness and distress, gain and loss; according to the Epics, these are various sides of the same coin. And when embarking on the spiritual path, we must go for broke.

As Krishna says in the *Bhagavad-Gita* (2.14), "The nonpermanent appearance of happiness and distress and their disappearance in due course, are like the appearance and disappearance of winter and summer seasons.

They arise from sense perception only, and one must learn to tolerate them without being disturbed." Otherwise, we are various shades of Ravana and Duryodhana. But, with *dharma*, with our sight squarely on spiritual progress, we can bridge the gap between heaven and earth, and approach the Lord in the mood of Arjuna and Hanuman.

CHAPTER 6

The *Bhagavad-Gita* and the Life of Lord Krishna

"The *Gita* is one of the clearest and most comprehensive summaries of the Perennial Philosophy ever to have been made. Hence its enduring value, not only for Indians, but for all mankind. . . . The *Bhagavad-Gita* is perhaps the most systematic spiritual statement of the Perennial Philosophy."

—Aldous Huxley

"One who knows the transcendental nature of My appearance and activities does not, upon leaving the body, take birth again in this material world, but attains My eternal abode, O Arjuna."

— Lord Krishna in the *Bhagavad-Gita* (4.9)

The Epics permeate the Indian subcontinent, and their characters, stories, and teachings are fundamental to the Hindu way of thinking. As important as the Epics are, however, there are two works associated with the *Mahabharata*, the longer of the two Epics, which are arguably Hinduism's most important religious texts today. The *Bhagavad-Gita*, a small section in the Sixth Book of the massive Pandava tale, is the first of these two. It is sometimes hailed as the "New Testament" of Hinduism, with Lord Krishna, its speaker, as Vishnu's most beloved manifestation.

It is Krishna, in fact, whose life is the subject of the *Harivamsa*, a text appended to the same Epic, and this will be the second of the two items discussed in this chapter. While the *Harivamsa* itself is not the most well known of Hindu texts, its subject—Krishna's life in Vrindavan, India—is at the core of modern Hinduism. Thus, this section will provide an overview of the *Gita* and a sampling of her verses, and it will also include a summary of Lord Krishna's life, not only as recounted in the *Harivamsa* but also as it appears in the Tenth Book of the *Bhagavata Purana*, which is the most complete version of the story. To elaborate on various aspects of Krishna's life, we will also draw on the insights of Hinduism's greatest teachers.

The *BHAGAVAD-GITA*: A SUMMARY

As we may remember from the *Mahabharata*, Krishna, the Supreme Person, had agreed to become the driver of Arjuna's chariot. Once on the battlefield, he sees his friend and devotee in illusion, paralyzed by the fear that he must kill his relatives and friends, who were in the opposing army. Feeling compassion, Krishna eloquently reminds him of his immediate social duty as a warrior, upon whom people are depending, and, more importantly, of his religious duty as an eternal spiritual entity in relationship with God. Their dialogue continues for 700 verses. The relevance and meaning of Krishna's teachings go far beyond the immediate historical setting of Arjuna's battlefield dilemma.

In the *Gita*'s many pages, Krishna and his devotee, Arjuna, discuss metaphysical concepts such as the distinction between body and soul (matter/spirit), the principle of nonattached action, the virtues of discipline, yoga, meditation, and the respective places of knowledge and devotion in spiritual life. Krishna teaches that perfection lies not in renunciation of the world, but rather in disciplined action, performed without attachment to results.

As the text moves on, Krishna shows Arjuna that he (and not Arjuna) is God, specifically by revealing his "Universal Form," a vision that includes everything in existence. After this, he shows Arjuna his identity with the mystical four-armed Vishnu form, and finally he again reveals his original two-armed form. He explains his many divine manifestations, such as Brahman (an impersonal force), Paramatma (also known as Supersoul, his localized aspect as he exists in all of nature and in the hearts of living beings), and Bhagavan (the Supreme Personality of Godhead). And he ultimately reveals that his personal feature supercedes his impersonal aspects.

Krishna explains the three qualities of material nature—goodness, passion, and ignorance—showing how an understanding of these three forces, along with the knowledge of the psychology behind divine and demoniac natures, can lead to enlightenment. He explains the different kinds of liberation and the primacy of surrendering to him with a heart of devotion. All of this and much more can be found in the *Gita*'s many verses.

WHY 'NEW" TESTAMENT?

It is often wondered why the *Gita* is called the "New Testament" of India. The reason, quite simply, is that it was among the first of Hinduism's sacred books to offer a new paradigm in spirituality. For its time, the book was somewhat revolutionary, proffering both contemplative and active forms of practice, whereas, prior to the *Gita*, adherence to contemplative forms was more common. That is to say, practitioners often performed yoga, solitary meditation, and studied, without a sense of service to the divine. This should be clearly understood.

In the first verses of the *Gita*'s third chapter, we are introduced to the two forms of spirituality: the contemplative life and the active one. The people of India in the time of the *Gita* tended toward acts of extreme asceticism. Aspiring spiritualists of the age felt that only by shaking off the burden of active worldly life could one approach a life of the spirit. Only by completely renouncing the material world could one advance toward the spiritual world. These ideas were gleaned from the Upanishads and other Hindu texts.

The *Gita*, however, chose to go further. It takes the doctrine of "negation," or of rejecting the material world, so dominant in ancient India, and augments it with a teaching of positive spiritual action. This latter teaching, to be sure, could also be found in the older texts as well, but the *Gita* brought out its special significance for the current age. Thus, Krishna teaches Arjuna not so much about renunciation *of* action but rather about renunciation *in* action. In fact, the *Gita* accepts both forms of renunciation, but Krishna describes the "active" form as more practical and more effective as well.

Whichever form, or approach, one chooses, says Krishna, detachment from sense objects is mandatory. The difference, then, lies only in one's external involvement with the material world. Krishna explains all of this in terms of yoga, or "linking with God" (the literal meaning of the word). He asserts that contemplative, or inactive, yoga is difficult, for the mind can become restless or distracted, especially in our current age, which was just about to begin when he spoke to Arjuna some 5,000 years ago. Rather, he recommends the active form of yoga, which he calls Karma-yoga. This is safer, he says, for one still strives to focus the mind, using various techniques of inner meditation, but augments this endeavor with practical engagement in the material world.

Krishna makes this clearer still in the *Gita*'s fifth chapter (in my own translation):

Both renunciation, or the contemplative approach, and the yoga of work, or Karma-yoga, can bring about the desired goal. But of the two, Karma-yoga is better. For the real renunciant neither hates nor hankers; being without duality, O mighty-armed one, he easily frees himself from bondage—for he is a true philosopher. The inexperienced person—as opposed to those who are learned—talk of philosophy and yoga as being different: If either approach is properly practiced, one can attain the result of each. The state attained by philosophers is reached by yogis, too: He who sees philosophy and yoga as one, truly sees. But renunciation is difficult to attain without yoga, O mighty-armed one, whereas the sage endowed with yoga attains the Supreme soon enough. (5.2–6)

It should again be underlined that while Krishna is endorsing both the contemplative and the active approaches to spirituality, saying that they lead to the same goal, he is unequivocally recommending the latter approach. In the next chapter, in fact, he elaborates on how to perform Karma-yoga, again emphasizing that it is superior to merely renouncing and philosophizing:

The true renunciant and yogi is he who is unattached to the fruit of work and yet performs the work that needs to be done—not he who lights no fire and performs no activity. That which is generally called renunciation . . . know that to be yoga. This is true for no one becomes a yogi without renouncing the desire for sense gratification. (6.1–2)

Such a teaching is especially useful for practitioners today, living in the modern world. Krishna is saying that we needn't go off to a forest to contemplate our navel. In fact, he says that such endeavors will most likely fail for most people. Rather, we can achieve the goal of yoga by learning the art of "unattached action," which is one of the *Gita*'s main teachings. In the *Gita*'s many chapters, he will explain this art to Arjuna and, by extenuation, to the rest of us. The *Gita* thus teaches how we can, in Western terms, be in the world but not of it. Indeed, it presents this as the topmost yoga system.

YOGA: *GITA* STYLE

Krishna explains that both processes of yoga, the contemplative and the active, begin with learning how to control the mind. In the modern world, this is known as "meditation."

By meditation (*dhyana*), one can learn to behold the Lord in one's own heart. This can be achieved by both the yoga of philosophy and by the yoga of works (Karma-yoga). (13.25)

Earlier in the *Gita*, Krishna elaborates on the importance of controlling the mind, which is essentially this same process of *dhyana*, or meditation:

When the yogi, by practice of yoga, disciplines his mental activities and becomes situated in true spirituality—devoid of material desires—he is said to be fully established in yoga. As a lamp in a place that is devoid of wind does not waver, so the true spiritualist, whose mind is controlled, remains steady in meditation on the transcendental self. (6.19–23)

Such meditation, Krishna admits, is difficult, but it can be achieved through arduous effort:

Of course . . . the mind is fickle and difficult to restrain. But by practice and by a renounced mood . . . it can be attained. For one lacking in self-control, yoga is nearly unachievable. But one who strives with self-control may eventually attain it by the correct means. (6.35–36)

In verses ten through fourteen of the *Gita*'s sixth chapter, Krishna indeed elaborates on the "correct means," and by his elaboration one begins to see how truly difficult it is to perform this kind of meditation: the yogi must learn to meditate in this way continually, without interruption, in perfect solitude. The *Gita* further tells us that he must fully restrain his mind and his desires, without wants or possessions. He must prepare a seat for himself in a clean place, neither too high nor too low, covered with cloth, antelope-skin, or grass. He must sit in this special place, says the *Gita*, and learn to make his mind one-pointed, restricting any deviated contemplation and distraction of the senses. He should practice such meditation for his own purification only—without any ulterior motive. Firmly holding the base of his body, his neck and his head straight and in one place, looking only at the tip of his own nose, he must be serene, fearless, and above any lusty thought. He must sit in this way, restraining his mind, thinking only of God, Krishna says, fully devoted to the Supreme.

Krishna calls this method Raja Yoga, for it was practiced by great kings (*raja*) in ancient times. The heart of this system involves control of the breath (*pranayama*), which, in turn, is meant to manipulate the energy in the body (*prana*). This, along with intricate sitting postures (*asana*), was an effective means for quieting one's passions, controlling bodily appetites, thus facilitating focus on the Supreme.

Nonetheless, this contemplative form of yoga, systematized in Patanjali's *Yoga-Sutras* (another Hindu book of knowledge) and popular today as Hatha-yoga, is too difficult for most people, especially in the current age of Kali-yuga. This is particularly true if they are going to try to perform it properly, as it is espoused in these original yoga texts, and Krishna says as much by the end of the *Gita*'s sixth chapter.

Still, he recommends elements of this contemplative yoga system along with the yoga of action, or Karma-yoga. And for most readers of the *Gita*, this can get confusing. Just which is he recommending—this austere form of disciplined sitting and meditation, or action in perfect consciousness? Does the *Gita* recommend Hatha-yoga, or doesn't it? Does this most sacred of texts accept the path of contemplation, or does it say that one must approach the Supreme Being through work?

Indeed, Arjuna himself expresses confusion in two different chapters of the *Gita*: Is Krishna advising him to renounce the world, Arjuna wonders, or is he asking him to act in Krishna consciousness?

STAGES OF YOGA

A thorough reading of the *Gita* reveals a sort of hierarchy, a "yoga ladder," if you will, in which one begins by studying the subject of yoga with some serious interest (this is called Abhyasa yoga) and ends up, if successful, by graduating to Bhakti-yoga, or "devotion" for the Supreme. All the stages in-between—and there are many—are quite complex, and it is at this point that most modern practitioners become daunted in their study of the *Gita*. Here we will briefly analyze only the crucial concepts of this yoga ladder, and, in so doing, bypass much of the *Gita*'s intimidating detail.

The question may legitimately be raised as to why the two approaches to yoga, the contemplative and the active (and all their corollaries) seem to be interchangeable in one section of the text, while they are clearly something of a hierarchy in another. The answer lies in the *Gita*'s use of yoga terminology, a lexicon that, again, can be confusing. The entire subject becomes easier to understand when we realize that the numerous yoga systems in the *Gita* actually refer to the same thing: they are all forms of Bhakti-yoga. The differences are mainly in emphasis.

It is called Karma-yoga, for example, when, in the practitioner's mind, the first word in the hyphenated compound takes precedence—not just in the physical placement of the word but in the conceptual placement as well. For instance, in Karma-yoga, one wants to perform work (*karma*), and is attached to a particular kind of work, but he wants to do it for Krishna. In this scenario, *karma* is primary and yoga is secondary. But since it is directed to God, it can be called Karma-yoga instead of just *karma*. The same principle can be applied to all other yoga systems.

Of all the yogas, however, the *Gita* teaches that Bhakti-yoga is the highest. This is because the first word in the hyphenated compound is *bhakti*, or devotional love. In love, one becomes selfless, and thus, instead of giving a prominent place to one's own desire, one considers the beloved first. Thus, the second part of the compound (yoga) becomes prominent—linking with God takes precedence over what the individual practitioner wants, even if that want, or desire, is love. In fact, the first and second words of the hyphenated compound become one. The devotee wants to love (*bhakti*), but he considers Krishna's desire before his own. And Krishna also wants to love. This makes Bhakti-yoga the perfection of the yoga process.

In other words, Karma-yoga emphasizes "working" for the Supreme; Gyana-yoga emphasizes "focusing one's knowledge" on the Supreme; Dhyana-yoga involves "contemplating" the Supreme; Buddhi-yoga is about directing the "intellect" toward the Supreme; and Bhakti-yoga, the perfection of all yogas, occurs when one has "devotion" for the Supreme. The main principle of yoga, in whatever form, is to direct your activity toward linking with God. This is enacted most effectively by loving him.

To summarize, we may first of all, then, observe that the *Gita* accepts many traditional forms of yoga and Hindu spirituality as legitimate. It claims that the main focus of these paths is the same—linking with the Supreme. However, the *Gita* also creates a hierarchy of sorts. Indulging some of the terminology, the hierarchical schema runs something like this: First there is study (Abhyasa-yoga), understanding (Gyana-yoga), and meditation (Dhyana-yoga), on the meaning of scripture. This leads to the contemplation of philosophy, and eventually wisdom (Sankhya- or an alternate form of Gyana-yoga), culminating in renunciation (Sannyasa-yoga). This, in turn, leads to the proper use of intelligence (Buddhi-yoga). When engaged practically, this is called Karma-yoga, and when imbued with devotion, Bhakti-yoga.

All of this involves a complex inner development, beginning with an understanding of the temporary nature of the material world and the nature of duality. Realizing that the world of matter will not continue to exist and that birth all-too-quickly leads to death, the aspiring yogi begins to practice external renunciation and gradually *internal* renunciation, which, ultimately, consists of giving up the desire for the fruit of one's work. From this, it is a short step to the topmost yogic path—performing the work itself as an offering to God.

This is synonymous with the method of detached action, leading to the "perfection of inaction," that is, freedom from the bondage of work. One becomes free from such bondage because one learns to act as an "agent" of the Supreme as opposed to his "competitor." That is, souls of this world tend to see themselves, at least on a subliminal level, as the center of action, unconsciously—and sometimes consciously—trying to usurp God's position. However, through this process, one learns to work for God, on his behalf. And from such work, one becomes purified, free from the misconceptions of false divinity. Further, the practitioner becomes reacquainted with his or her original position as an eternal servant of the Supreme. This is the essential teaching of the *Gita*, and in its pages Krishna methodically takes Arjuna (and each of us) through each step of this yoga process.

"Of all yogis," Krishna tells Arjuna, "you are the best." This is because Arjuna is linked to him through loving devotional service, the active form of spirituality found in the *Gita*. Krishna concludes by explaining the essential element of Bhakti-yoga that distinguishes it from all the rest: "Of everyone on the spiritual path, the one who is constantly thinking of Me within himself, meditating on Me within the heart—he is the first-class yogi."

EXCERPTS FROM THE *BHAGAVAD-GITA*[1]

Although the above might serve as an introduction to the teachings of the *Gita*, there is no substitute for the verse poetry in which Krishna's "song" beautifully manifests. What follows, then, is an English rendering of the *Gita*'s key verses by Carl Woodham, whose work does not seek to convey exact translation or to rigorously adhere to the Sanskrit original, but rather to capture the poetic flow and essential meaning of the text.

1.28–30
Arjuna:
Seeing all my loved ones on this field prepared to die,
All my limbs are shaking and my mouth is going dry.
My Gandiva bow keeps slipping through my trembling hand.
Skin ablaze and hair erect—I do not understand!
I cannot remain here, for my mind has gone to flight.
Only great misfortune can result from such a fight!

2.1
Sanjaya (the narrator):
Shedding tears of pity sat Arjuna, quite depressed.
Seeing this, Lord Krishna made the following request:

2.2–3
Krishna:
Tell Me why you give these unbefitting thoughts such worth,
Leading to dishonor and degraded future birth.
Don't give in to impotence with petty, weakened heart;
Rise, O mighty warrior—the battle soon will start!

2.9–10
Sanjaya:
Having spoken clearly of his sorrow and his plight,
Mighty Arjuna said firmly, "Krishna, I won't fight."
As Arjuna sat between the armies, sad and weak,
Krishna simply smiled at him and then began to speak:

2.11–15
Krishna:
Such a cultured speech, and yet your mind is filled with dread.
Learned persons mourn neither the living nor the dead.
Everyone has been alive throughout antiquity, and
Never in the future shall we ever cease to be.
Bodies change from young to old. At death the soul must leave,
Taking a new body, as discerning souls perceive.
Winter turns to summer just as sorrow turns to bliss;
Sages remain steady through perceptions such as this.
One who learns to tolerate misfortune or elation
Surely becomes qualified for endless liberation.

2.41–46
Krishna:
Earnest souls take up this path with single-minded aim.
Those without detachment have a shifting mental frame.
In the jumbled minds of those attached materially
Firm resolve to serve the Lord will never come to be.
Those possessing knowledge that is trivial and poor
Take the flowery Vedic words as heaven's open door.
Godly birth and wealth appear too tempting to ignore.
Wanting but a lavish life, they think of nothing more.
*Veda*s deal with matter and its threefold qualities.
Rise above dull matter and have no anxieties.
As a mighty reservoir replaces a small well
Higher Vedic teachings leave the lesser ones dispelled.

2.47–48

Krishna:

Always do your work, Arjun, but do not claim its yield.
Neither think yourself in charge nor flee the battlefield.
Balanced in your duty without care to win or lose,
Turn your work to yoga, as the learned sages do.

2.49–51

Krishna:

Stop all selfish actions and surrender to the Lord.
Only misers work with great attachment to reward.
Yogis rid themselves of work with good or bad reaction.
Strive, My friend, for yoga, which is called the art of action.
Stopping work that leads them to be born repeatedly,
Yogis gain the highest state beyond all misery.

2.56–57

Krishna:

Knowledge of the spirit, when completely understood,
Helps one become steady, whether times are bad or good.
Joy and sorrow never sway a steady-minded sage.
Sages are untroubled by attachment, fear or rage.

2.62–63

Krishna:

Dwelling on sense objects sets the blaze of lust afire.
Lust produces anger, born of unfulfilled desire.
Anger breeds confusion and bewilders memory,
Causing lost intelligence and endless misery.

2.64–66

Krishna:

Free from love and hatred and from sensual addiction,
Sages gain the mercy of the Lord without restriction.
His profound compassion leaves a pleased and peaceful mind,
Miseries diminished and intelligence refined.
Otherwise, the troubles of the mind will just increase.
How can you be happy when your mind is not at peace?

3.17–19

Krishna:

Those who find the soul within, with depth of realization,
Take delight and free themselves of earthly obligation.
Filling every purpose and completing every goal,
They depend on no one. Such is knowledge of the soul.
Do your duty faithfully and think not of reward.
Work without attachment leads directly to the Lord.

3.30
Krishna:
Doing all your work for Me with vigorous delight,
Give up thoughts of selfishness, compose yourself, and fight.

3.36
Arjuna:
Krishna, what imposing force will not let one desist from
Uninvited sinful acts, although one may resist?

3.38
Krishna:
Like a fire concealed by smoke, a mirror thick with dust, or
Embryos within their wombs, the soul is wrapped in lust.

3.40–42
Krishna:
Lust resides within the mind, intelligence and senses.
From it, one's bewilderment and ignorance commences.
Senses govern matter and the mind controls each sense, but
Soul surpasses all because it rules intelligence.
Knowing that the soul retains the ultimate position,
Set yourself to conquer lust—your deadly opposition.

3.43
Krishna:
Arjuna, control this lust, the symbol of all sin.
Slay this foe of knowledge so real learning can begin!

4.16–18
Krishna:
Now I shall explain to you both action and inaction.
Even sages fail to know this to their satisfaction.
Action and inaction and those actions that are banned
Surely are quite intricate and hard to understand.
Wise and active persons can behold, with proper vision,
Action in inaction—and the opposite condition.

5.1
Arjuna:
Krishna, kindly tell me clearly which is best to do:
Should I give up work, or should I simply work for You?

5.2–7
Krishna:
Mighty-armed, both paths are good for gaining liberation, but
Of the two, to work for Me transcends renunciation.
One who neither hates nor loves the fruits of his endeavor

Savors liberation from all worldly bonds, forever.
Detachment from matter and attachment unto Me
Are in fact identical, say those who truly see.
Thoughtful souls who serve Me come to Me without delay;
Others miss real happiness, renouncing work and play.
My servant is dear to all and to him all are dear.
His work brings no karma to distract or interfere.

5.18.21
Krishna:
Wise and humble sages see with vision, fair and equal,
Cows and dogs and elephants—and great or lowly people.
Those of equal vision, though residing on this earth,
Dwell in flawless spirit and transcend death and rebirth.
Tolerating pleasant things and things that bring them pain,
Knowing God and staying on the transcendental plane,
Such enlightened persons take no pleasure from the senses.
Focused on the Lord, their inner happiness commences,

6.26
Krishna:
Fleeting and unsteady minds meander here and there.
Yogis must retrieve their minds and govern them with care.

6.29–32
Krishna:
Yogis see all other souls with true equality,
Whether they are happy or awash in misery.
Yogis see Me in all souls and see all souls in Me.
I appear in everything enlightened yogis see.
One who sees Me everywhere, in everything that be,
Never loses sight of Me—nor is he lost to Me.
One who serves the Lord within—My own manifestation—
Certainly remains with Me in every situation.

6.47
Krishna:
Of all yogis, one with faith who fixes Me in mind,
Intimately serving Me, affectionate and kind,
Though perceived by others as a low and simple minion,
Is indeed the greatest yogi. That is My opinion.

7.7
Krishna:
No truth lies beyond Myself, so do not be misled.
Everything depends on Me, as pearls rest on a thread.

7.27–28
Krishna:
Everyone is born into delusion and remains
Overwhelmed by hate and lust they simply can't restrain.
Souls possessed of piety in this life and the last,
Worship Me, for all of their delusion has now passed.

8.3–5
Krishna:
Souls are called Brahman, Arjun. Their nature is to serve.
Karma, or their actions, brings the bodies they deserve.
This world is but matter and it constantly transforms.
Demigods are parts of My vast universal form.
I'm the Lord of sacrifice, residing in each heart.
There, as Supersoul, I watch the soul, my tiny part.
If you die with mind on Me, unflinching and devout
You will come to me at death. Of this there is no doubt.

9.15–16
Krishna:
Others seeking knowledge end up somewhat misinformed,
Taking Me as one, or all, or in My cosmic form.
But it is I who am the chant, the ritual, the *ghee*.
Fire, rite and healing herb are just the same as Me.

9.17–19
Krishna:
Universal father, mother, patriarch and Om;
Purity and Vedic knowledge-all are Me alone.
I sustain and shelter all. There is no better friend.
I'm the endless seed, both the beginning and the end.
I command the sky to clear and cause the clouds to swell.
Soul and matter come from Me, and life and death as well.

9.26–27
Krishna:
Cups of water make Me smile, though I could drink an ocean.
Fruits or flowers please Me, when presented in devotion.
All you do and all you give and all the food you savor—Offer
first to Me with love and you shall win My favor.

10.7
Krishna:
One who knows My opulence and power without doubt,
Links with Me in service, always steady and devout.

11.32

Krishna:

Time I am, the death of all, and I am here to reign!
But for you, the Pandavas, these men shall all be slain.
Rise and fight and win your fame, and claim your right to rule!
Even now your foes are dead, and you are but My tool.

12.1

Arjuna:

Tell me Lord, of these two paths, which one should I be on:
That of loving service, or the path to reach Brahman?
Some seek You impersonally and make Brahman their aim, the
All-pervading, changeless light that has no form or name.

12.2–7

Krishna:

Dear Arjuna, faithful souls who bow down at My feet, their
Minds absorbed in Me alone are surely most complete.
Formless meditation is quite troublesome, indeed, and
Though a sincere person may eventually succeed,
I shall swiftly rescue from the sea of birth and death
Faithful devotees who chant My glories with each breath.

18.65–66

Krishna:

Think about Me always and become My devotee.
Worship and give homage and you shall return to Me.
Giving up religious creeds, submit yourself to Me.
I accept your former sins. Have no anxiety.

18.67–69

Krishna:

Only speak these words of Mine to those who are austere.
Don't instruct those faithless souls too envious to hear.
If, instead, you teach My words among the devotees,
Your devotion is assured, and you'll return to Me.
Never in this world will any servant be more dear than
One who simply speaks My words and makes the meaning
clear.

18.70–71

Krishna:

I declare that one who learns this sacred conversation,
Worships Me with knowledge born of keen discrimination.
One who listens faithfully, with envy put aside,
Reaches higher planets where the sinless souls reside.

18.73
Arjuna:
Krishna, You can never fail. My fantasy is gone! Your
Kindness and Your wisdom give me strength to carry on.
I am firm and free from fear and quite prepared to act to
Carry out Your orders and defeat my foe's attack.

Overall, the teachings of the *Gita* are summarized in four nutshell verses. Krishna says: "I am the source of all spiritual and material worlds. Everything emanates from me. The wise who fully realize this engage in my devotional service and worship me with all their hearts." (10.8) "My pure devotees are absorbed in thoughts of me, and they experience fulfillment and bliss by enlightening one another and conversing about me." (10.9) "To those who are continually devoted and worship me with love, I give the understanding by which they can come to me." (10.10) "Out of compassion for them, I, residing in their hearts, destroy with the shining lamp of knowledge the darkness born of ignorance." (10.11)

As a result of becoming Krishna's devotee, one can expect to develop certain qualities. In the *Gita*'s twelfth chapter (verses 13–20), these qualities are enumerated by Krishna himself:

- The devotee is not envious of any living being;
- Cultivates a sense of friendship and compassion;
- Gives up the feeling of false proprietorship;
- Doesn't misidentify the self with the body;
- Is equal in happiness or distress;
- Is tolerant and forgiving;
- Strives for self-control;
- Is always content and grateful;
- Has strong determination on the spiritual path;
- Surrenders mind and intellect to God;
- Does not put anyone into difficulty;
- Is not disturbed by others;
- Is not thrown off by fear or anxiety;
- Is pure and efficient;
- Is disinterested in material results;
- Is indifferent to mundane dualities;
- Is equal to friends and enemies;
- Is unattached to honor and dishonor, fame and infamy;
- Is free from bad association and disinterested in useless talk;
- Is not attached to any particular living situation;
- Is steadfast in mind and fixed in knowledge;
- God is such a person's ultimate goal in all situations.

While the *Gita* describes these as much desired qualities, they are said to naturally arise in one who practices devotion to Krishna. A separate endeavor is simply not necessary. One should be a good devotee, say the texts, with consciousness focused on Krishna—everything else will fall into place.

WHO IS KRISHNA?

Krishna's martial character, as found in the *Mahabharata* and the *Bhagavad-Gita,* has many facets—he is seen as philosopher, statesman, charioteer, husband, friend, warrior, lord, and guru. While these images of Krishna are highly regarded by Hindus worldwide, his early life as a child and as a young lover is often held in greater esteem. Frolicking in the simple bucolic atmosphere of Vraja, in northern India, he captured the local people's hearts, and their descendents have been retelling his extraordinary pastimes ever since. It is *this* Krishna that is most loved in the Indian subcontinent.

He is God in the form of a beautiful youth, with an alluringly dark complexion that is reminiscent of newly formed rain clouds. His skin color is sometimes described as the deep, velvety blue of a peacock or a lotus. His large, elegant eyes are lotus-like, too, and they are often singled out in the writings of self-realized souls: "When will that merciful boy Krishna look upon me with his playful lotus eyes, which are soothing and cooling with loving emotion, reddish at the corners and dark bluish at the irises?" Or, "Above all his beautiful features, Krishna's eyes dance and move obliquely, acting like arrows to pierce the minds of Sri Radha and the *gopis*." The *gopis* refer to Krishna's cowherd girlfriends, amongst whom Radha is supreme. They love him more than life itself, making their affections paradigmatic. That is to say, all devotees seek to emulate their mood of pure and consummate devotion.

Krishna attracts souls with his mellifluous flute, which is always poised at his reddish lips, or firmly situated in his colorful sash. His dark blue cheeks are soft and smooth, his smile enchanting. His glistening yellow garments, the color of lightning, stand out against his dark skin, as his earrings dangle in time to his flute music. He wears an elegant peacock feather in his long, curly black hair and a fresh flower garland around his neck. As the ancient texts tell us, "Ornaments caress Krishna's transcendental body, but his form is so beautiful that it enhances the ornaments he wears. Therefore, Krishna's body is said to be 'the ornament of ornaments.'"

His mesmerizing beauty and his Godhood should be understood in conjunction with each other. The well-worn phrase, "Truth is Beauty," takes on new meaning as a result of Krishna's form. Since Krishna, as God, is the embodiment of Truth, his beauty follows as a matter of course. His name, in fact, means "the all-attractive one." This is significant. The idea is that God is a living being who attracts everyone, whether they know it or not. For those who are unaware of him as a person, they find attraction in him indirectly through his divine qualities, such as eternality, power, or knowledge.

Other names of God focus on particular attributes. Even the English word "God," for example, comes from the Germanic root *goot*, meaning "the good one." Certainly God is good, but He is also so much more. He is sometimes called Buddha ("the intelligent one"), to cite another example, because he is the most intelligent being in existence. But is God merely good or intelligent?

In the biblical tradition, he is called El, because he is "mighty, strong, prominent." God is strong, yes—the strongest of all—but isn't there more to him than that? Such names of God consider only a partial dimension of his totality, and they attract only devotees who are inclined toward goodness, intellect, or power, which is what those names mean.

The name Krishna, however, indicates God's all-attractive feature, hinting at his total Otherness and the fact that he has all positive qualities in full. This aspect of God's completeness, say Vaishnava texts, is only found in Krishna, or God in his original form.

In Hindu tradition, God is sometimes called "Bhagavan," a word that indicates "one who is full in six opulences"—strength, fame, wealth, knowledge, beauty, and renunciation. It is easy to understand how God has more strength than anyone else, and thus many of his names reflect his unremitting power, as in the name El, described above. Regarding fame, God is certainly well known, and it is clear that no one is more famous than He. Is God wealthy? As creator and proprietor of the cosmos, he owns everything in existence, thus exhibiting the ultimate wealth. Knowledge? An omniscient God will not be found wanting on this count, either.

But beauty and renunciation are difficult to understand from a Western point of view. For this, argues the Hindu, one needs access to the vision of God found in the Vedic scriptures and its corollaries.

Sure, God is commonly seen as beautiful in an abstract sense, but this mainly refers to his qualities of love and compassion, his inner beauty, if you will. And as far as renunciation goes, some may argue that he creates the world and then leaves it to us, to use as we see fit. He gives us free will, even if he remains the ultimate controller. This ability to relinquish the world into our care could be seen as a component of renunciation.

But when one acquaints oneself with Krishna or Rama, the qualities mentioned above take on unique characteristics, the likes of which are unknown in the Western world. Krishna's beauty is indescribable, as suggested a few paragraphs earlier. Volumes have been written about his unsurpassable beauty. And renunciation? His intimate friends in the spiritual world—the boys with whom he tends cows, or the *gopis*, his girlfriends, who dally with him on the banks of the Yamuna River—are heartbroken when he leaves Vraja, for their love for him is the very pinnacle of spiritual emotion, as is his love for them. His ability to leave them, which only increases their love, is the epitome of renunciation. Rama, too, is described as the most beautiful of males, and his kingdom the most magnificent in all of history. Yet he renounces every inch of it to honor the word of his father. He is ready to renounce the lovely Sita as well, for this will teach principle and righteousness.

All forms of Vaishnavism view Vishnu as the Supreme Godhead and Krishna as one of his most important manifestations. There are some Vaishnava groups, though, who view Krishna as the source of Vishnu, or as the original Personality of Godhead. As evidence for Krishna's supremacy, they often quote the *Bhagavata Purana* (1.3.28) or the *Brahma-Samhita* (5.1), which are quite clear regarding Krishna's unequalled position. Beyond scriptural quotation, Krishnaite Vaishnavas draw on the fact that Krishna is the embodiment of intimacy and love, qualities that, among all others, stand supreme. The other forms of Vishnu, and there are many, evoke awe and reverence, bringing to mind the powerful and majestic features of God. But Krishna, in his disarmingly playful way, eclipses their power with his bewitching smile, and surpasses their majesty with simple love. This is the conclusion of the Vrindavan school of Vaishnavism, and it has penetrated other segments of the Vaishnava world as well.

THE HISTORICAL KRISHNA

According to scriptural documentation, Krishna was "born" at midnight on the eighth day of the dark half of the month of Bhadrapada (August–September), in the year 3228 BCE. He displayed his pastimes for all to see for a little over 125 years and then left for his original abode. His "death" occurred in 3102 BCE, marking the beginning of the current age of Kali, characterized by conflict and degradation. Calculations may vary, based on astronomical and genealogical evidence, but these are the commonly accepted dates.

Of course, practitioners view him as "unborn," and, therefore, his appearance in the world is seen as grace, pure and simple, a magic show, of sorts, performed for our benefit. In other words, his life in the material world has a soteriological function in that it is meant to cure us of our spiritual amnesia, reminding us of our real life in the spiritual realm—encouraging us to go back home, back to Godhead. His eternal pastimes are, ultimately, imported from the spiritual world, and he sometimes manifests them here, just to entice us.

Precious little is known about the prehistoric worship of Krishna, though it is worth noting that even among the ancient Harappan relics, about which very little is known (see Antecedents, Chapter 1), there are seals with names related to Krishna, such as Akrura (Krishna's friend), Vrishni (his family), Yadu (his ancestor), and so on. Some of these seals date back almost 5,000 years.[2]

Early texts, too, mention him briefly, including the *Vedas* and the Upanishads. For example, his name appears in the *Rig Veda* (1.116, 117), though, due to usage and context, it is unlikely that these verses refer to the divinity we today know as Krishna. Nonetheless, there are scholars who take into account the cryptic nature of the Vedic literature, suggesting that the verses in question might in fact be about him, even if these same verses appear to be pointing in some other direction.[3]

Vedic references to Vishnu are less ambiguous, and these will be explored in the chapter on Vaishnavism. In the present context, it is worth noting that Vishnu's identification with Krishna goes back a long way, with highly suggestive statements in the *Vedas* themselves. For example, in one such Vedic text (*Rig Veda* 1.22.16–21), Vishnu is known as the "protector," a word that has many Sanskrit equivalents, such as *rakshana*. Yet this verse chooses to use *gopa*, a word that indeed means "protector" but that more commonly refers to a "cowherd." And while Vishnu is never visualized as a cowherd, Krishna certainly is. Such covert identification is not uncommon in Vedic texts.

When we get to the *Chandogya Upanishad* (3.17), which is from the sixth century BCE, at the latest, Krishna's Vedic presence is more definite, since here he is mentioned as the son of Devaki, who did appear as his mother during his earthly incarnation. This Upanishad, moreover, is part of the *Sama Veda*, thus giving him Vedic status.

Hala's *Gaha-Sattasai* is an early secular source telling us much about Krishna, and the *Harivamsa* is the closest thing we have to a full life story. Add to this Bhasa's *Bala-Charita*, another early record of Krishna's pastimes, and a full biographical narrative begins to emerge. It is difficult to date much of this literature, but it is clear that it took initial shape well before the Common Era. Naturally, the *Vishnu Purana* and the *Bhagavata Purana*, and the much later *Gita-Govinda*, are important sources, too. But this takes us well into the twelfth century CE.

Other early evidences of Krishna include Yaska's *Nirukta*, an etymological dictionary dating to approximately the fifth century BCE, where one already finds well-known stories about the cowherd divinity and his devotees. There is a brief reference to Krishna as "Vaasudeva," that is, the son of Vasudeva, in Panini's Sanskrit grammar, dated at about the fourth century BCE, too. In addition, there is a significant array of archaeological evidence for Krishna's pre-Christian existence. This evidence will be explored only briefly here, as numerous scholars have already treated it in greater detail.[4]

In the fourth century BCE, Megasthenes the Greek ambassador to the court of Chandragupta Maurya, wrote that people in the region of Mathura worshipped a divinity known as "Herakles," who is now usually identified with Krishna. This identification is plausible because the Greek author mentions particular regions as well as heroic acts that are easily associated with the Dark Lord. Also interesting is that Krishna was commonly called "Hari-kul-ish," or "God as the Supreme Controller," a name that could have been adapted as Herakles.

Then, in 180–165 BCE, the Greek ruler Agathocles issued coins with images of Krishna and his brother Balarama on them, offering significant numismatic evidence for the historicity of Krishna.

At Ghosundi, a town near Udaipur, there is an inscription dated at about 150 BCE. Here the words of an early Krishna devotee tell of his devotion for Vasudeva and Narayana, names related to Krishna. And in the first century BCE, the Greek soldier Heliodorus erected at Besnagar, near Bhilsa, a column with the following inscription: "This Garuda column of Vasudeva (Krishna), the God of gods, was erected here by Heliodorus, a worshipper of the Lord [Bhagavata], the son of Diya [Greek Dion] and an inhabitant of Taxila, who came as ambassador of the Greeks from the Great King Amtalikita to King Kashiputra Bhagabhadra ..." There is quite a bit of other evidence along these lines, too.[5]

Consequently, Krishna's historicity is now widely accepted, even in the academic world. That being said, most scholars naturally doubt the supernatural aspects of his earthly sojourn, including his many miracles, as they do with Jesus. Such subjects, of course, are a matter of belief and faith, or of realization, and beyond the reach of scholarly methods. Still, it is interesting to see that prominent authorities in the fields of Indology,

Hinduism, and South Asian Studies generally accept the historical veracity of Krishna's appearance. Here are but a few examples:

Bimanbehari Majumdar: "The western scholars at first treated Krishna as a myth.... But many of the Orientalists in the present century have arrived at the conclusion that Krishna was . . . a real historical personage . . ."[6]

R. C. Majumdar: "There is now a general consensus of opinion in favour of the historicity of Krishna."[7]

Horace H. Wilson: "Rama and Krishna, who appear to have been originally real and historical characters . . ."[8]

Thomas J. Hopkins: "From a strictly scholarly, historical standpoint, the Krishna who appears in the Bhagavad-Gita is the princely Krishna of the Mahabharata . . . Krishna, the historical prince and charioteer of Arjuna."[9]

Rudolf Otto: "That Krishna himself was a historical figure is indeed quite indubitable."[10]

Without any further ado, then, let us take a brief look at Krishna's life as revealed in the historical record.

KRISHNA'S LIFE[11]

Krishna appeared over 5,000 years ago in Mathura, India, to Devaki and Vasudeva in the jail cell of the tyrant Kamsa, who was a demon in human guise. That the Lord chose to begin his earthly sojourn in prison tells us much about Vaishnava thought: Life in the material world is tantamount to a prison sentence, but here we are trapped until we develop love for God. Only then can we know release from material suffering and attain the freedom to return to our spiritual home.

Krishna, of course, is not bound like an ordinary soul—he is not bound at all—and his birth in prison does much more than show the plight of common mortals. His story is complex. Mathura's throne was occupied by the Bhoja family, also known as the Vrishnis and the Andhakas, who were descendents of the Yadu dynasty. As an aside, Yadu is the name of one of the five Aryan families mentioned in the *Rig Veda*. The regions governed by the Yadu clan were in the southwest of the Gangetic plains, between the Chambal River, Betwa, and Ken, which, today, corresponds to the border areas of Uttar Pradesh and Madhya Pradesh. There, King Yadu founded the Yadava Dynasty, from which Krishna descends.

King Ugrasena was the last great emperor of the clan. But when his demon son, Kamsa, came of age, he jailed his father and usurped the kingdom. Kamsa's wicked activities go back to many lifetimes. At the dawn of time, says the *Mahabharata*, demigods and demons were at war in the heavenly regions of the cosmos. When the demigods began to get the upper hand, the demons decided to attack the earth instead. One by one, they invaded our planet by taking birth as princes in powerful royal families of the time.

As the earth became overrun by the materialistic activities of these kingly demons, the demigods earnestly sought Lord Vishnu's protection, who then assured them that he would tend to the ever-worsening situation himself. Accordingly, he told them to assist him by taking birth in the Yadu Dynasty, and that he would soon come to earth as Krishna, along with his brother (or primary expansion) Balarama, in response to their prayers.

Kamsa was one of those demons who repeatedly incarnated on earth to pillage and conquer for selfish ends. In his previous life, he had appeared as a villain named Kalanemi, who was eventually destroyed by Lord Vishnu. And because a vague memory of the incident carried over into this life, he was born with the premonition that Vishnu would slay him yet again. For this reason, when the sage Narada confirmed that this would in fact happen, and when a voice from heaven prophesied that his sister Devaki's eighth child would do the deed, he was not surprised.

Hoping to thwart his inevitable destiny, Kamsa imprisoned Devaki and her husband Vasudeva, killing each of their children as they were born. Her seventh pregnancy, however, was Balarama, the Lord's first expansion. By divine arrangement, this child escaped the fate of the first six, for he was mystically transferred to the womb of Rohini, one of Vasudeva's other wives who was staying in Vrindavan with his close friend, Nanda Maharaja.

When Kamsa saw that overdue Devaki was now childless, he assumed she had miscarried. What he didn't know was that Balarama was already born in the house of Nanda, waiting for the divine appearance of Krishna.

And then it happened. Krishna's birth was not ordinary. He appeared as God before Vasudeva and Devaki, his parents, in their Mathura jail cell. They saw him first in his majestic four-armed form as Vishnu, in full regalia, and then he assumed the form of a baby. As soon as they began to relish their newborn, the jail guards fell asleep as a result of Krishna's mystic potency, and the heavy prison doors flew open. Vasudeva knew what to do.

He picked up baby Krishna and carried him across the Yamuna, from Mathura to Gokula (in the Vrindavan area). Entering Nanda Maharaja's house, he saw that Mother Yashoda had just given birth to a baby girl, Subhadra, also known as Yoga-Maya, an embodied form of the Lord's spiritual energy. Everyone in Yashoda's house was also fast asleep, as per Krishna's arrangement.

Leaving baby Krishna in the girl's place, Vasudeva took the female child and returned to his cell in Mathura. He reentered the prison and shackled himself as before, so no one would know he had gone. An esoteric Vaishnava tradition teaches that Yashoda had actually given birth to twins, a boy and a girl. The boy was Krishna in his original form, and when Vasudeva arrived with his baby, who was actually an expansion of Krishna, the expansion merged into Krishna's original form, the son of Mother Yashoda.[12] Vasudeva then took the girl and returned to Mathura.

When Kamsa was informed of Devaki's new child (the young girl placed by her side in Krishna's stead), he savagely burst in to kill the infant. With heartless rage, he dashed the poor baby against the stone floor, hoping to smash its life from its body. It was at this point that the baby girl manifested her frightening eight-armed form. Yoga-Maya, says the texts, turned into Maha-Maya (Durga)—the goddess of the material spheres. "Fool!" she said. "You can't kill me. And know this too Kamsa: the child who will be your undoing is already born." With these frightening words, she resumed her form as a baby girl.

Some say that after Durga's intense display, Kamsa became somewhat contrite, releasing Vasudeva and Devaki from prison at that time. They named their little baby girl Subhadra and raised her in the Mathura area.[13] Others say that Krishna's parents weren't released from prison until much later, as we will see.

According to the most common version of the narrative, Kamsa immediately ordered the death of all children under 10 days old, hoping to avert his own. But because he only had jurisdiction in the immediate vicinity, Krishna was out of reach, safely ensconced in his new cowherd hamlet in Gokula.

It was soon after this that Kamsa sent out a bevy of demons, one by one, to hunt out Krishna and kill him. Some of them actually found him, but were killed before they could do him harm. The pastimes of Krishna and the demons convey the truth of good conquering evil—they report literal stories of Krishna's manifest actions and provide metaphors by which devotees live their lives.

For example, Putana (the witch), was the first of many demons to discover Krishna's whereabouts. She posed as a beautiful nanny, of sorts, entering Nanda and Yashoda's home compound to kill the divine child. Once there, she smeared her breasts with poison and took baby Krishna onto her lap in the hope that he would suckle them. The story ends with Krishna not only sucking the milk from her breasts but her life airs as well. And so she died, resuming her ghastly form as a demoness. Still, because she approached him in a mood of service, resembling a mother, he awarded her the form of liberation reserved for those who have parental affection for him.

In later Vaishnava teachings, Putana came to symbolize the pseudo guru—a master who poses as a learned, self-realized soul but who is actually more interested in exploiting his disciples. Such metaphorical readings of the demons and other aspects of Krishna's life permeate the Vaishnava tradition. Another example is Shakatasura (the cart demon), who represents the burden of bad habits, or Trinavarta (the whirlwind demon), who represents the false pride associated with mundane scholarship; there are countless others as well. Many nuances of Vaishnava philosophy have been evoked through this rich figurative approach to Krishna lore.[14] Still, God does more than kill demons.

The celestial cowherd stayed in Gokula for the first 3 1/2 years of his earthly life. But it soon became clear that Kamsa's evil comrades had discovered his whereabouts, and so Nanda and Yashoda, and the entire cowherd community of Gokula, relocated to nearby Chatikar, gradually moving to Vrindavan proper and then to Nandagram, the family's original ancestral home, as well. Records show that he lived in the Vrindavan area until he was 6 years, and 8 months old, and then in Nandagram until he was 10 years old. All of these locales are in the Vraja area of Uttar Pradesh.

It was in this new rustic setting that Krishna developed his reputation as "the Butter Thief," particularly at Chatikar. He and Balarama began to herd cows while there as well. The stories of Krishna and his stealing of butter are famous, as are his pastimes with his bovine friends. While Vaishnava texts report how this took place on our planet some 5,000 years ago, it is said that similar events recur repeatedly on other planets and go on eternally in the spiritual world. What follows, then, is but a taste of these charming and magical occurrences, even though countless variations appear in Hinduism's sacred texts.

Krishna would sometimes sneak into the houses of the cowherd women, the elderly *gopis*, and steal their yogurt and butter. Then he would run off to a nearby forest to enjoy the goods with some monkeys that frequented his hideout. When the *gopis* would catch him in the midst of his thievery, he would pretend to be innocent, saying, "Why do you call me a thief? Do you think butter and yogurt are scarce in my home?" Did he mean his home with Nanda and Yashoda in Vrindavan, or did he mean the universe? This is thought-provoking, since the entire cosmos is Krishna's home.

The *gopis*, however, would have none of this, and besides, the evidence (the remains of the stolen butter and yogurt) was all over Krishna's lips, and on the ground right in front of him. The *gopis* insist that Krishna fess up, but he simply chides them in return: "This butter and yogurt are useless anyway. Even the monkeys won't eat it." (Of course not: Krishna fed them so much that they couldn't eat any more!) In the end, the *gopis* were so charmed by Krishna that they forgave his mischief. More, it endeared him to them.

Krishna's mother, Yashoda, thought that little Krishna was stealing butter from the *gopis* because he wasn't satisfied with the butter in his own house. So, to improve her butter, Yashoda picked out several of her best cows and had them eat special grass, making their milk incredibly rich, fragrant, and flavorful. After collecting a bucketful of this milk, she began churning butter, with renewed dedication, for her transcendental child. Some might say that Krishna's initial thievery was meant to enhance Mother Yashoda's love as well as to charm the elderly *gopis*.

As Yashoda busily churned, Krishna woke up from his afternoon nap and felt hungry. He walked over to his mother and caught hold of her churning rod. Yashoda temporarily stopped churning and looked at her divine son with great love. Then she lifted him tenderly onto her lap and began to nurse him with her breast milk. At that moment she noticed that the milk on the stove was boiling over. So she quickly put Krishna down and rushed to tend the overflowing milk.

Krishna, angry because his mother had left him unsatisfied, picked up a stone, broke the container of freshly churned butter, and ran off to a secluded spot to eat it.

Meanwhile, Yashoda, having tended to the overflowing milk on the stove, returned to her churning area. Seeing the broken pot, she immediately understood that Krishna was the culprit and chased him down by following his butter-smeared footprints. As she finally located him, she beheld a most endearing sight: He was sitting on an overturned wooden mortar that was used for grinding spices, laughing as he gave butter to the monkeys, just as he had done after plundering the *gopis*' houses. Recalling, however, that she was disturbed by the recent acts of her naughty child, she bound Him to the mortar to punish him—but Krishna greatly relished her anger, for it was borne of motherly affection.

What is one to make of such stories?

First and foremost, it should be remembered that Krishna's "mischief" is far from ordinary. His life as an impetuous young boy is a gift to his devotees. Apparently, it can be exhausting while in the midst of it, but Krishna has a way of endearing himself in the long run—and this is his reason for engaging the devotees in these peculiar ways. Rather than evoking consternation, his rowdy pastimes ultimately serve a purifying function, healing and giving joy to all who take part in them. In short, these stories enable devotees to transcend the distance created by awe and reverence and situate them in a loving mood of divine intimacy.

Yashoda had such intense love for Krishna that she thought of him as her baby boy; she had little concern that he was the Supreme Personality of Godhead, and indeed, contemplating his divinity would only have reduced her affection. In the Vaishnava tradition, one begins with the idea that God is great, as in most religious traditions, where a sense of formality and respect is established toward an Almighty Creator. But as one advances in spiritual life, one becomes engulfed in a more intimate relationship. This takes one of five forms: it can be somewhat passive, or it can be active, as a servant, a friend, a parent, or a lover.[15]

Such relationships represent an unfolding, if you will, of our eternal relationship with God in the spiritual realm, a relationship that we forget during our millions of years' sojourn in the material world, but that we recall when we become self-realized. This is the teaching of Vaishnava mysticism, an extremely accomplished level of attainment (not to be imitated or accessed, say the texts, in a cheap way) only achieved by the grace of God and that of his pure devotees. Once attaining this level, the devotee is covered by a phenomenon known as Yoga-Maya, embodied in narrative traditions, we might remember, as Krishna's sister[16]—this is a sort of metaphysical curtain enabling one to relish any of the intimate relationships described above.

After all, awareness of Krishna's Lordship evokes a sense of majesty and subservience before the Supreme. To enable his devotees to rise beyond this stage, with the ability to engage in intimate, loving exchange with him, he masks his divinity. Imagine the *gopis* getting angry at Krishna for stealing their yogurt and butter if they were aware of his supreme position in the cosmic scheme of things. Or consider mother Yashoda: Would she bother to chase after him or enjoy motherly affection if she were conscious that he is God? Thus, in the higher stages of Krishna consciousness one lets Krishna's divinity fall to the wayside and instead enjoys an intimate relationship with him, which would be impossible if one were to think of him as the Supreme Being.

These truths are also evident in Krishna's numerous pastimes with his cows. After countless early episodes as a precocious young boy, along the lines of those described above, he and his cowherd friends, maybe 4 or 5 years old, began taking care of calves. When he turned 6 years, he and the boys were put in charge of some fully grown cows.

Ancient Vaishnava texts tell us that each day they would play together while the cows ate the soft grass in Vrindavan's forests and pasturing grounds. Krishna would warmly hug these docile creatures and play with them; his affection for them was the envy of all his cowherd friends. These cows were regarded as the most fortunate beings, associating with Krishna more than most of his human companions. The *Govinda-Lilamrita*, an esoteric Vaishnava text, tells us that sages from the spiritual world and from India's ancient past took birth as cows just to be close to Krishna in his earthly pastimes. The only living beings that received more attention from him, the *Lilamrita* informs us, were the younger *gopis*, the cowherd girls, who loved him with every inch of their hearts.

These details of loving exchange are elaborated upon in the Vaishnava scriptures, especially in the writings of the six Goswamis of Vrindavan, the intellectual systematizers of the northern Vaishnava tradition. In the esoteric books of the Goswamis we learn that Krishna's cows had names and distinct personalities, and he would call them with loving affection. This literature explains how Krishna and his cows would communicate by mooing, but that their real language was one of love, which is how Krishna ultimately communicates with all living entities.

The interrelationship between Krishna and his cows is extraordinary, and may be understood on various levels. While Vaishnava texts are clear that the stories should be taken as literal depictions of what actually transpires in the spiritual world, they are equally clear that there are metaphorical and symbolic dimensions to these stories as well. Hinduism scholar Barbara Powell eloquently paraphrases Vaishnava commentaries, insightfully expressing these latter ways of perceiving Krishna's mysterious life with the cows:

More than just a thief of butter, Krishna is the thief of love. The pots of butter represent the hearts of devotees. He breaks through the hard outer shell (ego, desire, ignorance, etc.) and releases the soft, sweet self within, the Atman. This He "devours".... It is often a painful process. The women of Vraja and the pots of butter are doubles; Krishna's breaking the pots corresponds to His breaking their hearts by prolonging the agony of the soul's yearning for Him, and the ladies' anger reflects the frustration of the soul struggling for Him. But like the butter inside which He devours, the women soften to Him, are overcome with love for Him, and surrender gladly to this love.[17]

Not only did Krishna destroy numerous demons, steal butter (along with the *gopis'* hearts), and tend cows, but he also engaged in other exciting pastimes too numerous to mention: His lifting of Mount Govardhan to protect Vrindavan's inhabitants from torrential rains; the mischief of stealing the *gopis'* clothes while they bathed in the Yamuna. These and other, similar episodes have been the subject of art, music, drama, and dance for millennia. The stories about the *gopis*, however, are particularly telling, revealing just who Krishna is—he is God as Divine Lover.

Ultimately, his affectionate interaction with these simple cowherd girls reaches its climax during his magical Rasa Dance,[18] before and after which he is said to have engaged in seemingly sensual behavior with them. The word "seemingly" is especially important here. The tradition is clear that Krishna has no prurient interest, nor does he have lascivious motives, at least not as commonly understood. His love for the *gopis*, and theirs for him, is pure.

The higher love described in these texts is sometimes compared to lust, specifically because it outwardly appears like sexual passion. However, the dichotomy between love and lust is an important part of Vaishnava philosophy, and commentators go to great pains to express the difference between the two, especially when discussing the love of Krishna and the *gopis*. The scriptures compare love to gold and lust to iron, one to heaven and the other to hell. The love of the *gopis* is like gold, and it is meant to serve as a model for the passionate attachment that all souls should have for God.

After dancing with the *gopis*, Krishna grew up fast. Now more than 10 years old, he and Balarama were soon invited to Mathura, where Kamsa, their demonic uncle, planned their death in a wrestling match against two large and powerful wrestlers. The demon sent Akrura, a great devotee (who was also Krishna's uncle), to fetch the divine brothers and bring them to Mathura. He reasoned that the boys would willingly go with someone so close to the family. Kamsa's assumption was correct, but what he didn't know was that pious Akrura had told Krishna about his entire plan. Krishna went anyway; it was time for Kamsa to meet his end.

The scene of Akrura bringing Krishna and Balarama out of Vrindavan is heartrending. The *gopis* and other loved ones followed along as far as they could, singing Krishna's glories and crying with a mood of intense separation as they watched the chariot move outside Vrindavan's border. Solace could have been theirs if they were aware that Krishna, in his original form, never leaves Vrindavan. Thus, as Akrura's chariot left the holy town's precincts, the Lord remained there in his unmanifest form, while his expanded facsimile, along with Balarama, continued the journey.

Once the boys arrived in Mathura, Kamsa tried to bring their lives to an end, but the wrestling match did not go as he had hoped. When his plan failed and the two divine brothers defeated his powerful men, he ordered the boys out of Mathura and the plundering of their cowherd villages. He also ordered the death of Nanda and Vasudeva.

But this was not to be. Krishna immediately killed Kamsa and reestablished the pious King Ugrasena, the demon's father, as emperor once more. With Kamsa out of the way, Krishna was able to release his parents from the shackles of Mathura's prison, too.

Krishna and Balarama then went to Ujjain and studied under Sandipani Muni, a great teacher of the time, learning the *Vedas* and the numerous arts and sciences associated with Vedic culture. After a while, they returned to Mathura, and enjoyed a peaceful life. These were happy days for Krishna and Balarama, at least initially.

In the years that followed, it became clear that not everyone was pleased with the recent course of events. The emperor of Magadha (modern Rajgir in Bihar), Jarasandha—who happened to also be Kamsa's father-in-law—vowed to bring ruin to Krishna. The emperor's two daughters, Kamsa's wives, were left disconsolate because of Krishna's action against their husband, and Jarasansha swore to get even. He repeatedly attacked Mathura with his massive armies, which included powerful demons such as Salva and Shishupal, but the young cowherd's small Yadava forces were able to defeat them every time.

This went on for 18 years, with Krishna finally deciding that his opposition's vast numbers were too great for his men. This being the case, Krishna led his troops to Dvaraka on the west coast, in modern Gujarat. It was a city that he had built (with the help of Vishvakarma, the architect of the demigods) to protect the Yadavas from Jarasandha—a perfect choice, for it was surrounded by sea, making it an impenetrable fortress. He had other concerns in Dvaraka, too, such as an ongoing relationship with the Pandava princes, and the soon-to-be marriage of Subhadra (his sister) and Arjuna.

Dvaraka was perfect for another reason as well. Had Krishna gone back to Vrindavan, which is where he really wanted to go, Jarasandha's troops would have followed him there, sullying Vrindavan's beautiful, rural atmosphere, possibly harming his family and friends, and if he had stayed in Mathura, it too would have been demolished. Thus, out of love for Vrindavan, and for its neighboring city, he specifically led his Yadava army to far away Dvaraka.

This became Krishna's kingdom for the rest of his eventful life. After some 18 1/2 years in Mathura, he would now spend almost 97 years in

Dvaraka. As time went on, Balarama married a princess named Revati, and Krishna married numerous queens. The foremost among them was the extraordinary Queen Rukmini, who was an expansion of Chandravali, one of his prominent cowherd maidens in Vrindavan. His other primary queen was Satyabhama, a manifestation of his unsurpassed lover, Sri Radha.

While in Dvaraka, both Krishna and Balarama established palaces, where they enjoyed married life (i.e., the love of their devotees) for many years. But Krishna, especially, always pined for his early days with Radha and for the atmosphere and friends of his cowherd village. Some esoteric texts, in fact, make much of his little-known return there.

Interestingly, Krishna had sent his cousin Uddhava, whose bodily features resembled his own, to Vrindavan, just to assuage the *gopis'* pain. Uddhava's sermon to them—saying that they should not grieve, knowing full well that Krishna is always in their hearts, and that they are, in some sense, always one with him—allows the *Bhagavata* to express the essential "oneness" that became popular in later Hinduism. However, the *gopis'* response to him reveals a higher teaching: "Yes, while all that you say is true, we still miss Krishna and will only be happy in his personal presence, serving him with all our hearts." This is the Vaishnava conclusion.

When Krishna and Balarama were in their nineties, the great Mahabharata war took place. This climactic battle, it is said, brought all major world leaders together for military confrontation. Lord Krishna, as we know, took the role of Arjuna's charioteer; the details of their exchange, and of the war, are explained above and in the prior chapter.

After the Mahabharata war, Krishna, Bhima, and Arjuna took care of unfinished business with Jarasandha, killing him and destroying his reign. Krishna also instructed his dear devotee Uddhava on the science of spiritual life, elaborating on the instructions he had given Arjuna on the Mahabharata battlefield. Having completed his mission to rid the world of its worst demons and to establish *dharma*, or religiosity, Krishna resumed his life in Dvaraka and eventually returned to the spiritual world.

Vaishnava texts explain a certain mystical symbolism in Krishna's story: They say that the six slaughtered children of Devaki are actually materialistic disqualifications (specifically: lust, anger, greed, illusion, madness, and envy). They also say that Kamsa represents the fear of such debilitating qualities, showing that fright, like everything else, has both useful and detrimental components. We are thus urged to have a healthy fear of things that distract us from the spiritual path, and until we develop such fear, systematically doing away with the above obstacles, Krishna will not be born to us—he will not manifest in our hearts.[19]

CHRONOLOGY OF KRISHNA'S LIFE

Birth

- Appearance at midnight, in the year 3228 BCE
- Taken by Vasudeva from Mathura to Gokula
- Stays in Gokula until 3 years and 4 months old
- Killed Putana, Shakatasura, and Trinivarta demons

3-6 years

- Moved to Vrindavan area
- Killed other demons and moved to Nandagram

7-10 years

- Lifting of Mount Govardhan
- Rasa Dance with the gopis
- Invited to Mathura for wrestling match
- Killed the wrestlers
- Killed Kamsa

10-28 years

- Lived in Mathura
- Initiated with Balarama into chanting Gayatri by Gargamuni
- Instructed with Balarama in *Veda*s and the sixty-four arts by Sandipani Muni
- Protects Mathura from many demons
- Makes an enemy of Jarasandha

29-125 years

- Establishes kingdom in Dvaraka
- Marriage to Rukmini and seven other principal queens
- Marriage to 16,100 princesses
- 161,080 sons born to Krishna
- Speaks *Bhagavad-Gita* at Mahabharata Battle (3138 BCE)
- Saves King Pariksit in the womb
- Kills Jarasansha (through Bhima)
- Instructs Uddhava

125

- Disappearance in 3102 BCE
- Start of Kali-yuga

CHAPTER 7
The Puranas and the *Bhagavata*

"The *Vedas* and the Epics are the two eyes of *dharma*, of duty, but the Purana is the heart . . ."

—*Devi-Bhagavata Purana* (11.1.21)

If the *Vedas* lay the foundation for all Hindu thought, and the Epics form the basic structures that are built on this groundwork, the Puranas are the fully constructed homes in which Hindus live. Puranic texts unabashedly present the Hindu deities in full, with elaborate detail and theology. Vishnu, Shiva, and the Goddess, in particular, are brought to life as never before. In fact, because comprehensive information about these divinities is not forthcoming in the Vedic literature, scholars assume that the Puranas are a later creation.

The scholarly consensus on Puranic dates, however, is not entirely accurate. The Sanskrit word *purana* itself means "ancient," and, as pointed out in our section on the *Vedas*, there were in fact ancient traditions that coexisted with the revealed word of God, the Veda, and these were considered the "Fifth Veda." So revered were these traditions that they were considered the essence of Vedic knowledge, in some ways surpassing the Veda itself, at least in terms of relevance and clarity. Along similar lines, the *Atharva Veda* (5.19.9), which is as early as 1000 BCE, if not earlier, mentions "the Purana" as part of its revelation. To be sure, there are many other references to it, too, in Vedic texts after that.

Many of the older Vedic hymns casually refer to any number of divinities, mortals, and events, without bothering to explain who they are, or what their actions represent. Thus, the texts assume prior knowledge and, implicitly, there were existing traditions in which these characters and events were explicated to a greater degree. As Hinduism scholar Klaus Klostermaier notes, "According to Puranic tradition, Brahma uttered the Puranas as the first of all scriptures; only after this did he communicate the *Vedas*."[1] It should be seen as no mere coincidence, therefore, that the Puranas provide much background information on the people and events only briefly mentioned in the *Vedas*.

The actual dating of India's scriptures, especially the Puranas, is a controversial subject. Unlike Egypt or Mesopotamia, where archeologists are privy to numerous relics, such as archaic tablets and inscriptions, most Indian documents were written on palm and other such leaves, which have a shelf life of a few hundred years, at best, particularly because of the subcontinent's tropical climate. For this reason, it is difficult to demonstrate that any of her literature is more than a few centuries old, though much of it clearly is.

Still, by applying linguistic analysis and by making comparisons to other literature whose dates are more certain, an entire field has emerged dedicated to the dating of India's sacred texts. Much ink has been spilled on this subject, and grants have been awarded to those who would make their theories public. This has been especially true when it comes to the Puranas. Unfortunately, there is little definite information outside of what the tradition already tells us.

For example, one of history's greatest Puranic scholars, R. C. Hazra, was unable to arrive at anything resembling a conclusive date: "It is difficult to say definitely how and when the Puranas first came into being, though their claim to great antiquity next only to that of the *Vedas* cannot be denied."[2] Ludo Rocher, another well-known Puranic expert, concurs, "I submit that it is not possible to set a specific date for any Purana as a whole."[3] Friedhelm Hardy, another respected authority in the field, goes even further, "On the whole, it is meaningless to speak of 'the date' of a Sanskrit *purana*, because many generations of bards, etc., have been involved in the accumulation of material which at some stage has been given a name . . .[4]

All this being said, let us reiterate that there is a living tradition in India assigning great antiquity to Puranic texts, based on chronologies, genealogies, and astronomical evidence found in the books themselves. More, the Puranas assert that its knowledge existed in oral form as the world was created, and that Vyasadeva, along with his disciples, compiled the main *Vedas* and their corollaries, including the Puranas, near the beginning of Kali-yuga (around 3102 BCE).

Despite scholarly assumptions about the rather late dating of these texts, then, let us work with the premise that these are ancient traditions, coexisting with the *Vedas*, as the texts themselves say.

WHAT ARE THE PURANAS?

The next two questions are, "Which texts make up the corpus of Puranic literature?" and "Is there a hierarchy of importance in these texts?" These questions are not as simple as they might sound.

The Puranas are primarily comprised of eighteen large books, profound in philosophy, and encyclopedic in scope. These works form three sets of six books, with each set associated with one of the main gods of India— Vishnu, Brahma, and Shiva. But there are also eighteen Upa ("following" or "subsidiary") Puranas, and numerous Sthala (or "regional") Puranas, too. So there is a considerable oeuvre of Puranic literature.

Here we focus on the eighteen main Puranas, for in their pages we find the essence of contemporary Hinduism. Rather than bore the reader with a list of these Puranas' names, it would be more fruitful to address their subject matter. While most Puranic literature covers only five general subjects, such as the genealogy of kings and the lives of saints, the "great" Puranas, as each of the main eighteen are called, deal with ten. These might be summarized as follows:

(1) primary creation, wherein the Lord creates the subtle elements of the material world, or the basic ingredients of existence; (2) secondary creation, where Brahma, the first created being, utilizes these ingredients for creating the material universes; (3) the way in which the Lord maintains the universe by using his multifarious potencies, moral laws, and created beings; (4) the intricacies of relationship, particularly between God and his devotees; (5) elaboration on the progenitors of humankind along with history of the world's major dynasties; (6) explanation of duties for living beings at various stages of existence, with particular attention to desire, which either binds one to the world or frees one to pursue the spirit; (7) detailed information about the Personality of Godhead and his various incarnations; (8) the winding up of all of God's energies, along with descriptions of universal annihilation; (9) various kinds of liberation and how to attain them; and (10) the ultimate end of knowledge, including a detailed description of Supreme. In some cases, the higher Puranas discuss the life and teachings of Krishna, the Supreme Personality of Godhead.[5] This tenth subject is the special focus of the *Bhagavata Purana*, discussed below.

Just as the three sets of the six major Puranas are associated with the three major manifestations of the Supreme: Vishnu, Brahma, and Shiva, the texts are also divided according to the three modalities of material existence, goodness, passion, and ignorance. The connection is logical, because Vishnu is associated with goodness (and its related quality of truth), Brahma with passion (the creative impulse), and Shiva and the Goddess with ignorance or darkness (destructive tendencies). In fact, the division of Puranic books into goodness, passion, and ignorance is, in some ways, more legitimate than separating them according to the deities with whom they are associated. This is so because all four deities are glorified in all of the texts.

Thus, one should give no credence to the mistaken idea that the "passionate" Puranas tend to glorify Brahma, and that those in "goodness" sing the praises of only Vishnu, and that the "ignorant" ones tell us about Shiva and the Goddess. Things are not so clear-cut. All Puranas extol both the virtues of Vishnu and Shiva, primarily, with only very few references to Brahma as a deity. The *Devi-Bhagavata Purana*, among others, emphasizes the Goddess, and the *Bhagavata*, the *Vishnu*, and the *Brahma-Vivarta* are known for their focus on Vishnu. But, more importantly, there is a certain oneness that the various deities share in these texts, with hierarchical considerations only understood by adepts. Ultimately, then, Puranic division is not about the deities. Rather, the texts are divided into three groupings according to the qualities and spiritual evolution of the people for whom the respective books are meant.

This tripartite classification is found in several places, most notably in *Padma Purana* (5.263.81) and in the *Matsya Purana* (290.13–15). The latter of these is a more interesting reference, since it identifies itself as one of the "ignorant" Puranas. This is significant. In recent decades, scholars have argued that the three divisions might have originally been a product of sectarian bias, and that Vaishnavas, or worshippers of Vishnu, sought to distinguish their own religion by relegating the others (i.e., Shaivism and Shaktism), to passion and ignorance. But this is clearly not the case, since the system of qualitative categorization is here seen to have been taught in one of the "Shiva" Puranas. More, it is clear from a thorough reading of the texts that the Puranas associated with goodness, passion, or ignorance tend to convey realities that are consistent with those qualities, respectively.

It follows that the scriptures associated with goodness convey higher truths, since, as pointed out in our Introduction, Vedic texts show a correlation between goodness and truth. This thesis gives additional nuance to scriptural statements such as, "the mode of goodness produces knowledge" (*Bhagavad-Gita* 14.17) or "goodness leads to realization of the Supreme."

(*Bhagavata Purana* 1.2.24) Such verses imply that literature in the mode of goodness is superior for acquiring knowledge of the Absolute Truth.

The *BHAGAVATA PURANA*

Whether or not we concede that, of the eighteen major Puranas, the six associated with goodness are best (i.e., that they give the highest knowledge), it is an undeniable fact that the most popular and loved of the Puranas is the *Bhagavata Purana* (also called the *Srimad Bhagavatam* or simply the *Bhagavata*). As fate would have it, of course, this is one of the eighteen major Puranas, and it is also in the mode of goodness, containing the considerable truths of the other Puranas and so much more.

Scholars tend to date the *Bhagavata* at about 900 CE, though the underlying assumptions for this date are necessarily tentative, as Hazra, Rocher, and Hardy indicate above. Still, there are many reasons why scholars claim the *Bhagavata* originates in the tenth century, not least because the work makes use of Alvar poetry. The Alvars were twelve poet-saints from South India, Vaishnavas who were said to have flourished in the eighth century, thus indicating that the *Bhagavata* came later. However, the dates of the Alvars are anything but certain, and tradition often places them in the prehistoric period. Likewise, much of the evidence for the *Bhagavata's* late date is circumstantial.

For several decades it has been acknowledged that the text is probably much older than previously thought, even if it was easy to accept the dates handed down by prior experts. Many scholars are now unearthing new evidence suggesting that the book is probably ancient, with sections that predate the Common Era.[6] Indeed, there are kernels in the *Bhagavata's* storehouse of divine narrative that can be traced back to the *Vedas* themselves.

A vast, encyclopedic work of over 18,000 Sanskrit verses (divided into twelve large sections, or books), the *Bhagavata* surveys a broad spectrum of factual knowledge, including history, psychology, politics, cosmology, metaphysics, and theology. The nineteenth-century American Transcendentalist Ralph Waldo Emerson once exalted the *Bhagavata* as a book to be read "on one's knees."[7]

The very title tells us much about the book. It translates as, "The Beautiful Story of the Personality of Godhead." In other words, this is a book that pulls no punches. It focuses on the essence of spirituality. In its own pages (1.1.2), it distinguishes itself as a spiritual work that accepts no compromise, totally rejecting the usual Hindu goals of "a pious life" in the material world, economic development, ordinary religiosity, and even liberation. This is a work that accepts nothing less then the ultimate goal of love of God. As the Purana says about itself, it is the ripened fruit of the Vedic tree of knowledge (1.1.3)—the essence of the *Vedas*, the Epics, and all other Puranas (1.2.3, and 1.3.42). Like all texts of this genre, then, it covers the ten subjects previously mentioned, but its special emphasis on Krishna as the Supreme Personality of Godhead virtually forces it to greater heights.

This superior quality was achieved through much hard work. As the story goes, Vyasa, who is seen in pan-Hindu tradition as the "literary incarnation of God," was the author. He received the knowledge through a lineage coming from God himself. At the dawn of creation it is initially revealed to Brahma, the first created being. Brahma conveyed the essence of this knowledge to Narada, and Narada passed it on to Vyasa, the compiler of the Vedic literature. Vyasa's place in the historical dissemination of primordial knowledge is significant. He divided the eternal wisdom of the Veda into four distinct sections. He then summarized the essence of Vedic knowledge into aphorisms known as the *Vedanta-Sutras*, terse philosophical codes that embody the truths of the *Vedas*.

At this point, however, Vyasa felt a sense of despondency—in his entire compilation and summarization of the Vedic literature, he had neglected to truly focus on the personal feature of the Absolute Truth. Narada, his spiritual master, confirmed that this was so, telling him that he (Vyasa) would only be satisfied if he would directly describe the name, fame, form, and activities of Krishna, the Personality of Godhead. Heeding the advice of his guru, Vyasa compiled the *Bhagavata*—the "king of books," the "spotless Purana"—as his own natural commentary on the *Vedanta-Sutras*.

Interestingly, he wrote the *Bhagavata* in the style of a novel, though he makes it clear that the text should not be seen as fictitious. He begins his work by telling the reader about the cursing and eventual death of Maharaja Pariksit, last of the great Vedic kings. He does this before explaining, in the Third Book (of the *Bhagavata*'s massive twelve), how the world was created and, gradually, how the world's entire early history, with legions of dynasties and wizened sages, led up to Pariksit's fateful curse. He starts the story in the middle and then goes back to the beginning, a common device in the writing of novels.

In other words, the *Bhagavata* is like a novel in its essential literary structure, but not in terms of the specific narrative it brings to light.

Why would Vyasa use the format of a novel to describe literal history? He uses it because it is effective—it captures the readers' attention and gets them involved in the story. By beginning with a penultimate event, such as the cursing of Pariksit and his related philosophical questions about the purpose of life, the reader perks up, anxious to discover what comes next. A similar device is used in the very first verse of the *Bhagavad-Gita*, when blind Dhritarashtra asks the virtuous narrator Sanjaya, "What did my sons and the sons of Pandu do, being desirous to fight?" After intriguing the reader in this way, the enticing dialogue between Krishna and Arjuna ensues.

At first blush, the *Bhagavata* can be somewhat intimidating, not only because of its formidable size but also because it can appear somewhat chaotic—with innumerable names, places, series of events, and deep philosophy—expressed in a difficult-to-comprehend manner. Why difficult to comprehend? First of all, though it deals with history, it is not chronological, as mentioned above. It skips around in time, according to thematic preference and subjects that interrelate in various ways. More, its teachings are couched in a tapestry of complex conversations between any number of teachers and disciples—so much so, that, in due course, the casual reader may well forget just who is talking to whom.

Nonetheless, perseverant readers will notice that such superficial confusion matters little. There is, ultimately, a systematic structure to the text, enabling readers to grasp its central message of love of God. More, it is possible to penetrate the *Bhagavata*'s barrage of teacher-student exchanges, but one must be determined to do so. There is a secret to untangling the web known as the *Bhagavata*: Such texts are properly studied "at the feet of a master" (*Upanishad*), within a Vaishnava lineage, just as Brahma, Narada, and Vyasa himself did. If it is approached in this way, the substance of the teachings emerges, outweighing the importance of just who speaks them, or the sequence of events.

The overall *Bhagavata* narration involves Suta Goswami, a renowned sage who was requested by Shaunaka Rishi, leader of thousands of sages, to speak on spiritual topics, particularly on the pastimes of Krishna, the Supreme Person. Readers of the *Bhagavata* quickly come to understand that Suta was in a unique position to do so, as he was in attendance at an earlier recitation when Shukadeva Goswami, son of Vyasa (compiler of the *Vedas*, and of the *Bhagavata* as well), had similarly spoken to a group of sages. And here is where we are introduced to the story of Maharaja Pariksit, the king who was cursed to die within 7 days.

So cursed, he had retired to the banks of the Ganges at Hastinapura (present-day Delhi). In this way, he would prepare for death by performing religious austerities. The resounding question, "What is the duty of a person who is about to die?" permeates this early section of the work. Meanwhile, a large gathering of holy men surround Pariksit by the Ganges, as Shukadeva, chief among them, sits down to answer this and other penetrating questions.

Essentially, then, the reader is given access to Suta's retelling of the conversation between Maharaja Pariksit and Shukadeva Goswami. Sometimes, however, this dialogue is interrupted with Suta's own answers to questions posed by Shaunaka. In other words, there are two conversations going on at once. Furthermore, Shukadeva, in making his point, sometimes relates conversations between other masters and disciples, such as those of Brahma and Narada, or of Maitreya and Vidura. So the reader must at times wade through three simultaneous dialogues.

But it is well worth the endeavor. Those who swim through the *Bhagavata*'s difficult waters quickly realize the value of this most unique treatise: Unlike any other, it gives more details about God and his kingdom than the mind can accommodate. So wide-ranging are its topics and so expansive are its spiritual perceptions that a thorough analysis would require a full volume of its own.

To sum up: Using the story of Pariksit as its central prop, again, the *Bhagavata* begins like many modern-day novels. With Pariksit's death, the end of a once glorious dynasty is at hand. But before this is revealed to the *Bhagavata*'s readers, the text takes us back—not just back to the beginning of Pariksit's reign, but back to the beginning of time, elaborately describing creation and the dawn of human civilization. Then, gradually, the *Bhagavata* winds its way through history, describing diverse dynasties and the incarnations of God that graced their genealogies. This includes, ultimately, the Tenth Book of the *Bhagavata*, which is its real crowning jewel: the life of Krishna, the Supreme Lord, as summarized in the prior chapter.

Finally, we end up at the Kuruksetra war—with the heroic Pandavas and their relationship with Krishna. The latter, of course, saves Pariksit while he is still in his mother's womb, as explained in our summary of the *Mahabharata*. This naturally leads to Maharaja Pariksit's curse, and his resolve to sit down and to fast until death—while hearing the *Bhagavata Purana*. The circular structure of the *Bhagavata* resembles not only that of a novel but also the cyclical nature of time and creation conveyed in the *Bhagavata*'s pages. This is a story that goes on forever, eternally repeating itself—thus hinting at its universal, transcendent, and timeless character.

BHAGAVATA PHILOSOPHY

What are we to learn from the *Bhagavata*? As with the *Vedas* and the Epics, there is more to the book than meets the eye. Its teachings are many, and any synopsis is bound to fall short.

Overall, however, it could be said that the *Bhagavata* focuses on three important components of the spiritual quest:

(1) *Sambandha* (relationship): This is the basis—that each individual being is essentially spiritual, not the body, and has an ongoing (if sometimes obscured) relationship with the Supreme Spirit, God.

(2) *Abhidheya* (method of attainment)—Once the foregoing is acknowledged, there must be some corresponding course of action, i.e., the proper methods by which one develops a relationship with the Supreme. The *Bhagavata* teaches how to act according to this relationship.

(3) *Prayojana* (ultimate perfection)—Once one's identity and relationship with the Supreme are established, and one's methods of pursuing that relationship are in place, the ultimate goal of love of God is easily achieved.

In pursuance of this ultimate perfection, the *Bhagavata* takes its readers through nine phases of spiritual life.

(1) *Faith*—In the beginning, an individual has tender faith in God and the scriptures, faith that can either be nurtured or trampled. Generally, this faith arises from contact with saints. The *Bhagavata*, therefore, tells the stories of paradigmatic devotees, hoping to inspire faith in its readers. It also outlines activities that are helpful on the path, and those to be avoided, so that faith will develop properly.

(2) *Association of Saints*—After faith begins to develop into strong realization, one naturally seeks a community of like-minded believers and also a spiritual teacher (guru) to help along the way. The *Bhagavata*, through both story and direct teaching, shows how to separate saints from swindlers, so that aspiring spiritual seekers can find a genuine guru, and how they can take best advantage of the community of devotees.

(3) *Engagement in Worship*—When true realization dawns, seriousness on the path follows as a natural result. Initiation from a bona fide spiritual master usually ensues at this point. Here, one learns the proper methods of devotion, including practices peculiar to one's psychophysical makeup. In the course of engaging in these practices, one undergoes various phases—initial enthusiasm, oscillating attentiveness and distraction, indecision, struggling with the uncontrolled senses, inability to maintain vows, and so on. The *Bhagavata*, through the examples of great kings and devotees, shows how to address all such issues and emerge as a more accomplished devotee.

(4) *Cessation of Unwanted Elements*—As one progresses on the spiritual path, one notices one's material fever going down. That is to say, the sages have devised numerous means by which a practitioner can gauge his or her spiritual advancement. Attraction to materialistic things will wane, and enthusiasm for

spiritual things will grow. Part of this procedure involves the dissipation of bad habits, which naturally fall to the wayside as the devotee grows in wisdom and learning.

(5) *Steadiness*—Overcoming laziness, distraction, and other bad habits, one comes to a stage of steadiness in practice. At this point, few obstacles can waver the advancing practitioner from his or her determined goal of love of God.

(6) *Taste*—Steadiness on the spiritual path leads to a higher "taste," one that is unknown in the material world. Sensual pleasures are alluring and can easily lead to mundane attachment. But one who has a higher taste can easily conquer them. Once conquered, a new world of spiritual pleasure opens up for the practitioner, rendering its material counterpart bland and unappealing.

(7) *Attachment*—Just as people, when conditioned by material nature, are attached to mundane pleasures, they can also develop a similar attachment to God and the spiritual pursuit. When a practitioner's taste matures, the Lord himself becomes the dominant object of desire. While on the prior level, some effort was required for focusing the mind on the Lord, but in this stage, spiritual endeavor becomes second nature.

(8) *Intense Emotion*—If one's attachment continues to grow, the dawning of true love begins to surface. At this stage, the naturally soft heart of the spiritual aspirant melts like butter in the presence of God, his devotees, and his scriptures. The practitioner now experiences an unquenchable yearning for the Supreme—this is a feeling that matures into ecstatic love for God. It is at this point that a devotee may realize a glimmer of his original identity in the spiritual world.

(9) *Ecstatic Love*—Finally, the seasoned practitioner attains the desired goal, sacred rapture, love for the Supreme. This love becomes like a powerful magnet attracting the precious metal of Krishna's heart. At this point, one's original relationship with God manifests in full bloom, and the flowering of its ecstatic love engulfs one's life. Expressing these various stages through the use of history, song, and philosophy is the *Bhagavata*'s singular brilliance.

All of this, of course, is set against the background of *bhakti*, "devotional love," which is the *Bhagavata*'s main theme. *Bhakti* is a word that implies "participation." In other words, *bhakti* is relational, joining *bhakta* and *bhagavan*, devotee and God. To be clear, *bhakti* is not just an emotional state: Without action, devotion has no meaning. Therefore, spiritual adepts, such as A. C. Bhaktivedanta Swami Prabhupada, have translated it as "devotional service."[8]

By so doing, he nuances the word in a more meaningful way—he connects *bhakti* with *dharma*, or duty, because he implies that a true devotee must "do" something, he must "act" for the divine; he must perform service. And he also connects *bhakti* with the notion of love—"if you love me, do something for me; don't just utter the words." Again, this connects devotion with active service.

Such service is summed up in one of the most important sections of the *Bhagavata* (7.5.23), in which the boy-saint Prahlad enumerates eight forms of active devotion:

- Listening to the stories and glories of God.
- Singing or reciting the names and glories of God.
- Recalling God and his divine activities.
- Serving his feet and those of the devotees.
- Ritual worship of God's forms or images.
- Bowing down to God.
- Service to his personality, incarnations, or devotees.
- Befriending him.
- Dedicating oneself to him, heart and soul.

All devotees model their devotional practices on one or more of these fundamental paradigms. The entire *Bhagavata*, in fact, is meant to assist in this endeavor, offering systematic methodology and illustrative stories to facilitate it.

In conclusion, tradition acknowledges four verses among the *Bhagavata*'s massive 18,000 that sum up its philosophy in a "nutshell." Talking to Brahma, in the world's earliest days, Lord Krishna says, "Brahma, it is I, the Supreme Person, who was existing before the creation, when there was nothing but myself. Nor was there material nature, the cause of this creation. He who stands before you is also me, as is everything else, and, after annihilation, only I will remain. (2.9.33) O Brahma, whatever appears to have any purpose, if it is not related to me—know that it has no reality. Know it as my illusory energy, a reflection that only resembles that which is real and true. (2.9.34) Brahma, know, too, that just as the universal elements enter into the cosmos and at the same time do not enter into the cosmos, similarly, I also exist within everything and at the same time I transcend everything. (2.9.35) A person who is searching after the Supreme, who wants to know and love God, must certainly endeavor for this in all circumstances, throughout space and time, both directly and indirectly." (2.9.36)

CHAPTER 8
Vaishnavism and the Practice of Hinduism

"Vishnu is the instructor of the whole world—what else should people learn or teach, except for Him, the Supreme Spirit?"

—*Vishnu Purana* 1.17

The roots of theistic Hinduism, as embodied in Vaishnavism, Shaivism, Shaktism, and other minor religious traditions, are found in the *Vedas*, but one must use a special lens to find them there. These traditions began to truly sprout in the gnarly pages of the Epics, with their vines eventually becoming more apparent in the Puranas. Finally, they came into full bloom with the writings of the great teachers, the systematizers of early Hinduism. It is on the basis of this cumulative tradition that the fruits of Hindu practice came into being.

According to the most respected teachers of the tradition, the truths found in the "later" literature are implicit in the older ones, and, if one adheres to any of the traditional lineages it becomes clear how this is so.

But the academic study of Hinduism often yields different results. Thus, for the benefit of those not studying within established traditions, it would be useful to briefly explore the older texts, to see what indications or premonitions they offer regarding the Hinduism we know today.

As a preface to that exploration, let us briefly look at just who Vishnu is. Without getting overly technical, he is the Supreme Godhead, the recipient of awe and reverence, the embodiment of majesty and divine excellence. His long black hair, large lotus eyes, deep blue complexion and glowing yellow garments show us where Krishna gets his charm, or, according to some, where Vishnu gets his. Unlike Krishna, who appears more as a simple cowherd, he is regal and obviously transcendent, self-consciously above everything else—he is power personified.

His four arms indicate his all-powerful and pervasive nature. In his four hands we find a conch, symbolizing creativity and victory; a *chakra* (or discus), symbolizing the powers of the mind—it is also a weapon with which he not only kills demons but slays misconception and doubt; a large mace, with which he evokes the fear of the unrighteous—it is also a symbol of strength; and a lotus, which represents liberation and the ability to rise beyond the material world.

He is usually depicted as reclining on the cosmic waters of creation, with Sesha, a serpent-like form of Balarama, guarding him, acting as his bedstead, with his soft skin and his many hoods rising high above him. From Vishnu's navel we see the world's first being, Brahma, ready to create on the Lord's behalf. Or, sometimes, Vishnu is depicted in a standing position, with Lakshmi, his consort, who is always serving him. By so doing, she shows all souls how to perform the most important form of yoga—devotional service. This is Vishnu, the Lord of all, and the Supreme deity of the Vaishnavas.

VISHNU IN THE *VEDAS*

Since our focus is on Vaishnavism, we begin with references to Vishnu in the *Vedas*. It should be said at the outset that Brahman, the amorphous divinity referred to in Vedic texts, has certain fundamental affinities with Vishnu. To begin, the words are related, if not etymologically then certainly in meaning. The word "Brahman" comes from the Sanskrit root *brih*, which means "expansion," or "to spread throughout the universe." The name Vishnu means much the same: "pervasive," to "expand."[1]

D. N. Shanbhag, a scholar of Hindu studies, has thoroughly analyzed the numerous scriptural instances in which the words "Brahman" and "Vishnu" have the same connotation, and he thereby concluded that all references to Brahman could also be read as references to Vishnu.[2] The great Medieval Vaishnava teachers, such as Madhva and Ramanuja, expressed the same realization.

Vedic references to Vishnu are few, but they are overflowing with meaning. This was the verdict of Indologist F. B. J. Kuiper, who was among the first Western academics to fully research the subject. After years of poring through the Sanskrit texts, amassing volumes of evidence, he made a claim that shook the academic world: that there is more to Vishnu in the *Rig Veda* than one might at first suspect.[3] His findings, indeed, ran contrary to what most Indic scholars had previously thought, since the negligible references to Vishnu in the *Rig Veda* tend to present him as a minor solar deity.

Kuiper concluded that Vishnu, when looked at closely, was the only deity to take his devotees beyond the material world. The normal trajectory of Vedic concern is heaven-earth, day-night, and gods-demons—but Vishnu goes beyond such dualities into a more transcendent domain.[4]

This is the true significance, he wrote, of Vishnu's "three steps," which are frequently elaborated upon in traditional Sanskrit literature. His steps encompass all that exists and goes beyond, into uncharted territory. Most Vedic gods are embodiments of celestial, terrestrial, and atmospheric forces, but Vishnu's three steps are symbolic of his ability to accommodate all three.[5] More, these steps are said to reach the highest abode, signifying unparalleled attainment.[6] Therefore, the *Katha Upanishad* (3.9) compares Vishnu's ultimate "step" to the culmination of the spiritual journey—it represents the point at which all souls reach their ultimate home.

Even comparisons with other manifestations of the divine tend to give Vishnu his due. The *Rig Veda* (7.40.5) tells us that Lord Vishnu is supreme, and that Lord Rudra (Shiva) depends on him for sustenance. Similarly, the *Aitareya Brahmana* (1.1) says that of all the gods, Agni is the lowest and Vishnu is the highest.

This latter reference is particularly important, since it is the very first of the *Brahmana* commentaries—it rivals the Veda itself in terms of antiquity, authority, and, according to the tradition, sanctity. These early texts tell us, too, that there was once a contest among the gods to determine who was the greatest. Vishnu, by his deeds, emerged victorious, and he is therefore referred to as the most excellent of all divinities.[7]

The *Vedas* themselves might be likened to a puzzle, using nondescript words like "Brahman" to address the Supreme, whose true identity only becomes clear when one is familiar with the entire Vedic corpus. As we have shown, Brahman can be identified with Vishnu, and, when all the pieces are put together, this truth materializes like the light of day.

For example, Brahman is usually addressed in impersonal terms, and "it" is said to be devoid of qualities. But Vaishnava commentators have argued that Brahman is merely devoid of *material* qualities, because the same texts that suggest its impersonal nature say that it partakes of "eternity, knowledge, and bliss." These are qualities of the spirit as opposed to matter, and matter's qualities are temporality, ignorance, and indifference. It is these latter qualities that Brahman does not possess.

But, more, what do eternity, knowledge, and bliss mean without the prospect of personality? Clearly, impersonal conceptions of the deity fall short, for they cannot explain just how, or in what form, the ultimate spiritual entity exists forever (eternity), perceives the world (knowledge), or feels love (bliss). Consequently, ultimate reality must be conceived as a new category of being altogether, possessing spiritual attributes even if devoid of material ones. Rather than seeing the Supreme as impersonal, therefore, Vaishnava sages prefer to view it as "supra-personal." In this way, they acknowledge that "he" is not a person like the rest of us, but he is not relegated to a lackluster impersonal existence, either.

Here's how the Vedic puzzle fits together: In the Brahmana literature, Vishnu is associated with "the sacrifice (yagya)," a word that, like "Brahman," is one of the many ways in which the texts allude to the Supreme. Throughout the *Vedas*, we are told of the mystic perfection of the Vedic sacrifice. The *Vedas* even suggest that the sacrifice should be worshipped and that it is representative of various Vedic deities, though we are not told exactly which one stands at the center.

As mentioned in our chapter on the *Vedas* (Chapter 4), however, the identification of Vishnu with the "sacrifice" in Brahmanical commentaries, which are part of the original Vedic literature, aligns him (and his alternate manifestations, such as Narayana, Krishna, and so on) with the Purusha-sukta. This is the primordial being who undergoes the ultimate sacrifice and therefore receives the title Purushottama ("the Supreme Person," or "God"), which is also a common name for Vishnu and Krishna. Thus, Vaishnavas have long held that the Purusha-sukta and other forms of divinity mentioned in Vedic texts are actually veiled references to Vishnu. For this reason, the earliest forms of Vaishnavism have used those names and forms in their worship of the Divine.

Brahmana literature might therefore be seen as penultimate pieces in the Vedic puzzle, awaiting the Epics and the Puranas for completion.

The Vaikhanasa texts of South India, too, are an important part of this Vedic conundrum, offering evidence for the early worship of Vishnu. They connect Vaishnavism to the *Vedas* through language, ritual, and practice. Michael Witzel, one of the Western world's leading authorities on the *Vedas*, has studied the Vaikhanasa Vaishnavas and their related literature, and has concluded that in terms of mantra style (both in meter and in language) they have a definite link to their Vedic past. Witzel goes so far as to say that this connection could indicate others, so that Vaishnavism could actually be seen as a Vedic religion.[8]

There is other evidence as well, such as that of the *Maha-Narayana Upanishad,* which clearly announces the supreme position of Narayana

(Vishnu), or the famous verses of the *Maha Upanishad* (1.1–4), appended to the *Sama Veda*: "In the beginning of creation, there was only Narayana (Vishnu). There was no Brahma, no Shiva, no fire, no moon, no stars in the sky, no sun." But such quotes lead us onto thin ice, for modern scholars relegate these texts to "later" compilations, unworthy of Vedic affiliation. That being the case, the texts are usually neglected in favor of those that are more certain, at least according to contemporary academicians. The vast majority of the Hindu world, however, supports the legitimacy of this Upanishadic literature, and this despite the cold opinion of recent scholarship.

WHAT IS VAISHNAVISM?

Given its Vedic past, Vaishnavism is among the most important "Hindu" religious traditions today, and, apropos of this, most Hindus are Vaishnavas of one kind or another. However, Vaishnavism is not dependent on its Vedic origins, and few Hindus would reassess their allegiances based on new findings in Vedic study. This is because the Vaishnava religion is strongly tied to the Epics and the Puranas, as already mentioned, and because personal experience supercedes book learning.

That is to say, while Hindus take their holy writ seriously, scriptures take a back seat to practical application and personal transformation. Religion is meant to bring practitioners closer to God, to make them better people, who are happy and productive. Hindus, like most others, are more concerned with the pragmatic value of their belief system. And Vaishnavism, for millennia, has provided such value for countless souls, sustaining itself by functioning properly, by awarding people the fruit of the religious quest. It works, and so people want it.

As commonly understood, Vaishnavism is a prototypical form of Hinduism focusing on Vishnu (or his many manifestations and incarnations) as the Supreme Being. It is a form of monotheism that perceives other deities as subordinate, viewing them as demigods, angels, or empowered beings. Thus, while Vaishnavas acknowledge the Rig Vedic idea that the many gods are just various faces on Brahman, they also assert that Brahman has an "original" face—the one belonging to Vishnu. A clarifying metaphor might run as follows: Just as one candle can be used to light others, and just as all candles thus lit would hold the same potency, so, too, is Vishnu the source of all divine emanations, even if these emanations are also various forms of the Supreme.[9]

Accordingly, Vaishnava tradition teaches that the worship of "other gods," such as Shiva, the Goddess, and Ganesh, is inappropriate once one knows the transcendental hierarchy outlined in the texts. Prior to that, such lesser worship may be useful in that it can help spiritual seekers raise themselves, albeit gradually, to the spiritual platform. Once on this platform, however, they will worship only Vishnu.

The Lord himself outlines this basic scenario in the *Bhagavad-Gita* (7.21–22), when, in his form as Krishna, he says: "I am in everyone's heart, and, if one wants to worship the demigods, I make his faith steady so that he can devote himself to any of those deities. I then award him the benefits that he thinks are bestowed by the demigods." Why would one want to worship demigods? Krishna explains this as well: "People in the material world desire success in fruitive activities, and therefore they worship the demigods." (4.12)

We see here the same principle found in Vedic sacrifices, that is, methods of worship designed to appease the gods and to create harmony and satisfaction in the material world. Such satisfaction, however, is material and therefore temporary. Consequently, Vaishnavism discards this motivated and goal-oriented worship and promotes only pure worship of the Supreme. Krishna concludes by denouncing the veneration of gods other than himself: "Those who worship other gods are actually worshipping me, but they are doing it in the wrong way." (9.23) In other words, Vaishnavism promotes the exclusive worship of the Supreme Godhead, whether in his original form or in any of his innumerable incarnations—but *not* the worship of those who might be considered removed expansions, like the many demigods.

The doctrine of *avatar* ("he who descends"), or "incarnation," is central to Vaishnava thought. This is when God "descends" into our world for purposes of his own, usually to destroy particularly virulent demons, to establish the path of righteousness, or to bring pleasure to his devotees. Actually, say the texts, he can destroy demons from afar, from his spiritual kingdom, and he can establish the principles of religion through powerful emissaries and religious reformers. Thus, the actual reason for his descent is to show his devotees his otherworldly pastimes, thus alluring them back to his supreme abode. Accordingly, he takes many forms, but his ten most famous incarnations, whose stories are elaborated upon in the various Puranas, are as follows:

1. The Divine Fish, Matsya, who saved the world from a deluge recorded in ancient Vedic texts.
2. The Divine Tortoise, Kurma, who offered his back as the pivot on which Mount Mandara rested. Here, gods and demons both churned various valuable objects from the ocean of milk, a famous story from the Vedic literature.

3. The Boar, Varaha, like Matsya, rescued the earth from a flood, raising it from watery depths on his tusk, for otherwise it would have been completely submerged.

4. The Man-Lion, Narasimha, came to earth to deliver the world from a demon, who had obtained from the gods a boon stating that he would be slain neither by a god, man, nor animal. Narasimha was not any of these, for he was a combination of all of them.

5. The Dwarf, Vamana, was Vishnu in the form of a dwarf. Here he was confronted with a demon king who had conquered the universe. On behalf of humankind, he begged from the demon for as much land as he could cover in three steps. His request was granted, but, much to the demon king's surprise, Vamana traversed the universe in these three steps, winning the world back for those who are righteous.

6. Rama with the axe, Parashurama, was Vishnu in the form of a hero. Here he destroyed the warrior class of men, who were exploiting others with their power.

7. Ramachandra, the great hero of the Hindu *Odyssey*, the *Ramayana*, taught, by his own example, the true meanings of fidelity, love, and duty.

8. Krishna, the playful lord of Vraja, is often viewed as the most perfect incarnation of Vishnu, and even as the source of all incarnations, including Vishnu. He displays his charming pastimes to allure humanity back to the transcendental realm. (See Chapter 6)

9. Buddha, the founder of Buddhism, is seen as an incarnation of Vishnu as well, though his primary accomplishment, according to Vaishnava texts, is that he bewilders those inclined to atheism. By doing so, say the Vaishnava sages, he gradually gets them to abandon harmful habits (such as meat eating) and to once again adopt Vedic teaching in earnest.

10. Kalki is the form of Vishnu who comes at the end of the present age, in about 427,000 years. At that time, all devotees will already be reunited with Vishnu in his heavenly kingdom. The remaining souls, whose lives, according to Hindu texts, are unfortunate, shortened, and riddled with disease, will be mercifully slain by Vishnu (as Kalki) so that they might be reborn in the next Satya Age, a pious time when the world is once again created anew.

This is just a brief sampling. According to tradition, incarnations and manifestations of Vishnu are as abundant as the waves of the ocean. Nonetheless, when considering these multitudinous aspects of the Supreme, there are two things to bear in mind: First, these incarnations and manifestations represent various sides of one overarching divinity—they are *not* many gods, as previously stated. And, second, the various forms of Vishnu are carefully delineated in the scriptures. Since the scriptures cannot, obviously, explicitly name all of the manifold incarnations and manifestations, these texts describe symptoms and definitive signs of divinity—so practitioners can avoid being deceived by would-be incarnations, a phenomenon that is not uncommon in India. Indeed, most people do not rigorously study their sacred texts, and therefore they could easily assign divinity to personalities who would otherwise be rejected by scriptural standards.

To avoid misconception, the texts advise affiliation with established lineages of knowledge, of which four stand out as representative of the rest: The Rudra, Sri, Kumara, and Brahma Sampradayas. These lineages were defined by historical reformers in the Vaishnava tradition, luminaries who revitalized the religion in South India, affecting northern provinces as well. The most prominent were Vishnu Swami (born ca. 700 CE), who systematized the Rudra lineage originating with Lord Shiva; Ramanuja (1017–1137 CE), who illuminated the Sri lineage; Nimbarka (ca. 1100 CE), the patriarch of the Kumara school of thought; and Madhva (1199–1278 CE), the stalwart philosopher who revolutionized the Brahma tradition. Others significantly contributed to these traditions—Vallabha (1479–1531 CE) was a prominent teacher in the Vishnu Swami school; the twelve Alvars, poet-saints of South India (ca. eighth century), added much to the Sri lineage; and Sri Chaitanya (1486–1533 CE), whom we will discuss in greater depth later, brought new life to the Brahma-Madhva tradition.

Vaishnavas of all kinds accept a threefold division of knowledge: (1) the scripture; (2) the words of saints; and (3) the teachings of one's individual guru. All philosophical speculation is gauged against the harmony found in these three sources of knowledge. If one of these is out of kilter, then something is amiss. In other words, the three sources of knowledge provide a sort of check and balance system for believers. For Vaishnavas, all truth must conform to the consensus of these three.

Once knowledge is received in this way, several articles of faith unfold as a matter of course. Though these articles have been expressed in numerous ways, they are perhaps best summed up by the nineteenth-century Vaishnava theologian, Bhaktivinoda Thakur (1838–1914):

(1) Vaishnavism sees itself not as a sectarian religion but as Sanatana Dharma, or the eternal function of the soul. In other words, all religions are but various expressions of Vaishnavism, to greater or lesser degrees. The soul is by nature an eternal servant of Vishnu (or Krishna, Rama, Allah, Jehovah, and/or other manifestations of God, depending on the lineage, tradition, or religion with which one identifies).

(2) God manifests variously—as an impersonal abstraction, as the soul of the universe, and as the Supreme Person in his spiritual kingdom. He also appears in Deity form, i.e., as the image worshipped in the temple, and he often interacts with humankind as so many incarnations (avatars), as already mentioned.

(3) Krishna, or Vishnu (or one of his direct incarnations), is the Supreme form of Godhead.

(4) Vishnu possesses infinite and multifarious energies, which are briefly mentioned in the world's sacred literature but are more fully described in the Vedic and Puranic texts of ancient India.

(5) The souls of this world are part of Vishnu's energies—they are technically called his "separated parts"—and their proper function is to serve him and to develop love for him.

(6) Certain souls are engrossed in Vishnu's illusory energy, which is considered his "material energy" (*maya*). By the practice of Vaishnavism, they can free themselves from the grip of such all-encompassing illusion.

(7) All spiritual and material phenomena are simultaneously one with and yet different from the Lord.

(8) Krishna, among all manifestations of Vishnu, is an ocean of intimacy, and one can derive the highest bliss by becoming reestablished in one's eternal relationship with him, which is now dormant.

(9) "Devotional service" (Bhakti-yoga) is the mystical path by which one can enter into a relationship with God—it supercedes all pious action, the cultivation of knowledge, and various mystical endeavors, such as yoga and meditation (though in its practice it subsumes various forms of yogic mysticism). The science of this holy devotion is detailed in books such as the *Bhagavad-Gita* and the *Bhagavata Purana*, but it is chiefly understood by associating with devotees who carry it in their hearts. The central practices of this path include singing the praises of God, chanting his names in a regulated fashion, offering food to him as a sacrament of devotion, and worshiping his image in the temple or in one's home.

(10) Pure love of God is alone the ultimate fruit of the spiritual journey.[10]

What do Vaishhnavas do? Their days are made up of various worship services, the studying of sacred texts, and rejoicing in the Lord. They are mainly vegetarian, preparing nonmeat delicacies as a form of yoga; they worship visible icons fashioned according to strict scriptural guidelines; they sing songs of praise; they meditate; and they work in the world— offering the fruits of their work to God. Specific details about these various activities will be revealed in upcoming chapters.

SHAIVISM

It is not that Vaishnavism is the only Hindu religion. Parallel traditions arose around other deities, such as Shiva and the Goddess. Shiva, in fact, is among the most widely worshipped deities in India. With names such as

Mahadeva ("the Great God") and Maheshvara ("the Supreme Controller"), he is venerated in ancient holy cities like Benares, where Shaivites (as his worshippers are called) devote their lives to him, viewing him as the Supreme Lord.

Shiva's worship goes back to Vedic times. Like Vishnu, his appearance in the *Vedas* is brief. There he is known as Rudra as opposed to Shiva. But, make no mistake—these two refer to the same deity. More, the Rudra-Shiva aspect of Godhead goes back to the Indus Valley Civilization, with a "Proto-Shiva" image called Pashupati appearing on an ancient seal. This makes Shiva one of the earliest divinities in India's current historical record.

Vaishnavas see Shiva as an alternate form of Vishnu. Sometimes this is expressed by saying that he is the greatest of Vishnu's devotees: "The *Bhagavata* is supreme among Puranas, just as the Ganges is the greatest of all rivers, Lord Acyuta [Vishnu] the best among deities, and Lord Shambhu [Shiva] the greatest among devotees." (*Bhagavata Purana* 12.13.16) According to Vaishnavas, then, Shiva may correctly be considered the greatest—at least among devotees.

Along these lines, there are countless stories in the Puranas indicating Shiva's subservient position as Vishnu's devotee. For example, there is the story of Vrikasura, a demon who practiced severe austerities and then asked Shiva for a boon—the power to kill at once any living being whose head Vrikasura merely touched. Shiva granted the boon, but was soon to regret his decision, for Vrika came after him to try out the newfound power. Lord Shiva ran to all parts of the universe to escape this power-mad devotee and finally ended up at the door of Vishnu's kingdom.

Hearing the words of a frightened Shiva, Vishnu devised a plan to help him. In accordance with this plan, Vishnu appeared directly before Vrikasura and told him that Shiva was not to be trusted. "Shiva is fond of joking and even lying," said Vishnu. "I am sure he is not telling you the truth. He was just teasing you. Touch your own head, and you will see that nothing will happen."

Vrika, of course, touched his own head and died. But the point of this story, in the present context, is Vishnu's superiority over Shiva, who could not resolve the problem on his own. After racing through the entire material cosmos to escape Vrikasura, Shiva sought refuge in Vishnu, the Supreme Personality of Godhead.

Shaivites, however, tend to see Shiva not merely as the greatest devotee but rather as God himself. Vaishnavas can accommodate this by emphasizing the Rig Vedic quote that all gods are one. They can also find substantiation for Shiva's divinity in their own texts. The *Bhagavata* (4.7.50), for example, says (through the words of Lord Vishnu): "Brahma, Lord Shiva, and I are the supreme cause of the material manifestation. I am the Supersoul, the self-sufficient witness. But impersonally there is no difference between Brahma, Lord Shiva, and Me."

In other words, all three divinities are one because they are all *avatars*, or descents of the Supreme, for the creation, maintenance, and annihilation of the material world. In this context, they preside over the modes of passion (embodied by Brahma, the creator), goodness (embodied by Vishnu, the maintainer), and ignorance (embodied by Shiva, the destroyer). All three of these *avatars* are considered aspects of the same principle of Godhead.

The *Mahabharata* too (*Anushasana-parva* 135) says that Vishnu and Shiva are nondifferent and even counts the names Sarva, Sthanu, Ishana, and Rudra (names traditionally identified with Shiva) among the thousand names of Vishnu. Such identification between Shiva and the deity of the Vaishnavas gives additional emphasis to the idea that all gods are just so many faces of Brahman.

But devotees of Shiva sometimes go even further, saying that Shiva surpasses Vishnu. They cite traditions in which Rama, for example, is seen as a devotee of Shiva. This would put an *avatar* of Vishnu in a secondary position and thus support the tenet of Shaivism that Shiva is Supreme. If we look a little closer, however, we find that Rama's worship of Shiva turns out to be a later tradition, not supported in Valmiki's *Ramayana*. Moreover, even these later traditions explain that Rama worshipped Shiva in accord with his identity: Rama was playing the role of a human being. People of his time worshipped the gods for material benefits, and Rama did not want to discourage them. It was a matter of etiquette, too. Rama wanted to become a greater devotee of Shiva than the evil Ravana was, and then ask Shiva for permission to defeat the villain.

The truth of the matter becomes clear when one carefully studies the *Ramayana*. Here one finds many stories about the glories of Shiva—his destruction of Daksa's sacrifice, his marriage with Uma (Parvati), his drinking of the ocean of poison, his killing of the demon Andhaka, his cursing of Kandarpa, But, ultimately, the sacred text makes Rama's supremacy indisputable. Rama—an incarnation of Vishnu—is supreme.

To clarify Shiva's position according to traditional Vaishnavism, the *Brahma-Samhita* (5.45) offers an analogy: "When milk is transformed by acids into yogurt, the yogurt is neither the same as nor different from the original milk. I adore the primeval Lord Govinda [Krishna, Vishnu], of whom Lord Shiva is such a transformation, specifically for performing the work of destruction."

Though milk and yogurt are essentially nondifferent, yogurt is a product of milk. One can use milk to make clarified butter (*ghee*), cheese, ice cream, or yogurt, but one cannot turn yogurt into milk. Clearly, then, Shiva's divinity is intimately connected with, even dependent upon, his relationship to Vishnu.

So, according to Vaishnava theology, Shiva is both God and yet different from God as well. Because of Shiva's intimate contact with the quality of ignorance and with matter (which is innately ignorant), the living beings in this world cannot receive the same spiritual restoration by worshipping him as they do by worshipping Vishnu.

But this is all from the Vaishnava point of view. Shaivites have a different story to tell. They trace their religion to the *Shvetashvatara Upanishad*, in which, possibly for the first time, Shaivite ideas are clearly formulated. These ideas are later developed in the *Linga* and *Shiva Puranas,* where we are introduced to many of Shiva's mystical pastimes as Lord of his devotees. These Puranas also specifically detail aspects of Shiva worship, such as installation of Shiva *lingas* (aniconic phallic symbols) and techniques for meditating on Shiva's various manifestations. They also describe Shiva's mystical abode, comparable to the highest heaven known as Vishnu's paradise.

Historically, the Pashupatas are the earliest Shaivite sect, and they are specifically mentioned in the *Mahabharata*. Shaiva Siddhanta, a form of Shiva worship found mainly in South India, is quickly becoming a world religion, particularly because of the efforts of the Shaiva Siddhanta Church, or the *"Hinduism Today"* people. Vira Shaivism (or the Lingayat religion), another Shaivite denomination, is gaining in popularity, too. These are Shaivite equivalents to Vaishnavism, with profound theological traditions and noteworthy history.

Although Shaivites tend toward impersonalistic philosophy, with an ultimate goal of merging into Shiva's essence, the Shaiva Siddhanta group emphasizes worship of a personal deity, thus setting up a significant parallel to Vaishnavism. In fact, during the eleventh century, a group of sixty-three Shaivite saints, known as the Nayanars, arose in South India—their work and teaching were analogous to those of the Alvars, their Vaishnava counterpart, whose poetry revolutionized Vaishnava thought.

However, in general, Shaivites might more realistically be compared to devotees of the Goddess, whom we shall soon explore more fully, for they usually envision the divine in horrific forms, as do devotees of the female Lord. In addition, Shiva is said to be the husband of Kali, Durga, and so on, the most popular forms of this feminine divinity. Ultimately, then, Shavism and Shaktism, worship of the Goddess, are kissing cousins.

Regarding the horrific forms of Shiva, the most common example is his manifestation as Bhairava. In this form of Shaivism, the Lord's devotees practice a form of asceticism in which they live in cremation grounds. Followers are sometimes known as Kapalikas ("skull men") because they carry a skull-topped staff and a cranium begging bowl. This is an austere form of religion, and few can practice it properly.[11]

SHAKTISM

Vaishnavas view the ultimate Goddess as Radha or Lakshmi, the consorts of Krishna and Vishnu, respectively. Sita, too, is a manifestation of the Supreme feminine deity. Thus, Vaishnavism sees itself as nonsexist, with equitable treatment of male and female forms of Godhead. In some Vaishnava traditions, in fact, the feminine divine is exalted above her male counterpart. In this sense, Vaishnavism often views itself as a form of Shaktism in which "higher" feminine powers are given their due.

More commonly, however, it is not the Vaishnava Goddesses who are being addressed in the religion known as Shaktism, but, rather, it is Shiva's wife, the goddess of the spheres. Still, just as the *Rig Veda* tells us that all the gods are one, it should be kept in mind that India's many goddesses share this trait, too, along with hierarchical considerations best left to more technical literature.

Durga is the goddess of material creation, though she is also known as Kali, Uma, Parvati and so on—with numerous forms and pastimes to express her various incarnations and moods. She is also Mother Earth, known in Sanskrit as Bhu, and the personified form of the Lord's energy; when manifesting as spiritual energy, she is called Subhadra, or Yoga-Maya, when her darker side is unleashed, she is known as Bhadra, or Maha-Maya, illusion personified.

The *Brahma-Samhita* (5.43) explains that the material world is her central avenue of concern—the venue for her service. This work outlines four levels of existence, contextualizing Durga's place in the Lord's creation. The highest level of existence, according to this particular text, is Krishna's own abode, the most profound manifestation of the kingdom of God. Just below that is Hari-dham (Vaikuntha), the dwelling of Vishnu—this is still the spiritual realm, but not quite as high as Krishna's original abode. Lower in spiritual geography is Mahesh-dham, the dwelling place of Shiva and his devotees. Finally, there is Devi-dham, the material world, where the Goddess (the Mother of the universe) exerts her control.

Devi-dham consists of fourteen divisions of planetary systems, which make up our visible cosmos. The *Brahma-Samhita* (5.44) states the following about the Goddess: "The Lord's external potency, Maya, who is by nature a shadow of the spiritual potency, is worshipped by all people as

Durga—the creating, preserving, and destroying agency of this mundane world. I adore the primeval Lord Govinda (Krishna), in accordance with whose will Durga conducts herself."

In the verse just quoted, the presiding deity of Devi-dham is identified as Durga, a goddess whose physical appearance is both frightening and symbolic. She is often depicted with ten arms that represent ten kinds of fruitive activities. She rides on a ferocious lion signifying her heroism, and is popularly known for trampling Mahishasura—a buffalo demon that is said to represent all vices. Durga is the wife of Shiva. She has two sons, Kartikeya and Ganesh, who are the embodiments of beauty and success, respectively. She holds a snake that evokes destructive time, and holds twenty diverse weapons, each representing various pious activities enjoined in the *Vedas* for the suppression of vices.

Durga incarnates in many forms, as mentioned above. Although these manifestations, such as Kali and Uma, are worshipped as distinct deities with specific characteristics, they are nonetheless aspects of the same Goddess. In other words, when people in India speak of a generic "Goddess," they are usually referring to one of several overlapping feminine divinities: Durga, Kali, Mahadevi, Mayadevi, and so on.

As Shiva's consort, Durga has various names: Parvati, Gauri, Uma, Devi, Bhavani, amongst many others. Her characteristics are diverse and manifest differently, depending on the aspect her devotee is focused on. Gauri, Uma, and Parvati are most benevolent and are generally portrayed as loving and kind. Durga is often represented as a heroic fighting goddess with violent and even bloodthirsty overtones. More intense still is her alter ego, Kali, who is the beneficiary of sacrificial animal offerings, though such offerings are now on the wane.

The Brahmin who actually performs the animal sacrifices is instructed to avoid causing the animal pain, and he must wait for the animal to acquiesce before cutting off its head with a single stroke. The blood is used as an offering to icons and to bless worshippers, and the meat is cooked and served to nonvegetarian worshippers and to the poor. Those Shaktas who are averse to the bloody sacrifice will use pumpkin or melon instead of killing animals. Sometimes, red flowers are used to simulate blood through its color—these have become popular and acceptable substitutes.

The Goddess is identified with *prakriti* (material nature) and *maya* (illusion). Indeed, two of her more popular names are Mulaprakriti ("the embodiment of primordial matter") and Maha-Maya ("the great illusion"). This is significant. As Krishna says in the *Bhagavad-Gita* (9.10): "The material energy [*prakriti*] is working under My direction, O son of Kunti, and is producing all moving and non-moving beings." Prakriti is Durga, and Krishna controls her by giving her direction. When one doesn't acknowledge that, Durga becomes Maha-Maya—the Great Illusion.

But, again, this is all from a Vaishnava point of view. In modern Shaktism, the Goddess stands on her own as the Supreme feminine Godhead. Like the other deities mentioned in this section, the Goddess goes back to pre-Vedic times and is the subject of many Puranic stories as well. Various Shakta traditions have grown up around her, incorporating elements of Shaivism (since Shiva is her spouse) and regional particularities too numerous to mention.

While most Shaktas claim the Goddess is Supreme, others argue that she is a vehicle through which one reaches the ultimate masculine deity, usually some form of Shiva. From this perspective, the Divine Mother becomes something of a mediatrix, which is much how Lakshmi is often viewed in the Vaishnava tradition. In this way, Shaktism is sometimes seen as a Shaivite subsect. Usually, such forms of Shaktism talk of merging into the Goddess's ultimate identity, creating a oneness between the Divine Feminine, Shiva, and the practitioner. Admittedly, this is less common than simple devotion to the Divine Mother as an independent divinity, a doctrine that is the heart and soul of numerous Hindus throughout the world. But it is often an underlying principle of even those forms of Shaktism in which the Mother is seen as Supreme, and so it is significant enough to mention here.

The most important scripture of the Shakta tradition, embodying both perspectives mentioned above, is the *Devi-Mahatmya*, which originates as chapters 81–93 of the *Markendeya Purana*, usually dated at about the fifth century CE. Here one finds a wealth of lore concerning the Goddess—how to worship her, venerate her, and please her. It teaches how to set up altars in her service, and how to live one's life according to her expectations. The text includes both esoteric and exoteric explanations of her divinity, and devotees normally recite portions of it on a daily basis.[12]

SMARTA RELIGION

Although there are many religious traditions that today fall under the broad category "Hinduism," we will concern ourselves here with merely one more. The Smartas are those who worship Hinduism's many gods as equal—the deities are distinct individuals, they say, who are all due our respect and worship, though, in an ultimate sense, they are all one, ala the statement of the *Rig Veda*. Overall, Smartas seem to hold polytheistic views similar to that found in Greek and Roman mythology.

Consequently, there are five major deities to whom the Smartas give their worship: Vishnu, Surya (the sun god), Ganesh (the elephant-headed son of Shiva), Durga, and Shiva. But there are others as well.

Many trace Smarta beliefs to Shankara, the famous eighth-century philosopher who held that ultimate reality is impersonal and that the goal of life was to merge with the Supreme. Shankara, it is said, was born into an India that was besieged by religious rebellion. During his time there was an upsurge of diverse religious traditions, such as Buddhism and Jainism, which were competing with long established Vedic and post-Vedic religious milieus. His goal was to bring all of these communities together by showing the richness of the original tradition. This way, he hoped, he might reconcile divergent views.

His approach was simple. He asserted that any of the established Hindu gods would do, and that any and all can be worshipped, and that devotees should do so according to the prescriptions given in their respective texts. The Epics and the Puranas, of course, were the main texts in question. Since these works are collectively known as Smriti, the community of devotees who rallied around him was eventually known as Smartas ("those who follow Smriti").

Shankara thus established the legitimacy of worshipping various deities, teaching that multiple loyalties were compatible with the teachings of the *Vedas*, since these deities are nothing but manifestations of one impersonal Brahman. By doing this, he successfully revived interest in the Vedic literature and its related traditions. But he created a Hinduism that was nonspecific to a fault. That is to say, later commentators would criticize him both for his impersonal view of the Divine—which, by the way, is accepted in pan-Hindu tradition, but usually as subservient to a Personal Absolute—and for establishing harmony between the gods.

At first blush, such harmony might appear desirable. But the sages had long determined the wisdom in keeping worship divided. Devotees of Krishna, for example, could develop unalloyed love for God only by having single-minded devotion, and by directing full attention to their chosen deity. Otherwise, a sense of unfaithfulness or infidelity develops, in which one's focus becomes compromised. An unsavory doctrine of competitiveness and betrayal follows close behind: "On which god should I place my attention?"

In fact, the nature of the mind and heart are such that a choice must ultimately be made. Even in mundane dealings, it is frequently seen that a man with several lovers will eventually lean toward the one he likes best. Our tendency is to compare and then to opt for that which satisfies our inner needs, according to our taste and conditioning. The scriptures, in their wisdom, ask us to be pointed in our devotions from the beginning.

True, the *Rig Veda*, again, echoes in the background—reminding us that all the gods are, in some sense, one. But such homogeneity needs to be understood from a certain perspective, and the Epics and the Puranas are quite clear that focused allegiances will yield a more concrete result.

Nonetheless, Shankara's "universalist" Hinduism became widespread, and much of modern India has embraced his polytheistic worldview. Even many Vaishnavas, who hold Vishnu to be Supreme, tend to see their Lord as an alternate aspect of Shiva or the Goddess. While there is no doubt a basis for this in scriptural Hinduism (and we may repeatedly refer to the *Rig Veda* for this) it needs to be understood under the direction of a bona fide spiritual master, where its various nuances and particularities can be assessed and grasped on a deeper level.

The Gaudiya Vaishnava saint, Bhaktisiddhanta Sarasvati Thakur (1874–1937), has expressed the Vaishnava view of Smarta philosophy in his work on Sri Chaitanya:

The *Brahma-samhita* has refuted Panchopasana [Hinduism's traditional worship of five gods: Vishnu, Surya, Ganesh, Durga, and Shiva]. Five *shlokas* of the *Brahma-samhita* have described the natures of the five deities: (1) "I [Lord Brahma] adore the primeval Lord Govinda [Krishna], in pursuance of whose order the Sun-god, the king of the planets and the eye of this world, performs his journey mounting the wheel of time." (2) "I adore the primeval Lord Govinda, whose lotus-like feet are always held by Ganesh on his head in order to obtain power for his function of destroying all the obstacles of the three worlds." (3) "I adore the primeval Lord Govinda, in accordance with whose will Durga, His external potency, conducts her function as the creating, preserving, and destroying agent of the world." (4) "I adore the primeval Lord Govinda, who transforms Himself as Shambhu [Shiva] for performing the work of destruction, just as milk is transformed into curd, which is neither the same as, nor different from, milk." (5) "I adore the primeval Lord Govinda, who manifests Himself as Vishnu in the same manner as one burning candle communicates its light to another candle which, though existing separately, is of the same quality as the first."[13]

CHAPTER 9
Underlying Metaphysics

"As the embodied soul continuously passes, in this body, from childhood to youth to old age, the soul similarly passes into another body at death."

(Bhagavad-Gita 2.13)

Hinduism encompasses numerous teachings, and a huge tome devoted to this one topic would not even scratch the surface. This work, to be sure, does not attempt to summarize Hindu thought, for such an endeavor would be lost in the quagmire of centuries of learning. We will, however, look at certain philosophical premises that underlie all the rest.

There are three basic ideas, in particular, that make the principles of Hindu practice abundantly clear: (1) the Hindu concept of identity, that is, of being a soul distinct from the body; (2) the teaching of *karma*—that every action has an equal and commensurate reaction; and (3) reincarnation, which opines that the soul transmigrates from body to body until it reaches perfection. All Hindu practice is set against the backdrop of these three teachings. More, these teachings are the fundamental truths learned from the scriptures and traditions that form the basis of early Hinduism, as outlined in the first half of this book.

IDENTITY BEYOND THE BODY

People generally identify with their gross and subtle bodies—the physical form and the mind/intellect that accompanies it. When asked who they are, most people respond with a name, a profession, a description of their religion (i.e., their inherited faith), or their political affiliations. Sometimes they identify with familial connections, their heritage, or their "roots." Others have a more psychological perspective: "I am sensitive; I would never hurt anyone; I am rational and honest, and I have close ties with others who have similar qualities."

Most readers would be able to identify with the above personality traits or with their endless variations. And at first it might seem appropriate to define ourselves by using such words and concepts, at least in a practical, everyday sense. But do we cease to exist if we change our name? If we lose our job? Or if we convert to another religion? If our sense of morals or ethics become compromised, do we then lose our identity? True, our identity may, in a sense, change, but aren't we still really the same person? The question remains: Who are we beyond these changeable, material designations?

This is the resounding question at the core of all Vedic texts and Hindu practice. If we are merely the material body—flesh, bile, mucus, and so on—what is life really all about? In fact, what value do we place on our body once it is divorced from the life spark within? Not much. It is then merely an empty shell. For the Hindu, life is about understanding our original identity, about nurturing our real selves, the being beyond the body and the mind.

Plato described existence in this world as *metasy*, "an in-between state." Living beings, to him, were a combination of matter and spirit, a spark of the eternal caught in a web of temporality, a quantum of knowledge drowning in an ocean of ignorance. Most forms of Eastern thought agree with this view. According to ancient India's Vedic literature, living beings are essentially spiritual, creatures that took birth in the world of matter due to a series of complex yet subtle desires. Such embodied souls are called in Sanskrit *tatashtha-shakti*. The root *tata* signifies the hypothetical line that divides land from sea. Sometimes the water covers the land, and then it recedes. Living beings in this world are sometimes covered by forgetfulness of their true nature, and sometimes, rarely, they are uncovered.

The process of uncovering the true self, which is known as self-realization, is the project of the believing Hindu.

The *Chandogya Upanisad* (8.7–8.12), an ancient Vedic text, relates a classic story about finding one's true identity. Implicit in this tale is not only the importance of knowing who one really is, but also how difficult it is to attain such knowledge. All Hindu traditions embrace this story in one form or another, for its metaphysical implications are prerequisite to Hindu practice.

This is the story of Indra and Virochana, two specially empowered beings from a higher planetary system. Indra was known as the king of heaven, and Virochana was the leader of celestial demons. At the dawn of creation, both approached Lord Brahma, the demigod deputed to create heavens and earth on behalf of the Lord, and asked how they might attain unparalleled happiness and complete satisfaction.

Lord Brahma told them that it is impossible to know true happiness until one knows who he or she really is—until one knows the soul. The energy within the body, Brahma told them, is eternal, for energy is not created or destroyed. More, it is free from birth, death, old age, and disease—it is also free from hunger, lamentation, sin, and material desire.

To realize the truth of Brahma's statements, Indra and Virochana stayed in his association for 32 years, practicing severe austerities and chanting the Lord's holy names. At the end of this period, they asked Brahma to tell them more about the soul. In response, Brahma said: "That person you are now seeing with your own eyes is the ultimate self, the soul, and know for certain that this being is fearless and immortal."

Indra and Virochana now felt they were on the verge of true enlightenment, and so with confidence they asked, "Is the soul the same person we see when we look in water or in a mirror? In other words, the reflection we see before our eyes—is this the soul?"

Brahma smiled and asked them to look into separate clay pots filled with water. He then asked them to elaborate on what they saw.

They told Brahma, "O Lord, we see the complete Self, the soul, just as it is, from the hair on our heads down to our shiny toenails."

Leaning over as if to whisper a secret in their ears, Brahma advised them to cut their hair and their toenails, and to decorate themselves with new clothes and ornaments as well. After this, he again asked them to look into the clay pots. "Now what do you see?" Brahma asked.

"We see that the two personalities in these reflections have cut their hair and toenails just as we have," Indra and Virochana enthusiastically responded, "and they are freshly dressed in new clothes and ornaments, too."

Brahma looked them squarely in the eyes and said: "These reflections are actually the fearless and immortal soul."

With this information, Indra and Virochana left Lord Brahma's presence with happy hearts—they now knew that they had seen the soul, their actual, ultimate selves.

Virochana, who was chief among the demons, went back to his people, exclaiming, "The body you see before you is nondifferent from the soul. He who worships his body properly attains happiness in this world and in the next. All his desires are fulfilled and he attains the pinnacle of enjoyment."

On the other hand, Indra, who shared Virochana's experience with Brahma, came to a different conclusion. On his return journey he contemplated all he had learned from Brahma, and he deliberated in the following way: "This body takes birth, dies, undergoes transformations, is subject to disease, and so on. How, then, can the body be the same as the actual self, which is immortal and without fear?"

Thinking in this way, Indra immediately returned to Brahma and proceeded to tell him about his doubt. Brahma smiled, inviting Indra to stay with him and study for deeper entry into the truths of the self.

Another 32 years pass, and Indra performs intense austerities in the company of his teacher, Brahma. Finally, Brahma tells him a secret: "That person who you understand to be the self in your dreams—it is this individual who is fearless and immortal. Indeed, the 'I' in your dreams is the actual soul for whom you are looking."

Hearing this, Indra left with confidence that he now understood the soul. But as he was returning home, he thought to himself: "The self in my dreams is temporary—he departs when the dream comes to an end. Moreover, he is a fictitious, ever-changing entity—in one dream he may be blind, in another have several heads, and in still another he may be a monster. I can't see how such a self can be the fearless, immortal soul. It just doesn't make sense."

With these thoughts in mind, Indra returned to Brahma, who encouraged his now perplexed pupil to stay on for some more years under his tutelage. If he does so, Brahma assured him, he will eventually understand the nature of the soul and thus attain ultimate happiness.

At the end of another cycle of 32 years, Brahma revealed to Indra that the soul lies hidden in the state of deep sleep, buried in the unconscious mind, where there is neither vision nor the experience of dreaming.

But, as before, Indra felt uncomfortable with his newfound knowledge, doubting its veracity and returning to Brahma for more complete instruction. "I must tell you, dear Brahma, my teacher, that this current notion of the soul falls short, just like the others. It cannot be reconciled with reason or logic: In deep sleep, there is no understanding of who one is, nor is identity being perceived on any level. In many ways, this deep sleep state clouds the issue of the self even more than the prior conceptions."

Brahma told Indra that he was nearly ready to truly understand the soul. After five more years of intense study and severe austerities, Brahma called him to his side: "Indra, now I will explain the ultimate truth about the actual self. The physical body, which is subject to death, is only the abode of the soul, who is concealed within. This soul is attached to the body, just as a bull is harnessed to a cart. Self-realization means to break free of this harness, and to realize the self within. In reality, it is the soul who desires—such as 'I shall look,' or 'I shall hear'—and these desires are fulfilled through the crude external senses. But the soul also has a transcendental life beyond the body, in relationship with God.

"I could not tell you these truths in the presence of Virochana, for his demoniac mentality could never understand the subtleties of the actual self, and he needed to identify with the body in order to relish the petty pleasures he desires. Moreover, I did not want to merely explain these things to you in terms of logic and argument, but, rather, I wanted you to stay with me and perform austerities, so you could realize the truth of the soul as an undeniable fact."

From this story we learn that the soul has three manifestations, if you will, which correspond to three sheaths of consciousness explained in the Vedic literature: (1) the gross, physical body; (2) the subtle body—this refers to mind, intelligence, and one's sense of identity; it is often divided into the two states of covered consciousness, as in the tale above; and (3) the Self, or the actual person within all external material coverings.

These truths are confirmed in the *Bhagavad-Gita*, more than in any other Hindu text: "For the soul, there is neither birth nor death. He has not come into being, nor does he ever come into being. He always exists, and he is not slain when the body perishes." (2.20) "As a person puts on new garments, giving up old ones, the soul similarly accepts new material bodies, giving up those that have outlived their usefulness." (2.22) "As the embodied soul continuously passes, in this body, from childhood to youth to old age, the soul similarly passes into another body at death." (2.13)

Such well-worn *Gita* verses tell us not only about the nature of the Self (that it is indeed separate from the body) but they also reveal much about the Hindu view of reincarnation. But before looking at this latter doctrine in any depth, it would be wise to briefly explore the related concept of *karma* (action and reaction), often misunderstood in the study of Hinduism.

KARMA: WHAT GOES AROUND, COMES AROUND

The word *karma* comes from the Sanskrit root *kri*, meaning "action." But it also implies the cyclical nature of action, causality, "what goes around, comes around." That is to say, *karma* refers to cause and effect, a metaphysical extension of Newton's Third Law of Motion: For every action there is an equal and commensurate reaction. It is a universal law, and it manifests in uncountable ways. As Mark Mathew Braunstein, author and scholar, noted:

The Eastern law of *karma* might be defined in various Western ways: scientifically as action and reaction, epistemologically as cause and effect, biblically and botanically as sowing and reaping, and even economically as supply and demand.[1]

In other words, *karma* refers to the inevitable result of old choices—old beliefs and old attitudes, leading to old actions. These acts, as a matter of course, create and re-create uncountable consequences, until, eventually, the perpetrator becomes outwardly conscious of the reasons for his actions and chooses to change them, if necessary. In this way, *karma* is not a punishment, as some mistakenly think, but rather an opportunity to correct old patterns, and thus to make our lives richer and more fulfilling.

Karma, then, is a teacher. Through understanding the consequences of our actions, we eventually learn to refrain from committing misdeeds. In this way, as a system of justice, *karma* helps us, albeit gradually, to learn from our mistakes, first on an unconscious level, and then with full consciousness of right and wrong. By acting in particular ways, lifetime after lifetime, we gradually develop a sense of direction, intuiting mistakes we made in the past. Over the course of time, as self-realization matures, we develop a distinct awareness of what is to be done, and what is not to be done.

Thus, *karma* helps individuals understand the error of their ways and to reform their behavior, even if it uses a "refining" method that takes a long time—sometimes many lifetimes. Still, once having learned the lessons that *karma* tries to teach, the acquired realizations become deeply embedded in the psyche.

To be clear: Karma teaches us every action carries with it a concomitant reaction—all actions have built-in consequences. And if we learn from these consequences, *karma* has served its purpose and we can move on in our journey toward spiritual perfection. In Hindu thinking, then, *karma* is the sum of all that an individual has done, all that he is currently doing, and everything he will do in the future.

Given *karma*'s all-encompassing nature, it might seem that there is little room for free will. Not so. Just as free will created our *karma*—after all, we chose to act in a certain way—it can change our *karma* as well. Consequently, *karma* is not fatalistic, though a superficial reading of it might suggest that it is. Rather, as human beings we have the ability to change our own behavior, thus changing consequences that at one time might have seemed irrevocable. That is to say, the doctrine of *karma* challenges us to overcome our conditioning, our inclination to act in particular ways, and it paves the way for a better future. But, it also teaches that if we don't work hard to overcome bad habits—inclinations acquired over numerous lifetimes—these very actions will manifest *karma*'s darker side, revealing stringent laws that are as binding as our tendency to cling to conditioning.

The idea was eloquently summed up by Manly P. Hall (1901–1990), prolific author and founder of the Philosophical Research Society (1934), who wrote: "*Karma* does not mean fatalism, but rather, compensation. When a man buys something on credit, he creates a debt, and the law declares that he must pay that dept. In a material, economic transaction this would not be regarded as fatalism, but as responsibility."[2]

Sarvepalli Radhakrishnan (1888–1975), philosopher, statesman, and former president of India, also offers insight into how *karma* might be seen in terms of fatalism, but that it more accurately represents an exercise of choice:

Life is like a game of bridge. We did not invent the game or design the cards. We did not frame the rules and we cannot control the dealing. The cards are dealt out to us, whether they be good or bad. To that extent, determinism rules. But we can play the game well or play it badly. A skillful player may have a poor hand and yet win the game. A bad player may have a good hand and yet make a mess of it. Our life is a mixture of necessity and freedom, chance and choice. By exercising our choice properly, we can control steadily all the elements and eliminate altogether the determinism of nature.[3]

Needless to say, *karma* is complex, with enough variables to allow for diverse interpretations. Actually, there are three basic forms of *karma*, which we will briefly outline below. This will be followed by six additional elaborations on the doctrine, two sets of three each—these will help to clarify the mechanism through which *karma* works. An understanding of all nine of these karmic dimensions are necessary to appreciate the concept as a whole, for they give insight into how *karma*'s laws are not irreversible and how it doesn't go against the principle of free will. To begin—and without the distraction of the complex Sanskrit terminology that usually accompanies these explanations—the overarching three categories might be broken down as follows:

(1) Ordinary *karma* means "good works," usually in accordance with scriptural recommendations and pious activity. Such *karma* yields good results.

(2) A second form of *karma* refers to negative works. Such acts naturally bring unfortunate reactions, usually commensurate with the initial act.

(3) The third kind of *karma* is actually known as "freedom from works." This is described in the *Bhagavad-Gita*—if one works as an agent of the Lord, one does not enjoy or suffer the fruits of one's acts. Rather, one transcends the duality of action and reaction and becomes situated in transcendence, even while in this life.

The second group of *karma*'s nine dimensions is more technical, addressing the period in which a given action may have occurred and how its consequences may or may not have reached maturity. In more simple terms:

(1) First, there is the accumulated store of actions from past births, both good and bad. These are yet to be worked out and often appear in this life in the form of desires—in other words, as conditioning and as inclinations.
(2) "Detained" *karma* comes next. This is the result of actions already worked out in a previous life. They appear in our present life in the form of what actually happens to us. They shape the events and conditions of our present experience, including the nature of our body, our personal tendencies, and our goals.
(3) And then there is our present *karma*, continuously made through our ever-present movements in the material world, creating what happens to us in the future.

The first of these three kinds of *karma*, the residue of one's total accumulated actions, is often compared to rice that has been harvested and stored in a granary. From that stored rice, a small portion has been isolated, husked, and prepared for cooking and eating. This is comparable to the second phase, where past actions are shaping the events of the present. Simultaneously, new rice, gathered from the most recent harvest, is being planted in the field—this will eventually yield a future crop and be added to the store of grain.

The final three karmic considerations tell us much:

(1) Flexible—This is *karma* that can easily be deflected.
(2) Middling—This is *karma* that can be overcome with intense effort.
(3) Fixed—There is no human endeavor that can obliterate this kind of *karma*. Rather, through spiritual practice one may evoke God's mercy, and thus become free.[4]

Most *karma* is binding, or "Fixed," according to the above list, only to be overcome by the grace of the Lord. In fact, the whole of Hinduism balances on this premise—that we've created an entangled web through lifetimes of selfish desire. And that only by daily devotions and heartfelt prayer might we not only recondition ourselves to a more pure and selfless demeanor but also attract the attention of the Lord. By so doing, we might clean away the *karma* of our past (both good and bad) and become situated in spiritual awareness.[5]

REINCARNATION IS MAKING A COMEBACK

If every action has an equal and corresponding reaction, what happens when a given person doesn't seem to get his due? How is it that a criminal, for example, might make it through his entire life without receiving appropriate retribution for his heinous act? The Hindu answer for this is reincarnation: If a villain doesn't pay for his misdeeds now, he can always pay for them in the future.

As a quantum of energy, the soul can neither be created nor destroyed—this is the First Law of Thermodynamics. So the soul goes on after death. But where does it go? In response, the Hindu asks the following question: Is heaven or hell an appropriate destination for most people? The answer: No. Most are not saintly, nor are they demonic. Rather, they are people who are working out their problems—discovering their assets and trying to overcome their inadequacies. Thus, a compassionate God would give them ample opportunity to correct their wrongs, to nurture their assets. This might take more than one life, which is where reincarnation comes in.

The earliest Vedic writings support this doctrine. The *Yajur Veda* (12.36–7), for instance, has this to say:

O learned and tolerant soul, after roaming in waters and plants, a person enters the womb and is born again and again. O soul, you are born in the body of plants, in trees, in all created animate objects, and in waters. O soul, blazing like the sun, after cremation, having reached the fire and the earth for rebirth, and residing in the belly of your mother, you are born again. O soul, having reached the womb, again and again, you auspiciously lay in your mother's body, as a child sleeps in her mother's lap.

The *Shvetashvatara Upanishad* (5.11) gives further insight into the nature of rebirth:

As the body is augmented by food and water, so the individual self, augmented by its aspirations, sense contact, visual impressions, and delusion, assumes successive forms in accordance with its actions.

The *Brihadaranyaka Upanishad* (4.4.1–4) goes still further in outlining just how reincarnation occurs:

[At the time of death] the area of his [the soul's] heart becomes lit and by that light the soul departs either through the eye, the head, or through other apertures of the body. And when he departs, the various life airs follow him to his next destination. . . . His knowledge and his deeds follow him, as does his previous wisdom.

Just as a caterpillar, when it reaches the end of one blade of grass, and after having properly approached another one, draws itself together toward the new blade, so the soul, after having thrown away the prior body and its ignorance, draws itself together, and latches onto the new body. And as the goldsmith, taking a piece of gold, turns it into another, more beautiful shape, even so does this soul, after having thrown away the old and useless body, makes unto himself newer and, hopefully, better bodies, according to his previous actions, ability and desires.

Thus, reincarnation is deeply ingrained in the Indian subcontinent. Overall, when it comes to rebirth, Hindus subscribe to one of three views:

(1) *The Early Vedic View.* This tradition maintains that most people are engaged in materialistic affairs, and that after death they go to the realm of Yamaraja, the nether regions, where their only hope for salvation lies in food and water offered by the deceased's children and grandchildren throughout the generations.

This traditional offering, a ceremony known as Pinda, is undertaken even today by most believing Hindus. It consists of a complex series of rituals wherein a ball of rice is offered to the deceased parent, allowing them entry into the association of the ancestors. Until that time (either 12 days or 12 months after death, depending upon which texts one refers to), the soul remains in a subtle ghostly form, and only this ceremony permits the departed soul to enter the next stage of existence.

After spending an unspecified time in this state, one "dies again" (possibly a reference to the soul's continuing journey toward its next incarnation through various intermediary way-stations) and passes through the various material elements (earth, water, air, fire, ether, and other, more subtle elements as well), eventually being "recycled" through the food chain and finally being born again in one of the 8,400,000 species that pervade the universe. This peculiar early Vedic view of transmigrating through the food chain is expressed by Vaishnava scholar and exemplary practitioner, A. C. Bhaktivedanta Swami Prabhupada as follows:

In the process of sacrifice [delineated in the *Vedas*], the living entity makes specific sacrifices to attain specific heavenly planets and consequently reaches them. When the merit of sacrifice is exhausted, then the living entity descends to earth in the form of rain, then takes on the form of grains, and the grains are eaten by man and transformed into semen, which impregnates a woman, and thus the living entity once again attains the human form to perform sacrifice and so repeat the same cycle. In this way, the living entity perpetually comes and goes on the material path. The Krishna conscious person, however, avoids such sacrifices. He takes directly to Krishna consciousness and thereby prepares himself to return to Godhead.[6]

The other 2 views Hindus subscribe to are as follows:

(2) *The Puranic View.* To this early Vedic view, the Puranas ("ancient histories") added the notion of unlimited types of heavens and hells where the dead are rewarded or punished according to their pious or impious actions. The Puranas describe that the soul wanders through these subtle spheres of existence before being reborn in another body, affording the chance to pursue self-realization.

(3) *The Samsara view.* This is the matured Hindu explanation of death, a culmination of the Vedic and Puranic concepts. *Samsara* teaches that, immediately after death, the soul is reborn into the material world and continues the cycle over and over again until achieving purified consciousness free from material desires. At that time, the purified soul returns to the spiritual realm, the spawning ground from which all souls originally come. There, one resumes one's natural, constitutional life in the company of God. Contemporary Hinduism, including Vaishnavism, Shaivism, Shaktism, and a host of other popular East-Indian traditions, hold this perspective, seeing it as the essential truth of all previous teachings.[7]

So the Hindu view is basically this: The soul, attempting to be the Lord of its own domain, leaves the spiritual realm, where God is supreme, and becomes an angelic being in Brahma's world (which is considered the highest heavenly planet of the mundane universe). From there, a small quantity of souls may return to their heavenly state. However, the majority, due to irrational passions associated with the body, and due to envy borne of life in a self-centered world, fall to the lowest species on lower planets. After this, they gradually evolve through each of the 8,400,000 forms of life, eventually reaching the human form, which is like a gateway to the spiritual world.

Born and reborn as humans with various levels of consciousness, the soul learns its lessons while accruing *karma* again and again. These many embodied lives are meant to teach us that divorcing ourselves from God is hellish and that our constitutional position involves returning to his kingdom as his servant. As the *Gita* (7.19) says,

After many births and deaths, he who is actually in knowledge surrenders unto Me [God], knowing Me to be the cause of all causes and all that is. Such a great soul is very rare.

CHAPTER 10
The Yoga of Eating

"Nonviolence is the highest duty and the highest teaching."
—Mahabharata (13.116.37–41)

Nonviolence, Cow protection, vegetarianism, and offering food to God—
these are the four subjects of this chapter. All are interrelated; all are
fundamental to the Hindu worldview. Interestingly, Hindu vegetarianism
is somewhat connected to the metaphysical underpinnings outlined in the
previous chapter: If we are not our bodies, and if animals are not theirs—
and if the soul transmigrates through the various species of life—then
who is to say that a slaughtered animal is not a former loved one, or a
relative? Or that the person who dines on animals' remains won't be a
sacrificed creature in his next life? Naturally, where bodily identification
is considered dubious, more attention is paid to the living being within.

Still, Hindus do not accept vegetarianism across the board. Shaktas,
for example, perform animal sacrifices, eating the remaining flesh as a
special benediction from God. Even here, however, Shaktas are mindful
of the mandate for nonviolence, and their methods of slaughter are akin
to the koshering laws of the Jews, in which they try to cause the least
amount of pain possible. To cite another example: There are pockets of
Vaishnavas who also engage in meat eating, usually due to necessity. This
is particularly true of those living in coastal areas, such as Jagannath Puri.
Here one might find Vaishnavas consuming "sea vegetables" (i.e., fish),
though such "delicacies" are never offered to the deities. Admittedly, these
exceptions are rare.

Overall, Hindus lean toward vegetarianism.[1] As evidence, one need merely observe how meat-oriented restaurants in India advertise to their vegetarian clientele—with a sign in the window saying, "nonvegetarian." In the West, where meat eating is more common, it's just the opposite. The sign might say, "special vegetarian dishes," for here meat is considered the norm.

Since Vaishnavas constitute the Hindu majority, vegetarianism is naturally the preferred diet in Hindu India. Indeed, there are some 500,000,000 Hindu vegetarians, or quasivegetarians, in the world today, including almost 80 percent of India's current Hindu population.[2] The practice has been exacerbated, too, by the influence of Buddhism and Jainism—both traditions emphasizing nonviolence. And so Hinduism has become known for nonviolence, for its sense of compassion for all creatures, for its harmless diet, and for its tasty cuisine. Let us look at all this a bit more closely.

HINDU NONVIOLENCE

Hinduism is among the earliest and strongest supporters of total nonviolence, including animal rights and all related issues. To this day, Hindus advocate the equitable treatment of our four-footed, feathered, and scaly kin. All living beings are considered brothers and sisters under God's fatherhood.

By the time of the *Mahabharata*, especially, nonviolence (*ahimsa*) was elevated to a central principle, as the opening quote of this chapter makes clear. This ethical mandate is summed up in the Sanskrit phrase, *sarva-bhuta-hita*, which means "kindness to all creatures" a doctrine embraced instead of the more limited *loka-hita*, or "kindness to one's own species." The former principle, says Hindu tradition, is a more inclusive ethic— one who is kind to all creatures is necessarily kind to their own species, but the converse is not necessarily so. Thus, practitioners, to this day, are encouraged to develop a more comprehensive ethical perspective.

The earlier Vedic tradition was a strong supporter of *ahimsa* and its concomitant love of all creatures. The following are but a few of the *Vedas'* hundreds of injunctions against meat eating, along with other quotes from corollary literature:

- One should not use their God-given body for killing God's creatures, whether these creatures are human, animal or whatever. (*Yajur Veda*, 12.32)
- One should be considered dear, even by those born in the animal kingdom. (*Atharva Veda*, 17.1.4)

- Those noble souls who practice meditation and other yogic ways, who are ever mindful of all beings, who protect all animals, are the ones who are actually serious about spiritual practices. (*Atharva Veda*, 19.48.5)
- A person who kills an animal for meat will die a violent death as many times as there are hairs on the body of that killed animal. (*Manu-Smriti*, 5.38)
- Having well considered the origin of flesh-foods, and the cruelty of fettering and slaying corporeal beings, let man entirely abstain from eating flesh. (*Manu-Smriti*, 5.49)
- By not harming any living being, one becomes fit for salvation. (*Manu-Smriti*, 6.60)
- God, Keshava (another name for Krishna), is pleased with a person who does not harm or destroy other nonspeaking creatures or animals. (*Vishnu Purana*, 3.8.15)
- The purchaser of flesh performs violence by his wealth; he who eats flesh does so by enjoying its taste; the killer commits harm by actually tying and killing the animal. Thus, there are three forms of killing. He who brings flesh or sends for it, he who cuts off the limbs of an animal, and he who purchases, sells, or cooks flesh, and, of course, there is a fourth: he who devours it—all of these are to be considered meat eaters. (*Mahabharata, Anu.* 115:40)
- He who desires to augment his own flesh by eating the flesh of other creatures lives in misery in whatever species he may take his birth. (*Mahabharata, Anu.* 115:47)
- Those who are ignorant of actual religious duty and, though wicked and haughty, account themselves virtuous, kill animals without any feeling of remorse or fear of punishment. Further, such sinful persons will, in their next lives, be eaten by the same creatures they have killed in this one. (*Bhagavata Purana*, 11.5.14)

Despite the above recommendations for a compassionate way of life, the Vedic disavowal of animal killing is anything but clear-cut. A significant tradition of animal sacrifice appears in Vedic texts, and even Brahmins—at least in certain quarters—at one time ate meat.[3] That being said, texts supporting animal sacrifice came with intimations about its lesser nature, suggestions that bloody offerings were an inferior form of worship—that, in fact, they coexisted with a superior vegetarian alternative.

This is similar to what went on in the Jewish tradition, where, in the Bible, God is depicted as saying, "I desired mercy, and not sacrifice; and the knowledge of God is more than burnt offerings." (*Hosea*, 6:6). Or, "'Of what purpose is the multitude of your sacrifices unto me?' said the Lord. 'I am full of the burnt offerings of rams and the fat of fed beasts; and I delight not in these.'" (*Isaiah*, 1:11)[4]

The *Sama Veda* (1.2.92) resonates like an Indic precursor to these biblical texts: "Ultimately, we endorse no sacrificial stake, no slaying of human or nonhuman victims—we endorse only worship that makes use of sacred mantras." Another striking example may be found in the *Mahabharata* (12.174–365), in which a sage named Kapila eloquently expresses his distaste for animal sacrifice, and points out that while such sacrifices, as part of the *Veda*, must be honored, there are higher forms of sacrifice—those that do not require the killing of animals.

Clearly, in both Vedic and biblical contexts, meat was only eaten if it was produced from the animal sacrifices. This was true, at least, in the higher echelons of society. Serious practitioners were advised never to eat flesh that was not part of the sacrificial arena. This is directly stated in the *Manu-Smriti* (5.31): "The holy sacrifice is the reason for eating meat. This, the tradition says, is clearly permitted. Doing it for any other purpose, however, is the activity of lesser beings."

The *Manu-Smriti* (5.56) offers a final word in this regard: "There is no sin in eating meat . . . but abstention brings greater rewards."

COW PROTECTION

Hindus have a special place in their hearts for cows, and it has been there since the beginning of their religion. According to the *Vedas*, Mother Surabhi—the primeval cow, the original prototype of all bovine entities—was churned at the dawn of creation, and her value was not to be minimized. Thus, Hindus have deep regard for her five products—milk, yogurt, clarified butter (*ghee*), urine, and dung—for these have objective virtue, as we will soon see. But there is no distinct "cow-goddess," as is generally supposed, nor are temples built in her honor.

The Vedic lexicon *Nighantu* offers nine synonyms for "cow," three of which—*aghnya*, or *ahi* (both meaning "not to be killed") and *aditi* ("not to be cut")—specifically forbid slaughter. These synonyms are found throughout the Vedic literature and are frequently used in the epic *Mahabharata* (*Shanti-Parva* 262.47): "The very name of the cows is *aghnya*, indicating that they should never be slaughtered. Who, then, could slay them? Surely, one who kills a cow or a bull commits the most heinous crime." This, in turn, was merely echoing the words of the *Rig Veda* (8.101.15): "The mother of the cosmic powers, the daughter of the beings of light, the sister of the sun gods, the navel center of truth. I speak to those who are aware: do not harm the cow, for, in so doing, you harm the Earth and all of humanity."

David Frawley, Director of the American Institute of Vedic Studies, writes, "The outer care of the cow reflects the inner care of the self: the cultivation of divine awareness, which yields the 'milk' of truth and pure perception."[5] This, of course, is paraphrasing Mahatma Gandhi, who said, "To me, the cow is the embodiment of the whole infrahuman world; she enables the believer to grasp his unity with all that lives. . . . To protect her is to protect all the creatures of God's creation."[6]

Hindu tradition's marked reverence and love for the entire bovine species might be traced to the fact that Lord Krishna is himself a cowherd boy. Indeed, an early Vaishnava prayer, called *Gita-Mahatmya* (verse 7) boldly declares, "The *Bhagavad-Gita*, which is the essence of all Upanishads, is just like a cow, and Lord Krishna, who is famous as a cowherd boy, is milking this cow. The hero Arjuna, to whom Krishna explains the *Gita*, is just like a calf, and learned scholars and pure devotees are those who drink the milk of this *Bhagavad-Gita*." The "cow," "cowherd boy," "calf," and "milk" imagery is significant, for it serves to stress the wholesomeness and purity with which the *Gita*, Krishna, Arjuna, and "learned scholars and pure devotees" are identified in Indian culture.

Scholar and author Lewis G. Regenstein observes bovine prominence in relation to the Krishna tradition:

Cows are important to Vaishnavas. They figure in an important way in two of the five major Hindu religious holidays. Janmastami, in August, is the birthday of Lord Krishna, who appeared five thousand years ago as a cow herder in the Indian village of Vrindaban. . . . Krishna demonstrated the necessity of protecting cows, and so is affectionately called Govinda, "One who gives pleasure to the cows."

Today, Govinda is the central figure of renown for the International Society for Krishna Consciousness, popularly known as the Hare Krishnas. They consider it "most sinful to kill and eat the flesh of these noble animals."

[The holiday known as] Gopashtami, falling in mid-November, is the day on which cows and bulls are brought into the temples . . . to be honored as sacred members of society. Since cows provide milk and bulls plow the fields, these bovines have traditionally been appreciated as important parts of the agricultural society of India.[7]

Here we are introduced to one of Hinduism's pragmatic reasons for revering the cow: agricultural necessity. In addition to reverence for Krishna, the people of India focus on the cow for a number of practical reasons, which is why philosopher and economist Jeremy Rifkin has written, "Our relationship to the cow has been both sacred and secular, spiritual and utilitarian."[8]

It was stated earlier that Hindus revere the dung and urine of cows as much as they do her milk. Here is why. Cow excrement is a cost-effective fertilizer. Through a form of organic composting, dung naturally generates methane fuel. Thus, cow manure is sun-dried into patties, creating a commonly used cooking and heating fuel without the cutting down of trees. This has been a precious resource to Hindus for millennia.

There is more. "Cow manure," writes Narasimha Dasa, an author and scholar of India's sacred traditions, "transforms desert soils, such as those in the Middle East and northern India, into fertile, humus-rich soils that retain moisture and support vegetation even with scarce rainfall."[9] The implications are significant—as the ground-cover vegetation becomes lusher and trees start growing, moisture retention increases the natural opulence of the land with beneficial microbes and plants, as well as with soil-building insects and animals. Manure, in fact, makes cow protection highly profitable even when milk production is low and the bulls are not fully engaged. In a sense, then, cow protection and bull protection are actually the same, even if people usually think that monetary profit is found in milk. Fact is, manure can be more profitable, because it leads to greater milk and grain production.

Cow urine, in its own way, is equally valuable: It is a natural and fully biodegradable cleanser and proven disinfectant (with an extremely high ammonia content). Her urine is also useful as an ingredient in any number of Ayurvedic (holistic) medicines. Rifkin, cited above, sums up the usefulness of the cow as follows:

To a great extent, the very survival of the Indian population depends on the contribution of this most useful of animals. The cows provide most of India's dairy requirements. The ox provides traction for 60 million small farmers whose land feeds 80 percent of the Indian population. Indian cattle excrete 700 million tons of manure annually, half of which is used as fertilizer to maintain the soil. The rest is burned to provide heat for cooking. Harris has estimated that cattle dung provides Indian housewives with the thermal equivalent of "27 million tons of kerosene, 35 million tons of coal, or 68 million tons of wood." Cow dung is even mixed with water and used as a paste to make household flooring. Each day small children all over India follow the family cow around on her daily rounds collecting her valuable excrement for a variety of household uses.[10]

Thus, because of her association with Lord Krishna, her symbolic value as representative of the entire natural world, her practical purposes in India's economy, and the magic of her byproducts, the cow is seen as a nurturing, invaluable creature to be loved, cared for, and respected. In fact, Hindus revere cows as one of their natural mothers, from whom they derive milk and sustenance in a variety of ways. And one doesn't eat their mother.

VEGETARIANISM

This brings us to vegetarianism. Again, not all Hindus subscribe to a nonmeat diet, but it is an important part of their tradition, particularly for Vaishnavas. So fundamental is vegetarianism to the Hindu way of life that one can now take a formal vow, known as *sakahara vrata* ("the vow of vegetarianism"), by logging on to http://www.hinduismtoday.com/in-depth_issues/veggie_vow/. The vow may be taken privately, before elders or parents, or as part of a temple ceremony. It reads, in part, like this: "I accept the principle of *sakahara* (vegetarianism) as the method by which I may acknowledge my compassion for all living beings. As an act of dedication, I am resolved this day to begin (or continue) the regular practice of eating a strict vegetarian diet and not eating meat, fish, shellfish, fowl or eggs." The standardization of such a vow speaks for itself.

Writing on behalf of the entire Hindu world, the late *"Hinduism Today"* guru, Satguru Shivaya Subramuniyaswami, explains Hindu vegetarianism as follows:

Hindus teach vegetarianism as a way to live with a minimum of hurt to other beings, for to consume meat, fish, fowl or eggs is to participate indirectly in acts of cruelty and violence against the animal kingdom. The abhorrence of injury and killing of any kind leads quite naturally to a vegetarian diet. . . . The meat-eater's desire for meat drives another to kill and provide that meat. The act of the butcher begins with the desire of the consumer.

Meat eating contributes to a mentality of violence, for with the chemically complex meat ingested, one absorbs the slaughtered creature's fear, pain and terror. These qualities are nourished within the meat-eater, perpetuating the cycle of cruelty and confusion. When the individual's consciousness lifts and expands, he will abhor violence and not be able to even digest the meat, fish, fowl and eggs he was formerly consuming. India's greatest saints have confirmed that one cannot eat meat and live a peaceful, harmonious life. Man's appetite for meat inflicts devastating harm on Earth itself, stripping its precious forests to make way for pastures.

The *Tirukural* candidly states, "How can he practice true compassion who eats the flesh of an animal to fatten his own flesh? Greater than a thousand *ghee* offerings consumed in sacrificial fires is not to sacrifice and consume any living creature."[11]

Additionally, it might be said that Hindus aspire to eat a healthy regimen in the "mode of goodness." This should be elaborated upon. The *Bhagavad-Gita* (17.7–10) teaches that food, like most other components of the material world, can be divided into three basic categories: ignorance, passion, and goodness.

Food in ignorance has the following qualities: it is stale, decomposing, putrid, overripe, impure, produces negative emotions, such as anger, greed, and jealousy, and contributes to ill health. Closely related to this are foods in passion. Heavy spices, onions, garlic, peppers, pickles, as well as meat, fish, and eggs, are usually included in this category. These are foods that will cause tension and overbearing demeanor. Finally, food in goodness is not irritating to the system and purifies the mind. It includes fruits, nuts, vegetables, and whole grains—foods that lead to health, strength, happiness, calmness, and compassion.

Needless to say, a vegetarian diet, properly prepared, partakes of the quality of goodness, and such a diet will bring goodness into the lives of those so nourished. Hindus, like everyone else, find themselves engulfed in a mixture of goodness, passion, and ignorance, but those who aspire for higher realms, and who want to live a full life of godly devotion, tend to lean toward foods in the mode of goodness. But, further still, they desire to offer all that they eat to the lotus feet of the Lord. It is this consideration to which we will now turn.

PRASADAM: THE LORD'S MERCY

Hindus believe that one should offer all foods as a sacrifice to God. This is based on the verse from the *Bhagavad-Gita*: "All that you do, all that you eat, all that you offer and give away, as well as all austerities that you may perform, should be done as an offering unto Me." (9.27) One should not conclude from this, however, that all things are appropriate for offering.

The *Gita* (9.26) specifies exactly what should be offered: "If one offers Me with love and devotion a leaf, a flower, fruit or water, I will accept it." There are other references in Vaishnava texts confirming that fruits, vegetables, grains, nuts, and dairy products are fit for human consumption. Followers of the *Gita* thus refrain from offering meat, fish, poultry, or eggs, for such edibles are not sanctioned by the scriptures nor by the Vaishnava prophets. According to Vaishnava tradition, then, submission to God's word invariably leads to vegetarianism.

The *Bhagavad-Gita* (3.13) further declares that one who lovingly offers food to God, according to scriptural guidelines, is freed from all sinful reactions and consequent rebirth in the material world: "The devotees of the Lord are released from all kinds of sins because they eat food that is offered first in sacrifice. Others, who prepare food for personal sense enjoyment, eat only sin."

The remnants of such devotional offerings are called *prasadam* (literally, "mercy"), which are enjoyed as food that has "first been tasted by the Lord," thus bestowing a purifying effect on those who eat it. This is a phenomenon that exists throughout India, in both Vaishnava and many non-Vaishnava temples. But more, countless Hindu households produce *prasadam* as well, as families prepare delectable vegetarian dishes for the Lord and offer it to him according to the rules and regulations of scripture.

This has been going on for centuries. The largest shrines, such as Sri Rangam in South India and Jagannath Mandir, the main temple in Puri (Orissa), are particularly famous for the distribution of *prasadam*. They freely distribute sanctified vegetarian foods on a daily basis, benefiting the multitudes (literally millions) that attend their worship services.

The food has its effect. When vegetarian food is offered back to God, it takes on a special quality, purifying all who devour it and all who share it with others. Accomplished devotees can actually taste the difference. Lord Chaitanya himself—accepted by Vaishnavas as the most current incarnation of Krishna—glorified *prasadam* in this way: "Everyone has tasted these material substances before. However, in these [now offered] ingredients there are extraordinary tastes and uncommon fragrances. Just taste them and see the difference in the experience. Apart from the taste, even the fragrance pleases the mind and makes one forget any other sweetness besides its own. Therefore it is to be understood that the spiritual nectar of Krishna's lips has touched these ordinary ingredients and transferred to them all their spiritual qualities."[12]

One of the most celebrated Vedic sages, Narada Muni, was inspired to embark on the spiritual path by tasting such delicious vegetarian offerings. His example in this regard is not uncommon. Vedic and post-Vedic texts tell of innumerable Narada Munis, people who achieved spiritual perfection by tasting *prasadam*.

In conclusion, the main reason for Hindu vegetarianism is that, according to scripture, God himself is a vegetarian—and devotees do not eat anything without first offering it to him as a religious sacrifice, as stated earlier. The massive scriptural texts of the Hindu tradition include recipes of food preparations that Mother Yashoda actually fed the Lord, and he is quoted as saying exactly which foods he likes best—foods that partake of goodness, cow's milk, and so on. He never eats food that comes from violence, particularly if that food would cost an animal its life. In other words, Vaishnavas, especially, naturally prefer to offer God those foods that he himself, in the scriptures, says he would like to eat, and then they accept the remnants as his mercy (*prasadam*). This, say Vaishnava texts, is "the yoga of eating."

CHAPTER 11

Idols, Deities, Worship, and Temples

"Seeing is not as simple as it looks."
—Ad Reinhardt (American abstract painter, 1913–1967)

One of the most misunderstood aspects of modern Hinduism is the worship of deities (i.e., visible images of God, his incarnations, and divine associates, made of material elements such as stone, marble, metal, and so on). These "statue-like" forms of divinity allow easy access to the Lord, who, in general, is beyond the purview of the senses.

At first, the deities can be provocative, particularly for a Westerner: "Is it 'a graven image,' the kind that is condemned in the Bible?" Outsiders might see the deity as both disturbing and sublime: Disturbing because they know that God is not a material object. "A statue might *represent* him," a person might think, "but it could never *be* him." This is simple logic and clearly delineated in the religious scriptures of the West (and in the East as well), which tell us not to worship concocted images, or idols. And yet those who see the deity generally find the beauty of his form, the elegance of his dress, and the enthusiasm with which he is worshipped as fundamentally alluring; it is sublime in the most direct sense of the word.

There are, indeed, Hindus who see divine images as merely a means to an end, a visible symbol leading to the "real" divinity, who is unmanifest. Usually, those with an impersonalistic bent hold this point of view. The vast majority of Hindus, however, do not view their deities in this way, and

Vaishnavas, in particular, tend to see the visible form in the temple as an alternate manifestation of God, with no qualifying caveat.

Is deity worship different than idol worship? Just what does deity worship mean? In what sense can this visible form be God? Why would rational people worship a material object as if it were divine? These are some of the questions we will address in this chapter.

GOD'S IMMANENCE

Hindus view God as having both transcendental and immanent aspects. The Lord exists in his spiritual abode (transcendence) and is likewise present in the hearts of all individuals (immanence). Another aspect of God's immanence is when he descends into our world as so many incarnations (*avatars*), as mentioned in a previous chapter.

Still another form of his immanence comes to us in the form of the Deity (Sanskrit: *murti*). God becomes manifest not only as incarnations but also in "material" images. Thus, Vaishnavism, in particular, sees the deity as the "iconic incarnation" of the Lord. One might argue that an unlimited God cannot be confined to material elements. But this can be countered by a rather simple response: God can do whatever he likes, and to deny him the ability to manifest in material elements (even though such elements are temporary and limited) is to deny his omnipotence.

Still, the Western world has always frowned upon deity worship, viewing worshippers of "idols" as people who bow down to mere "sticks and stones." The problem with such a negative view, however, is that worshippers of "sticks and stones" clearly do not think of themselves as such. No one would readily identify himself as an idol worshipper. (There are exceptions, of course, but this is because the English came to India with a missionary agenda, teaching the local people that the word for "deity" is indeed "idol," deliberately ignoring the latter word's negative connotations.) Clearly, then, "idolatry" is an outsider's term for the symbols and visual images of a culture that is foreign to them. Aware of this fact, novelist Theodore Roszak identifies the only proper location of idolatry: in the eye of the beholder.[1]

The Vedic literature itself maintains a sharp distinction between idol and deity. As Harvard scholar Diana Eck has written in *Darshan: Seeing the Divine Image in India:*

Just as the term *icon* conveys the sense of a "likeness," so do the Sanskrit words *pratikriti* and *pratima* suggest the "likeness" of the image to the deity it represents.

The common word for such images, however, is *murti,* which is defined in Sanskrit as "anything which has definite shape and limits," "a form, body, figure," "an embodiment, incarnation, manifestation." Thus, the *murti* is more than a likeness; it is the deity itself taken "form.". . .The uses of the word *murti* in the *Upanishads* and the *Bhagavad-gita* suggest that the form is its essence. The flame is the *murti* of fire, [etc.] . . .[2]

The deity is thus considered more than a likeness—he is God himself. How is that possible? To answer this, Srila A. C. Bhaktivedanta Swami Prabhupada (1896–1977), the founder and spiritual master of the International Society for Krishna Consciousness (ISKCON), a contemporary Vaishnava movement, explains the deity by way of an analogy:

A crude example may be given here. We may find some mailboxes on the street, and if we post our letters in those boxes, they will naturally go to their destination without difficulty. But any old box, or an imitation that we may find somewhere but that is not authorized by the post office, will not do the work. Similarly, God has an authorized representation in the Deity form, which is called *archa-vigraha*. This *archa-vigraha* is an incarnation of the Supreme Lord. God will accept service through that form. The Lord is omnipotent, all-powerful; therefore, by His incarnation as *archa-vigraha* He can accept the service of the devotee, just to make it convenient for the man in conditioned life.[3]

Prabhupada elaborates further:

The Lord in His *archa-murti*, or form made of material elements, is not material, for those elements, although separated from the Lord, are also a part of the Lord's energy, as stated in the *Bhagavad-gita*. Because the elements are the Lord's own energy and because there is no difference between the energy and the energetic, the Lord can appear through any element. Just as the sun can act through the sunshine and thus distribute its heat and light, so Krishna, by His inconceivable power, can appear in His original spiritual form in any material element, including stone, wood, paint, gold, silver, and jewels . . .[4]

Prabhupada's list of material elements is adapted from the *Bhagavata Purana* (11.27.12): "The Deity form of the Lord is said to appear in eight varieties—stone, wood, metal, earth, paint, sand, the mind, or jewels." Scriptures such as the *Bhagavata* give elaborate details on how such elements are transformed into divine substance (i.e., how their original spiritual nature is brought out). These scriptures also explain the theology behind the deity, and minutiae connected to its worship.

HOW TO SEE THE DEITIES

The Sanskrit texts called *Shilpa-Shastras* give exact prescriptions for the fashioning of deities. There are specifications for the proper stance of the deities, their hand gestures, bodily proportions, etc., so that the "image" is not merely a function of the "imagination" of the artist. Trained in scriptural specifications for divine forms, the *shilpins* (as the artists who create the images are called) enter into moods of deep yogic meditation, thus fashioning images not in accordance with fancy but in accordance with scriptural canon. After this, an elaborate ceremony, known as Prana-pratishta, is enacted, and through this, the Divine Lord is called upon to animate the material elements that are sculpted in his form. When the deity is ready to be worshipped and is placed in the temple, worshippers can come and have *darshan* ("seeing")—they see the Deity and, it is believed, *the deity sees them.*[5]

Vaishnavas basically view the deity in two ways. Primarily, the image is seen as an embodiment of the divine. The figure is infused with the presence of God. This makes it not simply a statue but the "abode" of the Lord, no different from his essential nature.

Secondarily, the image is a focal point for concentration. As Eck says, "the image is a kind of *yantra,* literally a 'device' for harnessing the eye and the mind so that the one-pointedness of thought (*ekagrata*), which is fundamental to meditation, can be attained."[6]

Ultimately, the image incarnation of the Lord is a divine "descent" by which the Lord entrusts himself to human care. The deity is a divine guest and he must be treated as such. Therefore, he is offered incense, flowers, lights, hymns, and food—all of this is pleasing not only to the devotee's senses, but also to the Deity. Moreover, this interaction establishes a loving exchange between devotee and God.

"[Vaishnava] worship," Eck writes, "... is certainly not an occasion for yogic withdrawing of the senses ... but it is rather an occasion for awakening the senses and directing them toward the divine. Entering the temple, a worshipper clangs a big overhead bell. The energy of the senses is harnessed to the apprehension of God. Thus, it is not only vision that is refined by *darshan,* but the other senses as well are focused, ever more sharply, on God."[7]

As Eck says, "The image, which may be seen, bathed, adorned, touched, and honored does not stand *between* the worshipper and the Lord, somehow receiving the honor properly due to the Supreme Lord. Rather, because the image is a form of the Supreme Lord, it is precisely the image that facilitates and enhances the close relationship of the worshipper and God and makes possible the deepest outpouring of emotions in worship."[8]

It has been said that God's willingness to incarnate in deity form constitutes the ultimate expression of his love for humanity. This was beautifully expressed by Pillai Lokacharya, a great teacher in the Ramanujite tradition of Vaishnavism:

This is the greatest grace of the Lord, that being free He becomes bound, being independent He becomes dependent for all His service on the devotee. . . .In other forms, man belonged to God. But behold the supreme sacrifice of Ishvara [Krishna] in the form of the *murti,* for here the almighty becomes the property of the devotee . . . He carries the Lord about, fans Him, feeds Him, plays with Him—yea, the Infinite has become finite, that the child soul may grasp, understand, and love Him.[9]

HOW IS THE DEITY WORSHIPPED?

Though more famous deities are usually housed in well-known temples, which Hindus frequently visit, such divine images are also installed in private residences for regular worship, usually performed once or twice a day. If a given family decides that regular deity worship might be too taxing for their daily schedule, they could perform services more sporadically, or offer homage to a facsimile—such as paintings of deities or paraphernalia offered to famous icons, like a dress or a set of beads. In these cases, standards of worship can be abbreviated or compromised. Overall, the most important part of deity worship is glorification, that is, the family gathers in their "deity room" and sings praises to God.

In addition, the deity is offered various items in sacrifice, such as food (see previous chapter), candles, incense, flowers, and so on. After the deity "enjoys" these offerings, remnants are left for the worshipper and his family and friends.

Traditionally, such worship is called *"puja"* and takes the shape of a formalized ceremony known as *"arati."* A list of the more standard items offered in *arati* would appear as follows:

1. A large conch-shell (to blow)
2. A cup of fresh water and a spoon (for purification)
3. Incense sticks (at least three)
4. Ghee lamp (usually five wicks)
5. Small conch-shell (for offering water) with a stand

6. Container of water to be offered
7. Cloth or handkerchief
8. Small plate of flowers
9. Lighter or matches
10. Whisk (a yak-tail *chamara* and/or a peacock fan)
11. Bell

Most Hindu households will have set aside such items for *arati*, though not all will perform the ceremony on a daily basis. Families might use all the offering paraphernalia, or only engage in a humble variation of the ceremony. Usually, scriptural rulebooks are consulted for proper procedure, with the offerings initially directed toward a picture of one's teacher or priest, and then toward the Lord himself, either as a deity, a picture, or some other representative item.

Arati is a ceremony replete with symbolism. The word *arati*, for example, literally means "before night," and this is not only because the first of these ceremonies begins in predawn hours. The waving of the *arati* lamp as an offering to the deity implies an end to the "night" of the practitioner's material sojourn—he or she is now situated in the light of God's devotion. *Arati* is a safe place to be, where "night" cannot reach us. But night has a tendency to engulf us again and again, and so *arati* is a reminder to be vigilant, before our materialistic night again rises to the fore.

Among all the *arati* paraphernalia, the devotee, first and foremost, offers his or her own heart. In the traditional *arati* ceremony, the flower represents the earth (solidity); the water and the accompanying handkerchief correspond with the water element (liquidity); the lamp or candle represents the fire component (heat); the peacock fan reminds us of the precious quality of air (movement); as does the yak-tail fan, which additionally brings to mind the subtle form of ether (space). The incense represents the purified state of mind, and one's intelligence is offered in the discrimination required with regard to timing, the order of the offerings, and so on. Thus, one's entire existence and all facets of material creation are offered to the Lord in the *arati* ceremony.

In Hindu temples, offerings are made at regulated intervals each day, every day, lasting for a specific period of time. These are usually impeccable ceremonies, performed by specially trained priests. Consequently, pious Hindus will attend to benefit from proximity to such auspiciousness and, sometimes, to learn how it is done. Depending upon what time of day a visitor enters the temple, he or she will witness one of eight *arati* ceremonies. With variations according to individual temple and the particular

Hindu tradition with which the temple is aligned, the eight appear as follows:

1. *Mangal Arati* —The deities are awakened from their night of rest, usually at about 4:00 AM, and they are offered various items for their pleasure. The deities appear in their night dress, with simple ornamentation. The devotees sing beautiful prayers glorifying the Lord specifically appropriate for this time of day.

2. *Shringar Arati*—The Lord is fully and elaborately dressed for his day's activities, as is his consort (usually Radha or some form of the Goddess). They are offered a morning snack as well.

3. *Raja Bhoga Arati* ("King's Feast") —This ceremony follows the noon offering, which is usually a large meal for the deities. Related rituals last for about 20 minutes. The deities are then prepared to take a short nap, with loving hymns chanted to help the deities rest.

4. *Utthapana Arati*—They are awakened from their nap in order to continue their daily activities. In the case of a Krishna deity, he will be encouraged to go out and to herd cows with his cowherd friends.

5. *Sandhya Arati*—During a specific twilight hour, the deities "return home" — and they rest from an active day. Usually a new meal is offered and beautiful prayers are sung for the deities' pleasure.

6. *Vyalu Bhoga Arati*—At this time, the deities are served their large evening meal; participants and guests are encouraged to partake of the purifying remnants.

7. *Shayan Arati*—The last offering takes place between 9:00 AM and 10:30 PM, and the devotees can see the deities for the last time of the day before the altar doors close. It is a comparatively short ceremony. At this time the Deities are dressed for bed and they retire for the evening; but do they really sleep?

In the Krishna tradition, at least, the answer is "very little."

8. Rasa-lila—The Deities take a short rest, but they should not be disturbed, for at this time, it is believed, they sneak out to enjoy a spiritual love affair— Radha and Krishna go out to enjoy a moonlit dance, only to return in the early morning hours just before Mangal Arati.

This last phase of the *arati* ritual reveals what the entire procedure is really all about, uncovering, as it does, the inner meaning of *arati* as a whole. On an esoteric level—at least according Krishna worshippers— these ceremonies are meant to provoke thoughts of the Lord's eightfold daily pastimes in the spiritual world. In other words, repeated attendance facilitates remembrance of God's kingdom. In fact, each of the eight *aratis* is constructed in such a way as to replicate Krishna's sweet pastimes in his otherworldly realm, which is beyond ordinary vision. There, say practitioners, Krishna's day is enjoyed in eight-part divisions of ecstasy, with carefree loving affairs and loved ones who tend to his every need.

TEMPLES: VENUE FOR DEITY WORSHIP

Hinduism is known for its many temples, where deities are honored and worshipped on a daily basis, using *arati* techniques as described above. Though hundreds of thousands of such shrines dot the Indian subcontinent, Diaspora Hindus have established newer and bigger temples throughout the world as well.

A Hindu temple is known as a Mandir. Although such shrines are usually dedicated to a central deity, other divinities may be worshipped there as well (with the understanding that God manifests in various forms). Most practicing Hindus maintain a Mandir, of sorts, at home, a special room set aside for daily religious practices. But a trip to a well-established public temple is always considered special. Thus, a section on deities and their worship would be incomplete without a brief introduction to the more famous temples associated with Hinduism's various traditions.

This, of course, tells us something about the important principle of pilgrimage, which is central to Hindu practice. Believers say that the purifying effect of even once visiting a sacred temple, a holy river, or some other place associated with the Lord or his devotees, is incalculable. Here, picked at random, are but a few temples that serve such purifying purposes:

(1) *Tirupati* is a temple town in the Chittoor district of Andhra Pradesh, India, deep in the foothills of Tirumala. "Venkateshwara," as Tirupati's presiding deity of Vishnu is known, means "Lord of the Venkata Hills." The title has an esoteric meaning as well: *Ven-kata* means "one who cuts or washes away a person's sins." And this is just what this deity does for all who approach his shrine.

Venkateshwara is a title, not a name. The deity here actually goes by the endearing name, Balaji or Bithala, and he is known throughout the entire Hindu world.

He has a dark complexion and four hands, as do most deities of Vishnu. In his two upper hands he holds a discus and a conch. With his lower hands, extended downward, he symbolically asks devotees to have faith in him, to surrender their life to the spiritual path. On either side stand Sridevi and Bhudevi, his spiritual and material energy, respectively.

Balaji is nearly 7 feet tall, feet firmly planted on a glistening lotus that is bedecked with rubies, diamonds, and gold, gifts from wealthy patrons through the centuries. The deity is often seen with a diamond crown, believed by some to be the most precious ornament in the world, bar none.

There are numerous written documents of luminaries, in particular, who have paid homage to Lord Venkateshwara throughout the centuries. Leaders from the Pallava Empire (ninth century CE), the Cholas of Thanjavur (a century later), the Pandyas of Madurai, and the kings of Vijayanagar (fourteenth century CE) were patrons who made known their devotion with temple endowments and offerings of wealth. Today, this is easily the wealthiest temple of all.

Tirupati, it is said, is the most visited temple in the world as well. It is estimated that more that 50,000 people visit every day—accounting for almost 19 million people every year, which doubles the estimated number visiting Vatican City.

To get there, one has to go through seven mountains, in an upward direction; an arduous task, to be sure. Regular buses go up to the top, and there is a paved path for particularly brave pilgrims who want to walk—either way, it is a long, austere journey to reach the temple. Once there, one can expect to wait in long lines—at any given time of the day—before actually seeing the deity.

But the wait, and the work, is well worth it.

An addendum: One distinct feature of a visit to Tirupati is the sea of shaved heads for miles around. No, it is not a Hare Krishna festival gone wild; it is a custom in which pilgrims offer their hair in sacrifice, as a symbol of their devotion. In fact, the volume of human hair at Tirupati is so considerable that it is actually sorted out and exported, to support the temple, making India the largest exporter of hair in the world.

(2) *Sri Rangam* is a small island town just off Tiruchirapalli in South India. Its border is created by the Kaveri River on one side, and by one of her many tributaries on the other. While Sri Rangam is an important pilgrimage site for Vaishnavas in general, it is particularly significant for those in the Ramanujite line of Vaishnavism, whose great teachers and poets wrote about the sanctity of the area in depth.

The entire town is focused on the deity of Ranganatha Swami, a reclining Vishnu form, lying on the soft, snake-like bed of Ananta, Balarama, as a hooded serpent. The deity is housed in one of India's most sacred and historic temples—significant not only for Vaishnavas but for all Hindus worldwide. This main temple at Sri Rangam is a major pilgrimage site and has been so for centuries.

Indeed, this is one of the largest temple complexes in all of India, covering almost 200 acres of land. The dome over the deity's primary altar is covered in gold and shoots up almost 236 feet into the sky. The entire temple environment is lavish, with an ancient-looking spiritual motif that inspires meditation and contemplation. It rivals any religious monument in the world.

Sri Rangam was the headquarters of the eleventh-century Vaishnava theologian Ramanuja, until he passed away at the age of 120. His tomb, prominently located on the temple grounds, is a major tourist attraction, reverentially approached by practitioners and sympathizers, who go there to offer worldly goods and to pray for benedictions. In 1326, the temple was attacked by a Muslim army led by Malik Kafur, who, it is said, killed more than 1,000 Vaishnavas. Knowing that the invaders were coming, and that they would try to destroy the deity, as they had in so many other Hindu temples, Ranganatha Swami was hidden behind a wall and a substitute deity was put in his place. When the Muslims entered the holy chamber, they indeed smashed the "Ranganatha Swami" standing before them and left. The original deity was returned to its rightful place in 1371.

(3) Closely related to Sri Rangam Temple in the south is the *Radha-Ramana Temple* in the north. Gopal Bhatta Goswami, one of the famous Six Goswamis of Vrindavan, established this temple for the Gaudiya Vaishnavas, though his ancestors hailed from the south and, in fact, were the head custodians of Sri Rangam in the sixteenth century. The tomb of Gopala Bhatta is found at this temple as well.

Sri Radha-Ramana, the deity around whom this shrine is built, is a Krishna deity, small in size, perhaps 12 inches in height. And while most such deities have a loving Radha icon at their side, this one does not.

There is, however, a golden plate next to Radha-Ramana, which has the name of Sri Radha engraved on it. Thus, the name of Radha compensates for her unmanifest presence. This is so because according to Vaishnava theology, the name and the person, when divine, are considered nondifferent.

Radha-Ramana is one of the few original deities of the Goswamis still in Vrindavan, for, as in Sri Rangam, Muslim armies invaded the sacred Vraja area, pillaging and destroying Hindu temples, forcing devotees to relocate their deities or to otherwise hide them. Most of these deities and valuables were moved to nearby Jaipur.

Though Gopal Bhatta started with a humble temple area, the present structure, somewhat more elaborate, was built in 1826 by Shah Behari Lallji, the grandfather of Shah Kundan Lall and Shah Fundan Lall, who built the famous Shahji Temple. Today, Sri Radha-Ramanji is among the most famous temples in Vrindavan.

(4) There are several other temples that could compete with Radha-Ramana in terms of both holiness and popularity, and the *Govindadev Temple* is certainly one of them. The red sandstone edifice, constructed in 1590 by military man and religious patron Man Simha, stands largely in ruins today, an empty husk compared to what it once was before the Muslim invasions. Yet Govindadev stands tall. He is a beautiful image of Lord Krishna, playing his flute—even if the original, established by the great Vaishnava sage, Rupa

Goswami, was brought to Jaipur, only to be replaced by the deity one sees here today.

Most impressive is the temple's massive, echoing exterior, along with the high, vaulted spaces of its somewhat ramshackle if also regal interior. One can only imagine what it looked like before being desecrated by unwanted soldiers.

In addition to the main temple, there are two additional shrines—one for Vrindadevi ("the Goddess of Vrindavan") and the other for Yogamaya, the Lord's sister.

In fact, this is the actual site where Rupa Goswami initially located a deity, a Yogamaya, and, later, the deity of Govindadev himself. Rupa lived here in simple quarters with the Lord of his life, as Gopal Bhatta did, just down the narrow street, with Radha-Ramana. He soon found a temple growing up around him, as wealthy merchants wanted to support his love of God and the deity worship that he established. After a while, a Radha deity was sent from Bengal, and a high standard of Radha-Govinda worship was developing for others to follow. Today, the Govindadev temple stands at the center of Vrindavan's spiritual culture.

(5) The *Meenakshi Temple* in Madurai is a huge temple complex dedicated to Lord Shiva, known here as Sundareshwara ("the handsome god"). His consort Parvati, or Meenakshi ("the fish-eyed goddess"), after whom the temple is named, is worshipped here as well. The original temple is said to have been built by a wealthy landowner named Kulashekara Pandya, perhaps in the seventh to tenth century CE, but was later developed into the beautiful temple we see today by a military clan known as the Nayaks, who ruled Madurai from the sixteenth to the eighteenth centuries.

The temple complex is contained within a high-walled enclosure, at the core of which one finds two sanctums for Meenakshi and Sundareshwara. These are surrounded by a number of smaller shrines and halls with majestic pillars.

The Meenakshi temple is larger than life; its visual imagery, architecture, and deities are overwhelming. In sheer size and grandeur it competes with most other temples. And, for Shiva and Goddess worshippers, its location is especially significant: Legend has it that Madurai is where Shiva and Meenakshi actually got married. As one might suspect, this is not a fact taken lightly by their devotees.

(6) The *Dakshineshwar Temple* is located in the Hooghly District of Calcutta. This is a Kali temple, made famous through its association with Sri Ramakrishna (1836–1886), the teacher of Swami Vivekananda (1863–1902), one of Hinduism's most renowned representatives.

The actual temple was constructed in the 1850s and is representative of Bengali temple architecture of the time, with its huddle of thin towers and a central dome soaring above the rest; it has a double-layered roof, with elegant steeples on each side. Nearby, across the Hooghly, is Belur Math, the headquarters of the Ramakrishna Mission, whose followers frequent this temple.

It is said that the Goddess herself came before one of her devotees, a queen named Rani Rashmani, and said to her, "Install my icon in a beautiful temple on the banks of the Ganges and arrange for my worship there. There is no need to go to Benares (where the worship of Shiva and the Goddess is popular). If you do so, I will manifest myself in the image and accept worship at that place."

Deeply affected by the dream, the queen immediately found and purchased land, and, soon after, began construction of the temple. The large temple complex has as its central shrine an image of the goddess Kali, but also has side altars for Shiva and Radha-Krishna. Devotees at this temple generally believe that all the gods are one, but they tend to favor Kali as the preeminent manifestation of the Supreme.

(7) The *Kalighat Temple* is located in the city of Calcutta on the banks of the river Hooghly (Bhagirathi), directly adjacent to the Dakshineshwar Temple. The present place of worship was built in 1809 on the site of an ancient structure dedicated to Lord Shiva, and it remains a Shiva-Kali temple to this day. It is, in fact, based on the name of this temple that the English devised the name "Calcutta," which is an anglicized form of Kalikata.

The temple is dedicated to the destructive side of Shiva, which, at least here, takes the form of Kali, his consort, also known as Sati, Durga, Parvati, and so on. The image of the Goddess in the dark inner sanctum is frightening to behold, with wild, tangled hair and ferocious eyes. Her most prominent feature is a distended tongue of bloody horror—there is a gold covering atop the tongue that is changed by devotees on a daily basis.

True to her terrifying form, this Goddess requires frequent animal sacrifice, and so, daily, temple priests attempt to satisfy her with the blood of goats. The altar's remains do not go to waste—the temple is busy throughout the year, particularly attended by the poor, who arrive in time for free food. Mother Teresa's Hospital for the Dying and Destitute is nearby and works in conjunction with the temple to help lepers and other unfortunate citizens in the vicinity.

(8) Jagannath Puri is home to one of Hinduism's most famous temples, *Jagannath Mandir*. The presiding deity is a wooden form of Krishna—although, as Jagannath ("Lord of the Universe"), he might be difficult to recognize, with large round eyes, truncated hands and strange shape. Enshrined alongside him are images of Balabhadra (Balarama) and Subhadra, his brother and sister, respectively. They, too, will look unfamiliar.

Why? According to tradition, the deities were fashioned by Vishvakarma, the architect of the demigods, and he wanted to meditate in perfect tranquility while he worked on them, without any disturbance.

When he was only halfway finished, however, King Indradyumna, who had commissioned him to make the deities in the first place, barged in, causing him to leave, with the deities unfinished. These incomplete forms are the deities we see in Puri today. But because love and devotion was in Vishvakarma's heart as he worked on the form of the Lord, Krishna agreed to appear in these images, even though they hardly look like him.

Other deities on the altar are Sudarshan, Madhaba, Sridevi, and Bhudevi—all forms of the Lord or manifestations of his spiritual energies.

Puri is located on the eastern coast of India, along the blue waters of the Bay of Bengal. The temple of Lord Jagannath, its major claim to fame, is still living and vibrant. Over the centuries its patrons have included kings, conquerors, gurus, devotees, and pilgrims.

Elaborate worship services are performed by 6,000 resident priests throughout each day of the year, with *prasadam* distributed to thousands of guests. There are over 400 temple cooks, so there are always food offerings for the seemingly endless crowds of people who go there.

The temple also sponsors more than twenty-four major festivals each year, the most important one being Ratha Yatra, or the Chariot festival, which occurs every summer. A spectacular event drawing hundreds of thousands from around the country, the festival centers on the procession of three colossal chariots, upon which ride the regal images of Jagannath, Balarama, and Subhadra. As they journey down the road, they are facilitated by pilgrims who take turns pulling the massive ropes attached to their chariots. In this way, their mercy is showered on all who attend.

(9) Interestingly, one of the most famous temples associated with Hinduism is not in India but in Cambodia: *Angkor Wat*. This is a huge temple complex originally built for king Suryavarman II in the early twelfth century. The largest and best preserved of similar temples in the area, it has remained, to this day, of religious significance. While it is now more revered by Buddhists than Hindus, its Khmer architecture and provocative history makes it an important ancient edifice upon which Hindu worship stands.

It is designed as a symbol of Mount Meru, home of the gods in the Vedic literature. In its grandeur and monumental appearance it evokes thoughts of bygone days of massive temple structures and Vedic kings who patronized religious architecture. The temple is particularly noted for its extensive bas-reliefs depicting Hinduism's many gods.

The inner walls shine forth with large-scale scenes from both the *Ramayana* and the *Mahabharata*. The northwest and southwest corner pavilions both feature much smaller-scale scenes, some of which remain unidentified but most are from the life of Krishna. In all, the temple structure is an extraordinary work of art—one of the great architectural masterpieces of all time.

A section on temples would not be complete without mentioning that Hindus view the body as a temple for the soul. This is more than poetic rhetoric. They see the Lord in the heart as a prominent manifestation of the Supreme, and the finite soul, who exists, as they say, "in the heart of hearts," as his servant. This indicates that we, the living entities, exist in the heart of the Supreme Lord, whose love for us is indescribable. Hindus are thus obliged to treat the body as a temple, in which both the Lord and the individual living being reside. This means eating food that partakes of goodness, the details of which have already been described, and to generally use the body in God's service, which is what all temples are ultimately for.

CHAPTER 12
Festivals and Holidays

"Hindus laugh and sing to the tune of the spirit. Their religion teaches joy and celebration. Every day is a festival or a holiday in which the Lord, in his multifarious forms, dances with his devotees. If any religion deserves the title, it is Hinduism: 'The festival religion.'"
—Bal Gopal Anand, Indian author and historian[1]

Hindus, it is said, have more festivals and holidays than there are days in the year. Because of their diversity of tradition and variation in celebration, it is impossible to actually assess the number of festivals and holidays observed by the average Hindu today. But scholars have isolated at least 1,000 that occur every year, acknowledging, of course, that there are many more.[2]

If the sizeable number of these festivals seems outrageous, the actual festivities are more so. Both melodious and cacophonous music, singing, dancing, elephants (where available), parades, dramatic performances, thousands of lit candles, and the throwing of colorful dyes on people in all directions—these are just some of the sensorial images one might expect at a Hindu festival. Suffice it to say, Hinduism redefines the phrase, "religious festival," with an enhanced sense of celebration, joy, and merrymaking that distinguishes it among world religions. Indeed, Hinduism is sometimes known as "the festival religion."

At their core, many Hindu festivals are not so different than those of other ancient religions—they are based on the cycle of nature or commemorate historical occurrences associated with God and his devotees. Often, they mark the transformation of seasons, rejoice in the harvest, and acknowledge the fertility of the soil. Others are dedicated to a particular deity, such as Krishna or Shiva. In addition to Hinduism's major festivals, celebrated throughout India, there are numerous regional festivals that are more or less confined to local areas.

Overall, Hindu festivals are intended to "purify, avert malicious influences, renew society, bridge over critical moments, and stimulate or resuscitate the vital powers of nature."[3] They include a wide variety of rituals, including worship, prayer, processions, magical acts, feasting, feeding the poor, and the other activities outlined above.

A list of some well-known Hindu festivals might run as follows:

- *Holi*— The festival of colors and the arrival of Spring (February–March)
- *Shiva Ratri*—A special celebration in honor of Lord Shiva (February–March)
- *Rama Navami*—The "Appearance Day" celebration of Lord Rama (April)
- *Krishna Jayanti*—Also known as Janmashthami, the "Appearance Day" celebration of Lord Krishna (July–August)[4]
- *Raksabandhana*—The renewing of bonds between brothers and sisters (July–August)
- *Kumbh Mela*—A major convergence of Hindu traditions occurring at rare intervals (July–August, the last one was in 2003). This is considered the world's largest religious festival.
- *Dassera*—The victory of Rama over the demonic king Ravana (September–October)
- *Navaratri*—The festival of the Goddess, a Shakta celebration (in Bengal), or, sometimes, part of the celebration of Rama's victory over Ravana (South India, September–October)
- *Diwali*—The festival of lights, New Year's Day (September–October)

Some Hindu holidays reflect more modern concerns, with several that even have nonreligious significance. For example, there are four well-known national holidays in India, which are honored by all Hindus, regardless of sectarian affiliation. Government institutions, too, acknowledge them in all Indian states:

- Republic Day, January 26
- Labor Day, May 1
- Independence Day, August 15
- Gandhi Jayanti, October 2 (This is the birth anniversary of Mahatma Gandhi, the political "Father of the Nation." Special prayers and celebrations are offered at Gandhi's tomb at Rajghat, Delhi, and parties are held throughout the country)[5]

But the vast majority of Hinduism's holidays are religious. Like in the West, most holidays are observed annually, but some occur only at rare intervals. And some, in fact, only take place in special locations. The huge Kumbha Mela, for example, when millions of Hindus gather at the confluence of the Ganges and Yamuna Rivers, takes place once every 12 years, though there are smaller Melas that occur more frequently. And these are in prescribed regions.

That is to say, the festival actually occurs four times every 12 years at special locations in the subcontinent. At the culmination of each 12-year cycle there is a "Great" Kumbha Mela at Prayag, attended by millions of people, making it the largest festival gathering in the world.

To be clear, festivals such as these are not merely festivals; they are also considered holidays. The huge Melas, at least, are holidays that are best celebrated in certain areas, and so numerous families take the day (or week) off of work and school to attend at the specific, sacred locations. Sometimes these holidays are re-created in other parts of the country (or in other parts of the world) but they are most effectively observed at their traditional settings.

IT'S ALL IN THE TIMING

According to Hindu teachings, there are particular days, or even moments, that lend themselves to efficacious results, which are designed for special purposes. Judging by alignments of stars and other technical considerations, there are moments that best serve the intention of auspicious acts— periods of time specifically meant for holy acts, including those acts that might be deemed holidays or festive occasions.

Hinduism bases its reckoning of time on a lunar calendar. Dates of holidays and festivals thus change from year to year. The Indian lunar year consists of 12 months, with an intercalary month inserted once every 3 years or so, which helps the Hindu calendar approximate solar dating standards.

A lunar month lasts from one new moon to the next, and is named according to the Indian month in which it begins. Therefore, the lunar month known as Bhadra, for example, will begin with the first new moon after August 16th, for instance, and continue from there. Though the exact procedure of calculating such dates is somewhat complex, especially when compared with the Western system, Hindus engage experienced astrologers and astronomers whose special task it is to assess the auspicious time periods associated with a given festival, and their calendars are prepared for them as much as a year in advance.

All Hindu calendars originate from the Jyotish Vedanga (one of the six Vedic adjuncts, said to have been composed just prior to the Common Era), though time sequence techniques and additional methods of calculation were added later, usually at the behest of astronomers and those accomplished in related sciences. In 1957, The Indian Calendar Reform Committee finalized the Indian National Calendar, along with a specific religious calendar—the Rashtriya Panchang, used by most Hindus worldwide. This calendar was created not only to determine standardized days for spiritual functions and religious festivals, but also to determine the holidays of government workers—and to standardize when shops should close and school children should have days off.

Interestingly, the Hindu calendar now incorporates solar reckoning, even if its calculation originates with texts and procedures originally given to lunar considerations. In other words, months are calculated according to the sun's position against fixed stars, or constellations, during sunrise. The sun's position is understood by diametrically opposed observations of the full moon. This can abrogate the need for leap year adjustments, but the number of days in any given month can vary by nearly 48 hours, and conversion of dates to Gregorian or day-of-the-week computations requires the use of an ephemeris. The average person therefore relies on the *panchangs*, or almanacs, produced by authoritative Hindu astronomers.[6]

The word *panchang* is derived from the Sanskrit *panchangam* (*pancha* = five, *anga* = limb), which refers to the five limbs of the modern calendar: (1) The lunar day; (2) the solar day; (3) the cluster of stars through which the sun rises; (4) the angle of the sun and moon; and (5) the half lunar day. Over time, various priests and scientists leaned toward diverse geographical centers, thus affecting numerous aspects of their astronomical calculation. This naturally resulted in a divergence of a few days, which is reflected in regional calendars. Even within the same region, there may be more than one competing authority, occasionally resulting in disagreement on festival dates by as much as a month.[7]

Given this confusing state of affairs, most people merely consult their local priests for the dates and times of religious holidays, thus avoiding the differences created by regional factors and other considerations. Still, if two Hindus, from various parts of the subcontinent, were to e-mail each other or to talk on the phone, it would not be uncommon for them to find that they celebrate the same holiday at different times—that one is in the midst a joyous festival while the other has to wait a day or two to observe the same celebration. Sometimes, a person might travel to different places just to enjoy the holiday a second time!

SOME SAMPLE FESTIVALS

Diwali, also called *Deepavali,* which means "row of lights," has become one of Hinduism's paradigmatic festivals. A celebration that symbolizes the victory of good over evil, lamps or candles are lit as a sign of goodness and hope. Generally, the festival is enacted for five consecutive days during late Fall, perhaps in October or November.

In some regions, fireworks play a big part in the festival. Whether fireworks or candles, however, the theme is the same—the burning flames are meant to remind practitioners of the famous Hindu prayer, in which they ask to be led from darkness to truth and light, to vanquish the ignorance that keeps people separated from God and the darkness that obscures the light of knowledge.

Diwali's 5 days, though celebrated variously according to religious tradition and locale, might be summarized as follows:

1. *Dhan-trayodashi* or *Dhan teras,* which refers to the importance of wealth. On this day, one is urged to be thankful for what one has, and not to hanker for greater material wealth or accomplishment. *Trayodashi* means "13th day." Thus, as the name implies, this day falls on the 13th day of the first half of the lunar month (in October). It is an auspicious day for shopping and for buying gifts for people.
2. *Naraka chaturdasi—Narak* indicates a new era of Light and Knowledge; *Chaturdasi* tells us that it occurs on the 14th day of the lunar month.
3. *Diwali*—This is the actual day of the festival, celebrated 2 days into the festivities.
4. *Varsha-pratipada* or *Padwa*—The beginning of the Hindu New Year—this is an important part of the Diwali celebration.
5. *Bhayiduj*—On this day, brothers and sisters meet to express their love and affection for each other.

While these are the traditionally accepted divisions surrounding the 5 days of Diwali, the holiday is actually saturated with religious meaning. Entrances to homes are colorfully decorated with traditional motifs of Rangoli design—an art form specifically used on Diwali. This is meant to welcome Lakshmi, the Goddess of wealth, Vishnu's consort, into devotees' homes, and to welcome prosperity along with her. In anticipation of Lakshmi's long-awaited arrival, small footprints are drawn with rice flour and vermilion all over individual dwellings, engaging children and other family members in the fun. Lamps—Diwali's signature—are kept burning all through the night, waiting for the Goddess's arrival. In Bengal, Kali/Durga, Lord Shiva's consort, is worshipped in place of Lakshmi.

In most of northern India, Diwali is also dedicated to the worship of Lord Rama. On this day, consciousness is focused on the day that Rama and Sita returned from their banished years in the forest and also from their battle with Ravana. When they arrived in their resplendent city of Ayodhya, the joy among the citizens was palpable—as if everyone had personally shared in Rama's pastimes of pain. Just as lights were lit to celebrate the triumphant return of Rama and Sita to Ayodhya, creating a beautiful atmosphere of divine victory over evil, so, too, do contemporary Hindus light their lamps with similar success in mind.

Northern Diwali celebrations also include Govardhan-Puja, commemorating the day that Lord Krishna raised a huge mountain like an umbrella, just to protect the inhabitants of Vrindavan from a devastating rainfall. This occurs on Diwali's 4th day, when celebrations also include Annakoot, meaning "mountain of food." In temples, especially in Mathura and Nathadwara, the deities are given a milk bath and dressed in especially elegant clothes, with ornaments reserved for this special time. After prayers and traditional forms of worship, the mountain of food is offered and the devotees take the remnants.

If Diwali is known as the archetypal Hindu holiday, *Holi* has also become famous in a similar way.

The day witnesses a colorful extravaganza signaling the arrival of Spring—the season of hope and new beginnings. Celebrated by men, women, and children alike, the most distinguishing feature of Holi involves the throwing of colored powder at all who wish to participate and, often, at those who don't.

Throughout India, bonfires both large and small are ignited on the day of Holi, as devotees reminisce about the famous boy-saint named Prahlad, one of Vishnu's greatest devotees. As the story goes, his demonic father, Hiranyakashipu, could not tolerate his son's pious ways, and was ready to kill him if he would not abandon his dedication to the Lord. It was Hiranyakashipu's prodding, in fact, that prompted the young saint's aunt Holika to throw the boy into a blazing fire.

Despite such torment, little Prahlad did not give up worshipping Vishnu. Rather, every act of treachery made him even more persistent in his devotions. But back to Holi: Holika had acquired the mystic perfection of not being affected by fire. So she grabbed Prahlad and entered the blaze hoping to kill him on Hiranyakashipu's behalf. Instead, by divine intervention, the wicked aunt perished and the virtuous Prahlad emerged without a mark on his body.

The Holi bonfire also represents devotion and knowledge, which burn away the mind's impurities, including egoism, vanity, and lust. The bonfire is also said to ignite spiritual love, mercy, generosity, selflessness, truth-fulness, and purity in the hearts of devotees.

On a more esoteric level, the festival is associated with the immortal love of Radha and Krishna. The young Krishna, it is said, would sometimes complain to Mother Yashoda about Radha's fair complexion—"Why is she so light, while I am so dark?" Feeling for her divine son's dilemma, Yashoda advised him to apply various colors on Radha's face, just to see how her complexion would change. When he enacted his mother's suggestion, Radha retaliated, throwing colored dyes back in Krishna's direction. This initiated a playful battle of throwing various dyes at each other. Thus, the throwing of colors on Holi is meant to remind practitioners of Radha and Krishna's love.

In another, related story, Krishna, the expert fighter, mischievously attacked the *gopis*, the cowherd maidens of Vrindavan, by throwing his most dangerous bomb at them: a volley of *ashoka* flowers. This caused a joyful fight between Krishna and his cowherd boyfriends, on one side, and the larger group of female *gopis*, on the other. Before long, all concerned were throwing fragrant red powder balls at each other, and squirting each other with deliciously scented colored water, too. As a result, a bombardment of colors covered all directions, and the Lord and his devotees reveled in pastimes of love.

These are the thoughts that properly engulf the mind on Holi. As the full moon rises, bonfires are lit, and joyous singing and dancing permeate the subcontinent, even as colors are sprayed and thrown in all directions. The reds, blues, yellows, and oranges of *kumkum* powder and liquid sprays transform devotees into modern art pieces on this most special day.

As an addendum, perhaps, Holi often occurs at exactly the same time as Gaura Purnima, the birth celebration of Sri Chaitanya Mahaprabhu (1486–1533), who is Krishna himself in the form of a perfect devotee. Although underplayed throughout much of India, Gaura Purnima is, in some ways, even more important than Holi. This is so because Sri Chaitanya is considered a preeminent form of Radha and Krishna combined in one form. Additionally, he appeared in Bengal, India, to inaugurate a form of *yoga* that centers on chanting the holy name of the Lord. This is considered the special means of self-realization in the current age of quarrel and illusion. But this will all be discussed more fully in the next chapter.

For now, it is significant that Holi and Gaura Purnima come together in a figurative sense as well: Devotees are called upon to "color" themselves with the Lord's name. Thus far, say Vaishnava texts, modern man has been colored by the worldly qualities of lust, anger, selfishness, greed, and so on. Our task is to remove these stains—to be bleached and cleansed by good deeds and by an intense desire for internal transformation. We need to dye our hearts.

The process of dying, say Vaishnava philosophers, is complete when we allow our hearts to be filled with God's name, satisfying the depths of our immortal longing for Krishna's love, forgetting all else, just like the color-soaked *gopis* of Vrindavan.

Rama Navami, which literally means "Rama's 9th Day," celebrates his "birth" in the material world. This birth took place on the 9th day of the Hindu month of Chaitra (March–April), which is how this holiday took on its name. In some parts of India, it is celebrated as a 9-day festival known as Vasanta Navaratri.

On this day, as on most days celebrating the birth of the Lord, devotees fast, after which they rejoice with a sumptuous feast. At most temples, images of Sita and Rama, and sometimes of Hanuman, too, are bathed and adorned with fresh clothes. Devotional songs are chanted in praise of Rama's heroic exploits, and readings and dramatic performances take devotees through the festival, as well as remind them of details of their Lord's manifest pastimes.

Most such festivals are somewhat formulaic, though specifics will vary according to the nature of the divinity being celebrated on any given holiday. For Rama, in particular, a huge party is held in Ayodhya on his appearance day, where thousands of devotees gather to sing his praises. Pondicherry, too, is a center for Rama devotees, with numerous Rama temples that gear up for the special day. Processions accompanied by huge floats of Rama, his wife Sita, his brother Lakshman, and his monkey-devotee, Hanuman, can be found in most Indian cities and villages, and devotions are renewed especially on his appearance day.

Perhaps the most popular Vaishnava festival of all is called *Ratha-yatra* ("*the Festival of the Chariots*"), briefly mentioned in the previous chapter when discussing its central deity, Lord Jagannath, a form of Krishna.

This is a summer, outdoor festival—a time when many pilgrims journey to Jagannath Puri, in Orissa, Jagannath's original hometown. And the festival, by far, is most impressive, to this day, in Puri, where hundreds of thousands, if not millions, attend the fabulous parade. Here we see three huge carts pulling their Lordships Jagannath, Balarama, and their sister Subhadra down a well-worn path filled with excited and enthusiastic devotees. If the trip to Puri proves impractical, however, the festival might easily come to you: Largely due to the efforts of the International Society for Krishna Consciousness (ISKCON), Ratha-yatra is now recreated in every major city of the world.

Although Jagannath, in his original temple, rarely comes out, and although the temple has a strict policy that disallows "non-Hindus" from entering, Ratha-yatra is a time when all bets are off and mercy is shown to all—the deities come out of the temple for the parade, and everyone is able to see them.

The actual construction of the carts begins 2 months before the festival day, on the 3rd day of the bright fortnight of Vaishakha (April–May). More than 600 trees, taken from local forests along the banks of the Mahanadi River, are used for the construction of the massive chariots. Applying the simple tools and procedures originated by their ancestors, devotee craftsmen and architects create the basic parts of the chariots, such as the wheels, for the Lord's festival. In actuality, Ratha-yatra is so all-encompassing that most of the townspeople will find themselves engaged in the event's numerous preparations, working together for the Lord's pleasure.

The actual festival starts a week or more before Ratha-yatra proper. Jagannath, Balarama, and Subhadra, are brought to another dwelling under the pretense of their having caught a cold, which, of course, allows devotees to tend to them and to bring them various healing food preparations, soothing them with song and dance as well.

As the Ratha-yatra festival draws near, everyone awaits the momentous event of the deities being brought out and placed on the carts. Massive in size, the divine forms are carried by several strong priests, specially trained to lift and move them.

Once the deities are on the carts, the King of Orissa comes and sweeps the road, a tradition that goes back many centuries. And then it begins. The English word "juggernaut" comes from the unstoppable force that is Lord Jagannath. Poetry in motion, the huge, ancient-looking vehicles slowly move down the road, being pulled by colossal ropes, held by seemingly numberless awestruck devotees. Countless faces move alongside the carts, with hands hoping to find a vacant spot—a moment in time where they might grab onto the ropes, to bask in Jagannath's glory, to be noticed by the Lord of their lives.

They want to pull the ropes, too, to serve, to assist in one of God's few visible adventures. This is, after all, the main message of Vaishnavism—that our real duty, our inherent nature, is that of a servant. As a part is meant to serve the whole, like a small cog in a large machine, humans are meant to serve the greater entity known as Jagannath. Being his part and parcel, our rightful place is at his side, assisting him in pastimes of love. Pulling the Ratha-yatra rope, then, means getting the Lord's attention, and letting him know that we acknowledge our identity as his servants.

But, for Vaishnavas, this rope symbolizes more than a desire to be noticed by the Lord; it represents something deeper than our constitutional position as an eternal servant of the Supreme—it is a rope by which the Lord is pulled into our heart, and, more, which can assist him in his Vrindavan pastimes.

It may be remembered that Krishna spent his latter years in Dvaraka, always pining for the sweet, simple days he had previously experienced in Vrindavan. The Ratha-yatra festival, according to Vaishnava texts, offers devotees an opportunity to pull Krishna back to the sweet rural atmosphere of Vrindavan, his preferred place of residence, in the company of his loving cowherd girls.

Seen in this way, Ratha-yatra becomes an esoteric festival indeed, by which one reaches the height of Hindu mysticism. Thus, by participating in this festival, chanting, and dancing, or helping to pull the ropes of the chariots, one becomes free of many lifetimes of *karma* and eventually attains the spiritual world.

CHAPTER 13
Sonic Theology

"The benefit that one attained in the Satya Age by meditation, in the Treta Age by sacrifice, and in the Dvapara Age by temple worship, can be had in the Kali Age merely by reciting the names of Krishna."
—*Bhagavata Purana* 12.3.52

Among the many existing forms of Hindu practice, calling upon the name of God is central, particularly in the current epoch of world history. This chapter will outline the basic philosophy, culture, and implications of such chanting.

To begin, the entire early tradition was steeped in mantras and verbal intonations of sacred sound. Brahmin priests performed sacrifices with the help of mantras, the proper pronunciation of which was crucial for maximum effect.[1]

Portions of the Vedic literature read almost like textbooks on chanting, informing devotees about an ancient art in which sound was used as a spiritual tool. The same concept reverberated in lands as diverse as Egypt and Ireland, which tell of a time when mystical vibrations were harnessed by spiritual adepts for the benefit of mankind.[2] Like the Bible, which states, "In the beginning was the Word (John 1.1)," the Vedic scriptures affirm that the entire cosmic creation began with sound: "By His utterance the universe came into being." (*Brihad Aranyaka Upanishad* 1.2.4) Vaishnava texts add that ultimate liberation comes from sound as well, in the form of chanting.[3]

Primal sound is referred to as Shabda Brahman—"God as word." Closely related to this concept is Nada Brahman—"God as sound." Both are fundamental Hindu precepts. *Nada*, in fact, is Sanskrit for "sound," and it is related to the term *nadi*, denoting "stream of consciousness," a concept that goes back to the *Rig Veda*. Thus, the relationship between sound and consciousness has long been recorded in Hinduism's religious literature.

Mantras, or sacred sounds, are used to pierce through sensual, mental, and intellectual levels of existence—all lower strata of consciousness—for the purpose of purification and spiritual enlightenment. The sounds of different letters, particularly Sanskrit letters, have been shown to affect the mind, intellect, and auditory nerves of those who chant and hear them. The seven energy centers (*chakras*) of the spinal column, it is said, all respond to specific mantras, bringing practitioners to elevated levels of awareness.

Most Hindu mantras are prayers, of sorts. There are literally millions of them, usually traceable to the *Vedas*, either in seed form or in full phrases, as they are chanted today. The "seed-form" mantras would be incomprehensible to most people; unless one is a Sanskritist, it is difficult to know what an ancient monosyllabic utterance represented in bygone eras. Otherwise, the full prayers, though in Vedic language, are easily translated into English. A famous one runs as follows: "Lead me from nonbeing into being, from darkness to light, from death to immortality."

OM: SOUND SUPREME

Hindu mantras often begin or end with OM, which is usually defined as an impersonal sonic representation of the Supreme. To truly appreciate the creative depth of this Sanskrit syllable, however, one must go back to the ancient Indic texts known as the Vedic literature, to the seed mantra, "Omkara." But before doing this, it would be worthwhile to know that OM is not a sectarian sound, nor is it peculiar to Hindu notions of divine mantras.

Indeed, the sacred syllable is evoked by the well-known Judeo-Christian utterance "Amen," which has been described as a variation on OM. Similarly, Muslims say "Amin." Many of our English descriptions of God, too, begin with OM—omnipresent, omnipotent, and omniscient. The prefix *omni* is a slightly disguised version of the Sanskrit syllable.

Although the divine OM is recognized in nearly all spiritual traditions originating in the East—from the Buddhists of Tibet to the Vedantists of Benares—few have penetrated its actual mystery, at least as it was originally expressed in the Vedic literature:

The goal, as declared in all the *Vedas*, at which all austerities aim, and which humans desire when they live a life of continence, can be summarized in one word: OM. This syllable is indeed Brahman, the highest spiritual truth. Whosoever chants this obtains all that he desires. This is the best support, the highest support, the ultimate end. Whosoever knows this support is adored in the world of Brahman. (*Katha Upanishad* 1.2.15–17)

The origins of OM, in fact, can be traced to the *Rig Veda*, the earliest of India's sacred texts:

One who chants OM, the sonic form of Brahman, Spirit, quickly approaches ultimate reality.[4]

Still, most practitioners today see the mantra merely as an exotic, impersonal utterance—an abstract feature of the Absolute, chanted by yogis and swamis in India (or by Westerners adopting an Eastern form of spirituality).

If one looks a little beneath the surface, however, one finds that OM is really so much more than this. It is described throughout the Vedic literature and by the great spiritual masters of India as the seed conception of theism. That is to say, as a tree or fruit begins with a seed, so, too, does everything begin with OM; even the Gayatri Mantra, considered by many as the ultimate mantra of Hindu Brahminism, begins with OM—the *Vedas* begin with OM, the Upanishads begin with OM, the Vedanta begins with OM, and the *Bhagavata Purana*, the cream of Vedic texts, begins with OM. Therefore, it can safely be said that the divine journey, or the search for transcendental knowledge, begins with OM.

In the *Bhagavad-Gita* (7.8), Krishna himself says, "I am nondifferent from the syllable OM." As such, this sacred syllable is known as the *maha-mantra*, or the supreme mantra, of the *Vedas*, and, in certain ways, can be considered equal to the more commonly known *maha-mantra* ("Hare Krishna, Hare Krishna, Krishna Krishna, Hare Hare/Hare Rama, Hare Rama, Rama Rama, Hare Hare"), at least if it is bestowed upon an aspiring disciple by one who is self-realized.

Thus, according to the most ancient texts on the subject, OM should never be thought of as impersonal. Rather, it is a sonic representation of the Supreme, identical to the Lord in both essence and character. It is not just sound, but it is God himself in the form of sound.

It is also said that OM is the sound of Krishna's flute: The ancient text known as the *Brahma-Samhita* reveals that when Brahma, the first created being, tried to articulate or verbally recreate what he heard when Krishna played his legendary instrument, Brahma uttered "OM."

The *Gopal-Tapani Upanishad* (2.54–55), another ancient text, also discusses OM—reinforcing its identity as the Supreme Divinity:

The letter "A" denotes Balarama, the divine son of Rohini, who is the substratum of the entire universe. The letter "U" denotes Pradyumna who is the supersoul of the universe. The letter "M" denotes Aniruddha, who is the supersoul of each individual being in the universe. And the "dot" above the "M" denotes Sri Krishna, the fountainhead of all Vishnu incarnations.[5]

Here readers are introduced to the original Sanskritic form of the mantra, which is actually AUM, as opposed to OM. The latter version of the word is really a loose transliteration.

The *Gopal-Tapani Upanishad* begins by interpreting OM as described above, but it moves on from there (2.56):

The wise and enlightened sages declare that the pleasure potency of God, Sri Radha, and all living beings are also contained in OM.[6]

Jiva Goswami, one of India's greatest philosophers, elaborates: "OM is a combination of the letters, A,U,M. The letter 'A' refers to Krishna. The Letter 'U' refers to Radha, and the letter 'M' refers to the ordinary living soul." Here, then, is the most evolved understanding of the mantra, at least according to many generations of Vaishnava savants. The mantra is thus summed up by Srila A. C. Bhaktivedanta Swami Prabhupada:

Omkara is a combination of the letters a, u, and m. . . . The letter *a* (*a-kara*) refers to Krishna, who is . . . the master of all living entities and planets, material and spiritual. . . . The letter *u* (*u-kara*) indicates Srimati Radharani, the pleasure potency of Krishna, and *m* (*ma-kara*) indicates the living entities (*jivas*). Thus, OM is the complete combination of Krishna, His potency, and His eternal servitors. In other words, Omkara represents Krishna, His name, fame, pastimes, entourage, expansions, devotees, potencies and everything else pertaining to Him. . . . Omkara is the resting place of everything, just as Krishna is the resting place of everything.[7]

While OM is clearly afforded a special place in the chanting of Hindu mantras, it is usually considered secondary when compared to actual names of the deity. Devotees of Shiva, for example, will recite their Lord's names more readily than chanting OM. Those who venerate the Goddess will prefer chanting her numerous appellations, and Vaishnavas, of course, would prefer the Thousand Names of Vishnu, a popular litany of holy names chanted regularly in Hindu temples, or other Vishnu-centered mantras.

THE POWER OF GOD'S NAMES

The spiritual sounds most lauded in Vedic texts are thus the names of God. These sounds are said to have powers that surpass those of any other uttered word. Vaishnava texts state that in much the same way that one can awaken a person who is sleeping by making a sound or calling out his name, man can awaken from his conditioned, materialistic slumber by calling out the name of God. In fact, the world's major religious traditions concur in regard to the importance of God's name.

For example, in the Bible, King David preached, "From the rising of the sun to its setting, the name of the Lord is to be praised." (Psalms 113.3); Saint Paul said, "Everyone who calls upon the name of the Lord will be saved." (Romans 10.13); Mohammed, in the Koran (87.2), counseled, "Glorify the name of your Lord, the most high;" Buddha declared, "All who sincerely call upon my name will come to me after death, and I will take them to paradise." (Vows of Amida Buddha, 18); and the Vaishnava scriptures repeatedly assert: "Chant the holy name, chant the holy name, chant the holy name of the Lord. In this age of quarrel there is no other way, no other way, no other way to attain spiritual enlightenment." (*Brihad-Naradiya Purana* 3.8.126).

Praise of God's holy name is found throughout the literature of the Vaishnavas, particularly in the *Bhagavata Purana*. Here are some examples:

Oh, how glorious are they whose tongues are chanting Your holy name! Even if originally lowborn dog-eaters, they are to be considered worthy of worship. To have reached the point of chanting the Lord's name, they must have executed various austerities and Vedic sacrifices and achieved all the good qualities of true Aryans. If they are chanting Your holy name, they must have bathed in all holy rivers, studied the *Vedas* and fulfilled all prescribed duties [if not in this life, then in previous ones]. (*Bhagavata Purana* 3.33.7)

My dear king, although Kali-yuga is full of faults, there is still one good quality about this age: simply by chanting the holy name of the Lord, one can become free from material bondage and be promoted to the transcendental kingdom. (*Bhagavata Purana* 12.3.51)

Devotional service, beginning with the chanting of the holy name, is the ultimate religious principle for the living entity in human society. (*Bhagavata Purana* 6.3.22)

The holy name of Krishna is the spiritually blissful giver of all benedictions, for it is Krishna Himself, the reservoir of pleasure. Krishna's name is complete in itself and is the essential form of all spiritual relationships. It is not a material name under any condition, and it is no less powerful than Krishna Himself. This name is not tinged by any aspect of material nature, because it is identical with Krishna. (*Padma Purana* 3.21)

And, finally, Krishna himself says,

> I dwell not in the spiritual kingdom,
> Nor in the hearts of yogis;
> Where my devotees are chanting,
> There, O Narada, stand I![8]

Because chanting the name of God is so much emphasized in Vaishnava texts, practitioners tend to include it in most forms of worship. One finds chanting at Hindu temples, while engaging in deity service, when offering food to God, and in private meditation. It permeates all forms of Hindu practice. Thus, deep meditation and great emotion accompany *japa* (soft chanting on beads, similar to the Christian rosary), *kirtan* (loud chanting, often in the form of song and dance), and *sankirtan* (congregational chanting, usually with an attempt to include others).

Sometimes this chanting is merely a combination of names, eloquently strung together through grammatical devices, appearing in Sanskrit or in regional languages. And sometimes it tells a story, weaving together pastimes of the Lord in any of his many forms. Melody plays an important part in both these kinds of *kirtans*, but some are accompanied by dancing, whereas a sit-down *kirtan* is often called a *bhajan*—this is usually more meditative and laid back. When perfected, the chanting, in any of its forms, leads to awareness of God's absolute nature (i.e., that there is no difference between the *nami*, "the named one," and the *nama*, "the name").[9]

This ultimate oneness between God and his name, of course, is something that virtually defines the unseen world, revealing a fundamental difference between matter and spirit: material substances are relative (i.e., in the material world a thing and its name are *not* one and the same). They are necessarily distinct. However, in the spiritual world, which is the exact opposite of the material world, the reverse must be true—an essential oneness engulfs all. A thing and its name are the same. This is not to say that there is no hierarchy in the spiritual world, with various gradations perceivable by spiritually realized souls, but rather that a sense of oneness and difference exist simultaneously. Elucidation on the absolute nature of Krishna and his name is the heart of Vaishnava mysticism, leading to love of God.[10]

For now, it need merely be pointed out that if God and his name are nondifferent, association with the name is the same as associating with God himself. This has certain implications. Proximity to God, say Hindu texts, results in purification, edification, and blissful feelings of love. Thus, by chanting, the devotee can expect to advance in spiritual life, developing a taste for the higher pleasures of spiritual attainment. Concomitantly, the practitioners' material fever is expected to diminish—that is to say, one's advancement in spiritual life can be gauged by how much one is foregoing material pleasures in favor of spiritual ones—and the supreme spiritual pleasure is chanting the holy name.

Great systematizers of the tradition, such as Ramanuja and Rupa Goswami, have delineated an elaborate science of the holy name, explaining step-by-step procedures for chanting. By applying these time-tested methods, devotees are able to gradually advance and ultimately attain spiritually developed consciousness. This is nowhere as apparent as in *kirtan*, where men, women, and children gather together to rejoice in the Lord.

Norvin Hein, Professor Emeritus at Yale University, was deeply touched when he personally witnessed an enthusiastic Vaishnava *kirtan* session, and in writing about it, he captures its most emotional components:

In the singing of verses like these, each line, separately, is incanted by the leader first, and the whole assembly repeats each line after him, one by one. As the verse is gone through again and again, the leader steps up the tempo. When the speed of utterance approaches the utmost possible, the whole group, in unison, begins to shout the lines, at the same time beating out the rhythm with sharply timed clapping of hands. The singers begin to sway and let themselves go in ungoverned gestures. Faces flush. From the line of instrumental accompanists the bell-like peal of small brass cymbals swells up with the rising shouting and pierces through it. The whole process approaches a crashing, breath-taking crescendo. The point of explosion is reached: eyes flash, mouths drop open, a tremor runs through the entire assembly. The Power, the Presence, has been felt![11]

CHAITANYA MAHAPRABHU: THE MASTER OF CHANTING

Though the phenomenon of chanting is fundamental to the Hindu way of life, and numerous personalities could be assigned prominent roles in establishing and developing the science of mantras, there is one luminous individual who stands out among the rest. This is Chaitanya Mahaprabhu (1486–1533), the doyen of chanting as a yogic practice.

Mahaprabhu and his accomplishments are viewed in various ways by scholars and devotees alike. Historian of Bengali culture, Edward Dimock, asserts that "the intense and unprecedented revival of the Vaishnava faith in Bengal" was due to "the leadership and inspiration of Chaitanya."[12] Vaishnava theologian A. K. Majumdar lauds Chaitanya as "the founder of the last great Vaiahnava sect."[13] And Indian historian S. K. De describes his contribution as "Vaishnavism *par excellence*."[14]

Just who is Sri Chaitanya, and what do existing records tell us about his actual life and doctrine? The subject is complex, and numerous volumes have been written for the sake of clarification.[15] Suffice it to say that he came to this world to inaugurate the Sankirtan movement—the movement centered on the congregational chanting of the holy name of Krishna. In so doing, he specifically taught the efficacy of chanting the *maha-mantra:* Hare Krishna, Hare Krishna, Krishna Krishna, Hare Hare/Hare Rama, Hare Rama, Rama Rama, Hare Hare. The actual meaning of the mantra will be discussed more thoroughly below. He taught that by chanting such mantras under the direction of a spiritual master, one can become "God-intoxicated," modified by divine love.

Thus, he established *bhakti*, or devotional love directed toward a personal God, as the highest goal of man. Many poets and theologians before him had alluded to this culminating devotional principle, and some even made it their central concern, creating a wave of *bhakti* that is today remembered as a significant movement in Medieval India. But Sri Chaitanya "broke open the storehouse," as it were, making it easily accessible to man, woman, and child.

With all of this, says the tradition, we are only introduced to the external reason for his appearance.

The internal reason is theologically elaborate. Put simply, in the descent of Chaitanya, God desires to taste the intense love of his own special devotees. This love is so profound that he wants to directly experience it from a Krishna aficionado's unique perspective. For this reason, he appears in this world as his own perfect devotee—as Chaitanya Mahaprabhu, Krishna in the mood of Radha—in order to fully taste this divine love, the most cherished goal of the Vaishnavas.

Thus infused with divinity, he inspired hundreds of thousands in his own lifetime, and many millions more after that. Christian theologian John Moffitt wrote of Chaitanya in glowing terms:

If I were asked to choose one man in Indian religious history who best represents the pure spirit of devotional self-giving, I would choose the Vaishnavite saint Chaitanya, whose full name in religion was Krishna-Chaitanya, or "Krishna consciousness." Of all the saints in recorded history, East or West, he seems to me the supreme example of a soul carried away on a tide of ecstatic love of God. This extraordinary man, who belongs to the rich period beginning with the end of the fourteenth century, represents the culmination of the devotional schools that grew up around Krishna. . . . Chaitanya delighted intensely in nature. It is said that, like St. Francis of Assisi, he had a miraculous power over wild beasts. His life in the holy town of Puri is the story of a man in a state of almost continuous spiritual intoxication. Illuminating discourses, deep contemplation, moods of loving communion with God, were daily occurrences.[16]

Though Sri Chaitanya trained theologians, whom he instructed to open temples and write massive treatises on the science of devotion, which they did, he left the world only eight Sanskrit verses of his own, four of which are specifically about chanting:

(1) Glory to the Sri-Krishna-Sankirtan, which cleanses the heart of all the dust accumulated for years and extinguishes the fire of conditional life, of repeated birth and death. This Sankirtan movement is the prime benediction for humanity at large because it spreads the rays of the benediction moon. It is the life of all transcendental knowledge. It increases the ocean of transcendental bliss, and it enables us to fully taste the nectar for which we are always anxious.

(2) O my Lord, Your holy name alone can render all benediction to living beings, and thus You have hundreds and millions of names, like Krishna and Govinda. In these transcendental names, You have invested all Your transcendental energies. There are not even hard and fast rules for chanting these names. O my Lord, out of kindness You enable us to easily approach You by Your holy names, but I am so unfortunate that I have no attraction for them.

(3) One should chant the holy name of the Lord in a humble state of mind, thinking oneself lower than the straw in the street; one should be more tolerant than a tree, devoid of all sense of false prestige, and should be ready to offer all respect to others. In such a state of mind one can chant the holy name of the Lord constantly.

(4) O my Lord, when will my eyes be decorated with tears of love flowing constantly when I chant Your holy name? When will my voice choke up, and when will the hairs of my body stand on end at the recitation of Your name?

CHANTING THE 'HARE KRISHNA" *MAHA-MANTRA*

As stated, Sri Chaitanya emphasized the chanting of the Hare Krishna *maha-mantra*, also known as "the great chant for deliverance." He uncovered scriptural evidence stating that this was the most powerful of incantations, for it includes the potency of all other mantras. And he showed, in his own life, the blissfully transformative effect bestowed on its chanters.

Statements about the mantra's singular potency can be found in the *Brahmanda Purana* (*Uttara-Khanda* 6.55), *the Kalisantarana Upanishad*, and in many other Vedic and post-Vedic texts.

Breaking down this sacred mantra into its component parts, the word "Hare" refers to Lord Hari—a name for Krishna that indicates his ability to remove obstacles from his devotees' path. In a more esoteric sense, the word "Hare" is a vocative form of "Hara," which refers to Mother Hara, or Sri Radha, the divine feminine energy—Lord Krishna's eternal consort and transcendental counterpart.

"Krishna" means "the all-attractive one," referring to God in his original form. Etymologically, the word *krish* indicates the Lord's attractive feature, and *na* refers to spiritual pleasure. When the verb *krish* is added to the affix *na*, it becomes *krishna*, which means "the absolute person, who gives spiritual pleasure through his all-attractive qualities."

"Rama" refers to both Balarama (Krishna's elder brother) and Lord Ramachandra, the incarnation of the Lord discussed at length in the *Ramayana*. It is also said, however, that "Rama" can refer to Radha Ramana Rama, which is another name for Krishna, meaning "one who brings pleasure to Sri Radha." Overall, the *maha-mantra*, composed solely of the Lord's most confidential names, embodies the essence of the divine. As a prayer, the mantra is translated in the following way: "O Lord, O divine energy of the Lord (Radha)! Please engage me in Your service."

The selflessness of this mantra—imploring God to be engaged solely in his service, rather than asking for individual needs—situates it in a unique category, even among the best of prayers and the most powerful of mantras. But, to chant it in its purest form is no simple matter. There is an elaborate science to chanting, and the tradition urges its readers to study this science closely. Otherwise, the fruits of the mantra may not be obtained.

There is another side, however: One can simply chant with a sincere heart, crying out to God with a sense of spontaneity. This, too, say Vaishnava stalwarts, may afford the fruits of Chaitanya's religious process.

ISKCON

If all this talk of chanting Hare Krishna seems somehow familiar, it's because of its association with the Hare Krishna movement, the shaven-headed and *sari*-clad enthusiasts seen in most major cities (and airports). The association is legitimate: during his lifetime, Sri Chaitanya predicted that the holy names of Krishna would spread to every town and village in the world. This prophecy lay unfulfilled for 400 years, until the time of Bhaktivinoda Thakura, a great spiritual master in the direct line of disciplic succession from Chaitanya himself.

In 1885, Bhaktivinoda wrote,

Lord Chaitanya did not advent himself to liberate only a few men in India. Rather, his main objective was to emancipate all living entities of all countries throughout the entire universe and preach the Eternal Religion. . . . There is no doubt that this unquestionable order will come to pass . . . Very soon the unparalleled path of *Hari-nama Sankirtan* [the congregational chanting of the holy name of the Lord] will be propagated all over the world . . . Oh, for that day when the fortunate English, French, Russian, German, and American people will take up banners, *mridangas* [drums], and *karatals* [hand cymbals] and raise *kirtan* [chanting] through their streets and towns! When, oh when, will that day come?"[17]

Bhaktivinoda's vision became a reality in less than a century. In 1965, a humble Vaishnava monk, Srila A. C. Bhaktivedanta Swami Prabhupada (1896–1977), arrived in New York's East Village, the heart of the countercultural movement of the1960s. Within a year, Prabhupada, tenth in the line of spiritual masters from Sri Chaitanya, had founded the International Society for Krishna Consciousness (ISKCON). Very quickly, the chanting of Hare Krishna spread, first across America, then on to England, and then throughout the world.

In one sense, Chaitanya Mahaprabhu is one among many manifestations of God (*avatar*); the Hare Krishna mantra is among a plethora of sacred chants; and Bhaktivedanta Swami Prabhupada is yet another guru, even if these three are exemplary in each of their respective categories. Indeed, the Hindu tradition knows many *avatars*, mantras, and teachers. It could be said, in fact, that the whole of Hinduism comes down to which manifestation of the divine one holds dear, which mantra one chants, and which lineage one chooses to align oneself with.

CHANTING TODAY

Prabhupada's mission still thrives, and, in the present context, has given the world popular *kirtan* performers whose CDs sell in significant numbers and whose concerts fill huge auditoriums. But it is not only Prabhupada's disciples who enliven crowds with tones from heaven: no one movement has the monopoly on *kirtan*, which is God's gift to humankind.

Along these lines, an interesting development has occurred over the last decade or so: Chanting that clearly originated in a Hindu context is now permeating the Western mainstream, affecting a revival in India as well. This has been a long time in coming. The 1960s saw an awakening of the mystic East on Western shores. Vegetarianism, nonviolent ethics, yoga, and meditation—all have enjoyed spates of Occidental popularity in the last 40 years, often influenced by ISKCON directly, if not indirectly.

The latest in this Hindu penetration of the modern world, as stated, is chanting. Kirtan is gaining momentum all across the United States, and in Europe as well. Yoga studios, once confined to silent meditation, now broadcast melodious mantras through their loudspeakers, and have special sales on CDs; health food stores and restaurants now popularize the latest *kirtan* to people through soft music and New Age magazines. Parts of upstate New York, formerly known as the "Borsht Belt" for its catering to Jewish comedians in the 1940s, the 1950s, and the 1960s, is now being redesignated the "Bhajan Belt."

Less than 10 years ago, few were aware of the virtues of *kirtan*, even in the yoga community. Today, *kirtan* events attract yogis and nonyogis alike. Business people relieve stress by listening to *kirtan* CDs and Grammy-winning artists sample *kirtan* performances on their disks. Krishna Das, whom *Yoga Journal* recently dubbed "The Pavarotti of Kirtan," and Jai Uttal, an extremely gifted *kirtan* leader, are arguably the most popular of the genre. They are disciples of the late Hindu ecstatic Neem Karoli Baba and have no connection to ISKCON or its lineage, though, interestingly, both admit that the Vaishnava tradition influenced and inspired their initial attachment to sacred chant.[18]

Popular books now contemporize Hindu mantras by explaining them in modern language. In *Chanting: Discovering Spirit in Sound*, for example, author Robert Gass says that *kirtan* is "singing our prayers, vocal meditation, the breath made audible in tone, and discovering spirit in sound." He reminds us that "Religions and armies, tribes and nations, political marches and sports teams have all recognized and made use of the power of chant to touch our collective minds and hearts—for better and for worse. Something happens when we chant together, when we choose to give our voices, our energy and our hearts to a common song and to each other."[19] His words merely echo Hinduism's ancient Sanskrit texts.

Conclusion

We have attempted to convey a taste, a drop, of the ocean known as Hinduism. To do more would be impossible. The full story, due to its enormity, variety, and spiritual depth, resists comprehensive treatment. In this sense, Hinduism is comparable to the great Ganges River, which, it is said, originates in the spiritual realm and flows wherever God is worshipped in any of his innumerable forms.

One can approach the Ganges from many angles, but never from each of them simultaneously. Still, by chemically analyzing even one drop of Ganges water, one can discover its chemical composition as a whole. That was our reasoning in *Essential Hinduism*, where we focused on Vaishnavism as representative of all the rest.

The river's many tributaries and streams are home to varieties of flora and fauna, adding color, if also confusion, to a much analyzed body of water. In this book we splash and play in that river's shallows, but let it be known: even the boldest and most experienced swimmers could not plumb its depths.

In addition, Hindu sages have long realized that the rivers of life are not simply out-flowing—they do not move downhill without expectation of upward return. All rivers and individual beings will eventually revisit their source. In the earth's ecosystem, most rivers pour into lakes and oceans, whose waters are eventually drawn up into the atmosphere. Soon, clouds are formed, only to again shed moisture upon the earth, completing life's self-sustaining cycle.

In the "Hindu ecosystem," if you will, the process that returns spiritual waters to their source is called sacrifice—the "making sacred" of thoughts and deeds so that the divine within us will flow through, facilitating the individual soul in his/her journey home. Therefore, Hinduism teaches to be mindful of our thoughts, to seek truth, to love and serve others, to pursue God, and to allow life's higher currents to bring us their precious boon: the love that nurtures the god-plant in our heart of hearts, watering the Tree of Life and the Tree of Knowledge. This is the essence of Hinduism.

By exploring that sacred river, we may come to know ourselves.

Though Hinduism, as we have shown, is a highly intellectual tradition, with elaborate scriptures and sophisticated theological exploration, *Essential Hinduism* has underlined at least one overriding principle: that devotion and "heart over head" sensibilities permeate the tradition, particularly in Vaishnavism.

One seventeenth-century text, the *Chaitanya-Charitamrita* (*Madhya-Lila*, 9.93–102), makes this abundantly clear in its story of an unnamed illiterate Brahmin in South India. The portion of the text that focuses on this Brahmin appears below in its entirety.

> This is the story of a Vaishnava Brahmin from the land of Ranga.
> He would go to the temple every day to recite the *Bhagavad-Gita*.
> During recitation, he would feel great bliss
>   and his eyes filled with tears as he read all eighteen chapters.
> His reading, however, was imperfect,
>   for his Sanskrit left a great deal to be desired.
> And so, people would make fun of him.
> Nonetheless, in his state of bliss,
>   he was unconcerned that some would laugh and mock him.
> Totally absorbed in reading the *Bhagavad-Gita*,
>   visible signs of bodily ecstasy, such as tears, quivering,
>   perspiring—all these would engulf him while reading.
> Witnessing this, the great Master (Chaitanya) became overjoyed.
> Sri Chaitanya asked him, "Dear Brahmin, please indulge me.
> What is the cause of your unequaled happiness?"
> The Brahmin said, "I am a fool and clearly uneducated.
> I do not know the meaning of these intensely philosophical words,
>   or whether I am reading the *Gita* correctly or not.
> I am simply abiding by the order of my teacher. And I see this:
> Krishna is in Arjuna's chariot,
>   holding the reins in His divine hands.
> He sits with His devotee, appearing dark and exquisitely beautiful.

He is offering Arjuna His elaborate teachings,
    but, more importantly, He offers His compassion.
And just visualizing Him, in this situation,
    causes a wave of bliss to overtake me.
As long as I read this, however imperfectly, I can have a vision of
    Him.
For this reason, I cannot cease reading the *Gita*."
The Master said, "You are the proper authority
    of the *Gita*. You know it better than the greatest of scholars.
You know the essential meaning of the *Gita*,
    for you view it with your heart as opposed to merely your
        intellect."

This short story confirms that Hinduism's spiritual tradition ultimately values a heart steeped in devotion over any other metaphysical commodity, be it philosophical acumen, intellectual prowess, or yogic perfection. The South Indian Brahmin rightly perceived that Krishna came into our world out of love, to become his devotee's charioteer—and that God became his servant's servant. This, said the South Indian Brahmin, is the real teaching of the *Bhagavad-Gita*. It is also the real teaching of Hinduism.

Notes

Introduction

1. See Diana L. Eck, in her book *Darsan, Seeing the Divine in India* (Chambersburg, PA: Anima Books, 1981), p. 19. The hierarchical model is also mentioned in L. Dumont's classic work, *Homo Hierarchichus* (Chicago, IL: University of Chicago Press, 1970).

2. See Schweig's essay "Krishna, the Intimate Deity" in Edwin F. Bryant and Maria L. Ekstrand, Eds., *The Hare Krishna Movement: The Postcharismatic Fate of a Religious Transplant* (New York: Columbia University Press, 2004), p. 19.

3. See Shashi Tharoor, *India: From Midnight to the Millennium* (New York: Arcade Publishing, 1997), p. 321.

4. See Stanley Wolpert, *India* (Los Angeles, CA: University of California Press, 1999, reprint), p. 251.

5. The 1966 Supreme Court ruling is discussed in Ramesh Pandit, *Who Speaks for Hinduism?* (Toronto, Canada: Powerfont Press, 2001).

6. See Alain Danielou, *The Myths and Gods of India* (Rochester, VT: Inner Traditions International, 1991, reprint), p. 12.

7. The three relevant books here are Gerald Larson, *India's Agony Over Religion* (Albany, NY: State University of New York Press, 1995), p. 20; and Agehananda Bharati, *Hindu Views and Ways and the Hindu-Muslim Interface* (New Delhi, India: Munshiram Manoharlal, 1981). See also K. Klostermaier, "The Response of Modern Vaishnavism" in Harold G. Coward, Ed., *Modern Indian Responses to Religious Pluralism* (Albany, NY: State University of New York Press, 1987), p. 129.

8. Brahma, Vishnu, and Shiva predominate over creation, preservation, and dissolution, respectively. Their function as one unitary Godhead can easily be

remembered by thinking of them as the *G*enerator, *O*perator, and *D*estroyer—or the entity known as G.O.D.

9. Some may think that equating Vishnu with goodness is a Vaishnava conceit, but, in fact, it is a pan-Hindu idea, and even Puranas that are traditionally associated with Shiva, such as the *Matsya* (53.68–9), acknowledge this correlation.

10. See Gavin Flood *An Introduction to Hinduism* (Cambridge, UK: Cambridge University Press, 1996), p. 104.

11. For more on the significance of this, see http://www.jsboard.co.uk/etac/etbb/benchbook/et_03/et_mf05.htm.

12. Klaus Klostermaier, *A Survey of Hinduism*, 2nd edition (Albany, NY: State University of New York Press, 1994), p. 145.

Chapter One

1. For more on the Indus Valley Civilization, see the work of Michael Witzel, Subhash Kak, and David Frawley. Particularly see David Frawley, *Gods, Sages and Kings: Vedic Secrets of Ancient Civilization* (Salt Lake City, UT: Passages Press, 1991).

2. For more, see Klaus Klostermaier, *Hinduism: A Short History* (Oxford, UK: Oneworld Publications, 2000), pp. 9, 36, 42. See also Arvind Sharma's article, "Method in the Study of Hinduism" in his edited volume, *The Study of Hinduism* (Columbia, SC: University of South Carolina Press, 2003), p. 57.

3. Recent work on the date of the Buddha suggests that he lived about one century later than generally supposed. The research of Richard Gombrich and Heinz Bechert is especially pertinent. See Bechert, "The Date of the Buddha Reconsidered" in *Indologica Taurinensia*, 10 (1982), pp. 29–36.

4. See also Ram Prasad Chanda, *The Indo-Aryan Races* (New Delhi: Indological Book Corporation, 1976).

5. Recent scholarship pushes Zarathustra's lifetime back another 6,000 years, which, if true, might very well indicate a much earlier date for the *Vedas* than previously supposed. For more on this, see Edwin Bryant, *The Quest for the Origins of Vedic Culture: The Indo-Aryan Migration Debate* (New York: Oxford University Press, 2001), pp. 130–131.

6. "The Collapse of the Indus-Script Thesis: The Myth of a Literate Harappan Civilization," a recent article by Steve Farmer, Richard Sproat, and Michael Witzel in the *Electronic Journal of Vedic Studies* (2004), is found online at http://users.primushost.com/~india/ejvs/issues.html.

7. The Indus script is not, of course, unique, and its value should not be exaggerated. There are other undeciphered scripts that could shed light on the ancient world. If one Googles "undeciphered scripts" on the Internet, for example, the informative http://www.omniglot.com/writing/undeciphered.htm emerges, along with alternate listings. Here we learn of many indecipherable or partially indecipherable scripts, such as the Vinxa/Old European, Proto-Elamite, Old Elamite,

Phaistos Disk, Etruscan, Rongo Rongo, and many others, including that of the Indus Valley.

8. Details on these theories can be found in Edwin Bryant, *The Quest for the Origins of Vedic Culture*, op. cit. See also Bryant's volume coedited with Laurie Patton, *The Indo-Aryan Controversy: Evidence and Inference in Indian History* (Richmond, VA: Curzon, forthcoming).

9. For more on this see Shukavak Das "Bhaktivinode and the Problem of Modernity" in the *Journal of Vaishnava Studies*, 5(1) (Winter 1996–1997), pp. 127–150; also see Edwin Bryant, *The Quest for the Origins of Vedic Culture*, op. cit., pp. 53–54.

10. For a good overview of the debate, see Klaus Klostermaier, "Questioning the Aryan Invasion Theory and Revising Ancient Indian History" in *ISKCON Communications Journal*, 6(1) (June 1998), as well as Edwin Bryant's response to Klostermaier's paper in the subsequent issue, 6(2) (December 1998).

11. By way of evidence, one need look no further than the two most widely used Hindu textbooks today: Klaus Klostermaier, *A Survey of Hinduism* (Albany, NY: State University of New York Press, 1994, reprint) and Gavin Flood, *An Introduction to Hinduism* (Cambridge, UK: Cambridge University Press, 1996). Here we find that Klostermaier categorically rejects the Aryan Invasion theory (pp. 35–36), indicating that the premises of the theory have been systematically dismantled. Yet Flood leans more toward an acceptance of the theory, at least in modified form (pp. 31–35). He suggests that it was perhaps a gradual "migration" as opposed to an "invasion," though he admits that the matter is far from settled.

12. Accordingly, there have been recent works, such as the one by David Weir, *Brahma in the West: William Blake and the Oriental Renaissance* (New York: SUNY Press, 2003).

13. See the following Web sites for this *stotra* and its significance in the Shankarite tradition: http://www.vidya-ashramvidyaorder.org/shankara.a.html, http://www.advaita-vedanta.org/avhp/advaita-parampara.html, and http://www.svbf.org/sringeri/guruparampara.html.

Chapter Two

1. Sri Aurobindo, "Indian Spirituality and Life" in *The Arya* (August 1919). Also called "The Three Fundamentals of the Hindu Religion."

2. Ibid.

3. This list of Hinduism's eleven essential principles is a revised version of a similar list found in *Hinduism Today*, a modern magazine on contemporary Hinduism. See the original list online at http://www.himalayanacademy.com/basics/nineb/. The Varnashrama social system is elaborated upon later in this chapter.

4. For the Persian origins of the term see S. Radhakrishnan, *The Hindu Way of Life* (New York: Macmillan, 1962), p. 12. Also see Klaus Klostermaier, *A Survey*

of Hinduism (Albany, NY: State University of New York Press, 1994), p. 31. Some argue that in the sacred *Avesta*, the scripture of the Zoroastrians, we find the first instance of the word "Hindu." Others say that the original version of the word (*Hind'ush*) is first found in two inscriptions from Iran (on the monuments of Darius), which are from 486 BC.

5. C. J. Fuller, *The Camphor Flame: Popular Hinduism and Society in India* (Princeton, NJ: Princeton University Press, 1992).

6. Pandit Rajmani Tigunait, *Seven Systems of Indian Philosophy* (Honesdale, PA: The Himalayan International Institute of Yoga, 1983), pp. 4–5.

7. Hans Kung, *Christianity and the World Religions* (Garden City, NY: Doubleday & Company, Inc., 1986), pp. 140–141.

8. See Heinrich von Stietencron, "Hinduism: On the Proper Use of a Deceptive Term," in *Hinduism Reconsidered*, Eds., Gunther-Dietz Sontheimer and Hermann Kulke (New Delhi, India: Manohar Publishers, 2001), p. 33.

9. See Gabriella Eichinger Ferro-Luzzi, "The Polythetic-Prototype Approach to Hinduism," in *Hinduism Reconsidered*, Ibid., pp. 294–295.

10. John Stratton Hawley, "Naming Hinduism" in *The Wilson Quarterly* (The Woodrow Wilson International Center for Scholars, Smithsonian Institute, Summer 1991), pp. 22–23.

11. Buddhists, of course, are the followers of Siddhartha Gautama. Jains, who emphasize *ahimsa*, or "harmlessness," come in the lineage of Mahavira, who flourished during the time of the Buddha (500 BCE). And Sikhs, a tradition founded by Guru Nanak in the sixteenth century, is an interesting blend of Hindu and Islamic doctrine. These three traditions do not trace their theology to the *Vedas* and are thus considered Hindu heterodoxies, if Hindu at all. We will treat these three traditions, especially Buddhism, in a separate chapter.

12. See *Cuttack Law Times* (1970), p. 1.

13. Hans Kung, op. cit.

14. Pandit Rajmani Tigunait, op. cit., p. 5.

15. Quote from Hans Kung. Cited in Axel Michaels, *Hinduism Past and Present* (Princeton, NJ: Princeton University press, 2004), p. 12.

16. Wendy Doniger, "Hinduism By Any Other Name," in *The Wilson Quarterly* (The Woodrow Wilson International Center for Scholars, Smithsonian Institute, Summer 1991), p. 36.

17. See Richard King, "Orientalism and the Modern Myth of 'Hinduism'" in *NUMEN*, 46 (Leiden, Netherlands: Brill, 1999), p. 182.

18. See Neal Delmonico, "Reassembling the Giant: The Development of Monotheism in Vaisnava Theology" in the *Journal of Vaishnava Studies*, 13(1) (Fall 2004), p. 174. Delmonico correctly asserts that one should be leery when using words that originate in other religious milieus. But he adds that, given all such due cautions, monotheism is an appropriate label for much of the religion in India today (p. 156).

19. I am indebted to Graham M. Schweig for this terminology. For more on this, see his essay "Krishna, the Intimate Deity" in Edwin F. Bryant and Maria

L. Ekstrand, Eds., op. cit., pp. 13–30. When discussing Vishnu, the deity of Vaishnavism, polymorphic monotheism is perhaps the best description of divinity, though lesser deities are acknowledged as well. The implications of this idea will be discussed at length in our Vaishnavism section.

20. See Axel Michaels, op. cit., p. 207.

21. There are, of course, other options, such as pantheism and panentheism. But monotheism and polytheism are the only two that recognize God in personal terms.

22. For arguments that the Christian trinity is a form of polytheism, see Rabbi Ben Baker, *Judaism and Other Religions* (New York: Bantor Books, 1984), pp. 30–35. See also Jim Scheinerman, *The Unique Nature of Judaism* (San Francisco, CA: Alchreft Publishing, 2000), p. 2.

23. See R. C. Zaehner, *The Bhagavad-Gita* (London, UK: Oxford University Press, 1969), p. 187.

24. L. J. Biallas, *World Religions: A Story Approach* (Mystic, CT: Twenty-Third Publications, 1991), p. 158. For a discussion of the Arundati concept see G. A. Jacob, *Handbook of Popular Maxims* (Bombay, India: Tukaram Javaji, 1907), pp. 5–6.

25. For elaboration, see Graham M. Schweig, "Sri Chaitanya's Philosophy of *Acintya-Bhedabheda-Tattva*" in T. D. Singh, Ed., *Synthesis of Science and Religion* (San Francisco, CA: The Bhaktivedanta Institute, 1987), pp. 420–429. The harmony between the One and the Many is made explicit in the ancient Vedic text known as the *Taittiriya Aranyaka* (3.133).

Chapter Three

1. The verse most quoted in regard to these three manifestations of the Supreme is found in the *Bhagavata Purana* (1.2.11). See also Steven J. Rosen, *The Hidden Glory of India* (Grodinge, Sweden: Bhaktivedanta Book Trust, 2002), pp. 42–45.

2. See Alain Danielou, *The Myths and Gods of India*, op. cit., p. x.

3. See Sri Aurobindo, *India's Rebirth* (Paris, France: Institut de Recherches Evolutives, 2000, 3rd edition).

4. For more on Frithjof Schuon's Vedantic view, see his book, *Language of the Self: Essays on the Perennial Philosophy* (Bloomington, IN: World Wisdom Books, Inc., 1999, revised translation).

5. See Seyyed Hossein Nasr, "The *Philosophia Perennis* and the Study of Religion" in Frank Whaling, Ed., *The World's Religious Traditions* (New York: The Crossroad Publishing Company, 1986), pp. 181–200. Nasr points out (p. 196) that the *philosophia perennis* is "the Sanatana Dharma of Hinduism or the *al-hikmat al-khalidah* of the Islamic tradition known also under its Persian name *jawidan-khirad*."

6. Nitya Dharma is an alternate way of saying Sanatana Dharma, a phrase used later in this work—both *nitya* and *sanatana* mean "eternal."

7. G. W. F. Hegel, *Philosophy of World History*, part 1, section 2, quoted in Axel Michaels, *Hinduism: Past and Present* (Princeton, NJ: Princeton University Press, 2004), p. 16.

8. Before confusion sets in, we should point out that Hinduism recognizes four extremely similar words, all variations on "Brahman." For our purposes, we will spell and explain these words as follows: (1) "Brahman" refers to the overarching soul of the universe, or God in his most abstract feature; (2) "Brahmin" refers to the social order comprised of intellectuals and priests; (3) "Brahma" refers to the first created being, existing on the topmost planet in the material universe; the demigod presiding over the mode of passion; (4) "*Brahmanas*" refer to a class of literature associated with the ancient Vedic texts.

9. Hinduism scholar, Vasudha Narayanan, underscores these facts in her recent study, *Hinduism* (New York: Oxford University Press, 2004), pp. 101, 104–105. Here she points out that later in the epic it is again made clear that "propensity" rather than "birth" is how one should actually measure class status, at least according to early Hindu tradition.

10. In India, the term "Untouchable" is now considered an insult. People who live as Untouchables, and those who have sympathy for them, prefer the terms Harijans ("children of God") or Dalits ("downtrodden").

11. For more on Marx and the Indian caste system, see *The Collected Works of Marx and Engels*, vol. XII (New York: International Publishers, 1979). The specific essay entitled "The Future Results of British Rule in India" was first published in the *New York Daily Tribune* (August 8, 1853); it was reprinted in the *New-York Semi-Weekly Tribune*, 856 (August 9, 1853). It is also available online at http://www.marxists.org/archive/marx/works/1853/07/22.htm.

12. See Shukavak N. Dasa, *Hindu Encounter with Modernity* (Los Angeles, CA: Sri Publications, 1999), pp. 211–214.

Chapter Four

1. See His Divine Grace A. C. Bhaktivedanta Swami Prabhupada, *Beyond Birth and Death* (Los Angeles, CA: The Bhaktivedanta Book Trust, reprint 1979), p. 7.

2. The prominence of Vishnu in the Veda is the subject of much debate. In the section on Vaishnavism, later in this book, this subject will be revisited in some depth.

3. See *Agni: The Vedic Ritual of the Fire Altar*, vol. II, Eds., J. F. Staal and P. MacFarland (Berkeley, CA: Asian Humanities Press, 1983).

4. For more on the tension between animal sacrifice and nonviolence in the *Vedas*, Steven J. Rosen, *Holy Cow: The Hare Krishna Contribution to Vegetarianism and Animal Rights* (New York: Lantern Books, 2004), pp. 19–27.

5. See Max Muller, *The Six Systems of Indian Philosophy* (Varanasi, India: Chowkhamba, 1962, reprint), p. 35.

6. See Barbara A. Holdrege, *Veda and Torah: Transcending the Textuality of Scripture* (Albany, NY: State University of New York Press, 1996), p. 346.

7. See A. L. Basham, *The Sacred Cow: The Evolution of Classical Hinduism* (Boston, MA: Beacon Press, 1989, reprint), pp. 7, 9.

8. See Jan Gonda, "Vedic Literature (Samhitas and Brahmanas)" in *A History of Indian Literature*, vol. 1, fasc. 1 (Wiesbaden, Germany: Harrassowitz, 1975), p. 62.

9. This translation is my own, adapted from Walter H. Maurer, *Pinnacles of India's Past: Selections From the Rigveda* (Amsterdam, Netherlands: Benjamins, 1986), pp. 271–272.

10. See Brown's essay, "The Sources and Nature of Purusha in the *Purusasukta (Rigveda* 10.90)" in *Journal of the American Oriental Society*, 51 (1931), pp. 109–118.

11. See Boris Oguibenine, "On the Rhetoric of Violence" in *Violence/Non-Violence: Some Hindu Perspectives*, Eds., Vidal, Tarabout, and Meyer (New Delhi, India: Manohar Publishers, 2003), p. 69.

12. Other parallels are brought out by Rev. Dr. John Dupuche in "In Theology @ McAuley," Issue 3, at http://dlibrary.acu.edu.au/research/theology/ejournal/Issue3/Dupuche.htm. See also M. S. Vasanthakumar, "Expound Christ from Non-Christian Texts" in *Dharma Deepika* (July–December, 2000), pp. 5–20.

13. These insights are attributed to the research of Abraham Eraly, especially in his book, *Gem in the Lotus: The Seeding of Indian Civilization* (London, UK: Weidenfield & Nicolson, 2004), p. 161.

14. Ibid.

15. See Brian K. Smith, *Reflections on Resemblance, Ritual, and Religion* (New York: Oxford University Press, 1989), p. 20.

16. See Barbara A. Holdrege, "Veda and Torah: The Word Embodied in Scripture," in Hananya Goodman, Ed., *Between Jerusalem and Benares: Comparative Studies in Judaism and Hinduism* (Albany, NY: State University of New York Press, 1994), pp. 109–110.

Chapter Five

1. 1. W.L. Smith, *Ramayana Traditions in Eastern India: Assam, Bengal, Orissa* (Stockholm, Sweden: University of Stockholm, 1988), p. 92. See especially C. Kirk, *The Nature of the Greek Myths*, p. 94, cited in W.L. Smith, Ibid.

2. For more on the concept of a "shadow" Sita, see Wendy Doniger, *Splitting The Difference: Gender and Myth in Ancient Greece and India* (Chicago, IL: University of Chicago Press, 1999), pp. 8–79. The story of an illusory or shadow Sita does not appear in Valmiki's Sanskrit epic. However, it can be traced to the ancient *Kurma Purana*. It was also used as a device in Tulsidas's *Ramcharitmanas*, and it is certainly part of the larger Rama tradition.

3. Ranchor Prime, *Ramayana: A Journey* (Great Britain: Collins & Brown Ltd., 1997), p. 7.

4. The *Ramayana* is nicely summarized in H. Daniel Smith, *The Picturebook Ramayana: An Illustrated Version of Valmiki's Story* (Syracuse University, NY:

1981); Ranchor Prime, Ibid.; and Krishna Dharma, *Ramayana: India's Immortal Tale of Adventure, Love, and Wisdom* (Los Angeles, CA: Torchlight Publishing, 1998). The summary here is based on my own readings of these sources and is a sort of amalgamation of Rama stories popular in the Indian subcontinent, incorporating many regional accounts, such as Tulsidas's *Ramcharitmanas*, as much as Valmiki's original Sanskrit *Ramayana*.

5. I base this summary on my own reading of the *Mahabharata* as well as on the summaries by Chakravarthi V. Narasimhan, trans., *The Mahabharata* (New York: Columbia University Press, 1998, reprint); the Introduction to Winthrop Sargeant, *The Bhagavad Gita* (Albany, NY: State University of New York Press, 1984); and Barbara Powell, *Windows into the Infinite* (Fremont, CA: Asian Humanities Press, 1996).

6. Pandit Rajmani Tigunait, *Yoga on War and Peace* (Honesdale, PA: The Himalayan International Institute, 1991), p. 77.

7. Angelika Malinar, "The Bhagavadgita in the Mahabharata TV Serial: Domestic Drama and Dharmic Solutions," in Vasudha Dalmia and Heinrich von Stietencron, Eds., *Representing Hinduism: The Construction of Religious Traditions and National Identity* (New Delhi, India: Sage Publications, 1995), pp. 443–444.

8. Winthrop Sargeant, *The Bhagavad Gita*, op. cit., p. 24.

9. Linda Johnsen, "Krishna: The Cowherd King," in *Yoga International*, 3(3) (November/December 1993), p. 34.

10. Winthrop Sargeant, op. cit.

11. Ibid., pp. 27–33. This rendition of the 18-day battle is drawn from a close study of the *Mahabharata* and is augmented by Sargeant's summarization of each day.

12. This is explained in His Divine Grace A.C. Bhaktivedanta Swami Prabhupada, *Collected Lectures on Bhagavad-Gita As It Is* (Los Angeles, CA: Bhaktivedanta Book Trust, 1991), vol. 1, p. 211 (August 1, 1973); and vol. 2, p. 301 (August 29, 1973). See also Satsvarupa dasa Goswami, *Vaishnava Behavior/The Twenty-Six Qualities of a Devotee* (Port Royal, PA: Gita-nagari Press, 1983), p. 90; and *Truthfulness, the Last Leg of Religion* (Gita-nagari Press, 1989), pp. 96–97.

13. For more on Arjuna's dilemma and violence in the Epic tradition see Steven J. Rosen, Ed., *Holy War: Violence in the Bhagavad Gita* (Hampton, VA: Deepak Heritage Books, 2002).

14. See Madhvacharya, *Mahabharata-Tatparya-Nirnaya* (trans., B. G. Rao, Bangalore: 1941), quoted in V. S. Sukthankar, *On the Meaning of the Mahabharata* (Bombay, India: The Asiatic Society of Bombay, 1957), p. 55.

Chapter Six

1. Excerpts From Carl Woodham, *The Song Divine* (Badger, CA: Torchlight Publishing, 2000). Reprinted with permission. Other significant *Gita* translations are A. C. Bhaktivedanta Swami Prabhupada, *Bhagavad-Gita As It Is* (Los Angeles, CA: Bhaktivedanta Book Trust, 1972) and Graham M. Schweig, *Bhagavad Gita:*

The Beloved Lord's Secret Love Song (San Francisco, CA: Harper San Francisco, 2006).

2. See the work of Professor N. S. Rajaram, particularly his "Search for the Historical Krishna," at http://www.veda.harekrsna.cz/encyclopedia/historical-krsna.htm.

3. Benjamin Preciado-Solis, *The Krsna Cycle in the Puranas* (Delhi, India: Motilal Banarsidass, 1984), pp. 11–17.

4. See R. P. *Chanda's Archaeology and the Vaishnava Tradition* (Memoirs of the Archaeological Survey of India, No. 5, 1920). Also see Edwin F. Bryant, *Krishna: The Beautiful Legend of God* (London, UK: Penguin Books, 2003), pp. xvii–xviii.

5. Benjamin Preciado-Solis, *The Krsna Cycle in the Puranas*, op. cit., pp. 20–37.

6. Bimanbehari Majundar, *Krishna in the History and Legend* (Calcutta, India: University of Calcutta, 1969), pp. 1, 279.

7. R. C. Majumdar, Ed., *The History and Culture of the Indian People,* vol. I (Bombay, India: Bharatiya Vidya Bhavan, 1980), p. 303.

8. Horace H. Wilson, trans., *The Visnu Purana* (Delhi, India: Nag Publishers, 1989), p. ii.

9. Thomas J. Hopkins et al. in Steven J. Gelberg, Ed., *Hare Krishna, Hare Krishna: Five Distinguished Scholars on the Krishna Movement in the West* (New York: Grove Press, 1983), p. 144.

10. Rudolf Otto, *The Original Gita*, cited in Bimanbihari Majumdar, op. cit., p. 5.

11. Traditional versions of Krishna's full life story can be found in the *Bhagavata Purana* (10–11); the *Brahma-Vivarta Purana* (*Sri-Krishna-Janma-Khanda* 4); the *Padma Purana* (*Patala-Khanda* 69–99); the *Vishnu Purana* (5); and of course the entire *Harivamsa*.

12. This unique aspect of the story comes from prominent Gaudiya Vaishnava theologian Rupa Goswami. See his *Sri Laghu-Bhagavatamrita*, trans., Kusakratha Dasa (Los Angeles, CA: The Krsna Library, vol. 101, 1990), part 1, texts 453–457.

13. See Krishna Dharma, *Beauty, Power, & Grace: The Many Faces of the Goddess* (San Rafael, CA: Mandala Publishing, 2004), p. 24. Some say that Subhadra was a later daughter of Vasudeva and Rohini, conceived after Vasudeva was released from Kamsa's prison (making her much younger than her brothers Krishna and Balarama).

14. For more on a metaphorical reading of Krishna's world, particularly in relation to the demons, see Bhaktivinoda Thakur, *Shri Chaitanya Shikshamritam* (Madras, India: Sree Gaudiya Math, 1983, reprint), chapter 6, part 5, pp. 215–218.

15. The paradigmatic individuals representing these five levels of intimate relationship are Prahlad Maharaja, who, through loving prayers, enjoys a neutral or passive relationship with God; Hanuman, Rama's chief companion, who demonstrates an unwavering attitude of service toward his master; the Pandavas, who exemplify the perfection of friendship; Nanda and Yashoda, the very emblems of divine parenthood; and Radha and the *gopis*, who are exemplary in conjugal love.

16. Not to be confused with Maha-Maya, the ordinary variety of illusion that keeps one distanced from ultimate reality. Both Maha-Maya and Yoga-Maya take the form of Krishna's sister.

17. Barbara Powell, *Windows into the Infinite: A Guide to the Hindu Scriptures* (Fremont, CA: Asian Humanities Press, 1996), p. 308.

18. For an elaborate treatment of the Rasa Dance, see Graham M. Schweig, *Dance of Divine Love—India's Classic Sacred Love Story: The Rasa Lila of Krishna* (Princeton, NJ: Princeton University Press, 2005).

19. This symbolism is explained by Srila A. C. Bhaktivedanta Swami Prabhupada, trans., *Srimad Bhagavatam*, 10th canto, part 1 (Bombay, India: Bhaktivedanta Book Trust, 1987, reprint), chapter 2, text 8 (purport), pp. 128–129. As an addendum, Krishna brought the six murdered children back to life, reunited them with Mother Devaki, and then returned them to the spiritual world.

Chapter Seven

1. Klostermaier, *A Survey of Hinduism* (Albany, NY: State University of New York Press, 1994), p. 94.

2. R. C. Hazra, "The Puranas," in H. Bhattacarya, Ed., *The Cultural Heritage of India* (Calcutta, India: The Ramakrishna Mission Institute of Culture, 1957–1962), vol. 2, p. 240f.

3. Ludo Rocher, *The Puranas: A History of Indian Literature,* vol. 2, fasc. 3. (Wiesbaden, Germany: Otto Harrassowitz, 1986), p. 103.

4. Friedhelm Hardy, *Viraha-Bhakti—The Early History of Krsna Devotion in South India* (Delhi, India: Oxford University Press, 1983), p. 486.

5. *Bhagavata Purana* (2.10.1 and 12.7.9).

6. See the breakthrough work of Dennis Hudson, particularly his article, "The Srimad Bhagavata Purana in Stone: The Text as an Eighth-Century Temple and Its Implications," in the *Journal of Vaishnava Studies*, 3(3) (Summer 1995), pp. 137–182; see also Edwin F. Bryant, "The Date and Provenance of the *Bhagavata Purana* and the Vaikuntha Perumal Temple," in the *Journal of Vaishnava Studies*, 11(1) (Fall 2002), pp. 51–80.

7. Quoted in Richard Daley, *Ralph Waldo Emerson, The Transcendental View of the American Transcendentalists* (New York: Pendare Press, 1999), p. 12.

8. For more on Bhaktivedanta's Swami's use of the word *bhakti,* see Graham M. Schweig, "Universal and Confidential Love of God: Two Essential Themes in Prabhupada's Theology of *Bhakti,*" in the *Journal of Vaishnava Studies*, 6(2) (Spring 1998), pp. 95–96.

Chapter Eight

1. For more on these terms in the present context, see Frances Dore, "Impressions on Hinduism and the Scientific Approach," in T. D. Singh, Ed., *Synthesis of Science and Religion* (San Francisco, CA: The Bhaktivedanta Institute, 1987),

p. 159. Also see Michael W. Myers, *Brahman: A Comparative Theology* (Richmond, Surrey: Curzon Press, 2001).

2. See D. N. Shanbhag, Ed., *Purna-Prajna-Darsana. Saya-Nama-Dhaviye Sarva-Darsana-Samgrahe* (Bangalore, India: Dvaita Vedanta Studies and Research Foundation, 1992). p. 6.

3. See F. B. J. Kuiper, "The Three Strides of Vishnu," in Ernest Bender, Ed., *Indological Studies: In Honor of W. Norman Brown* (New Haven, CT: American Oriental Society, 1962), pp. 147–148.

4. Ibid.

5. Ibid.

6. See *Rig Veda,* 1.22.20.

7. See *Shatapatha Brahmana* (14.1.1), *Taittriya Aranyaka* (5.1).

8. Michael Witzel, "The Vedic Literature," in Steven J. Rosen, Ed., *Vaishnavism: Contemporary Scholars Discuss the Gaudiya Tradition* (Delhi, India: Motilal Banarsidass, 1994, reprint), pp. 19–26.

9. *See Sri Brahma-Samhita* 5.46, Ed., Srila Bhaktisiddhanta Sarasvati Thakur (Los Angeles, CA: The Bhaktivedanta Book Trust, 1985, reprint), pp. 87–88.

10. This is a loosely translated version of Bhaktivinoda Thakur's "Ten-Rooted Truth of Vaishnava Wisdom." For a more literal translation, see his *Gauranga-Lila-Smarana-Stotram—Auspicious Meditations on Lord Gauranga,* trans., Kusakratha dasa (Los Angeles, CA: The Krsna Institute, 1988), verse 75. Of course, various Vaishnava sects will articulate their basic teachings in various ways, emphasizing one particular point mentioned in this list, or omitting another. Overall, however, Bhaktivinoda's summation should give the reader a basic idea of what Vaishnavas believe.

11. For more on Shaivism, see Gavin Flood, "Saiva," in Sushil Mittal and Gene Thursby, Eds., *The Hindu World* (London, UK: Routledge, 2004), pp. 119–139.

12. For more on Shaktism, see Kathleen M. Erndl, "Sakta," in Sushil Mittal and Gene Thursby, Eds., *The Hindu World* (London, UK: Routledge, 2004), pp. 140–161.

13. Bhaktisiddhanta Sarasvati, *Shri Chaitanya's Teachings* (Madras, India: Shree Gaudiya Math, 1934), pp. 309–311.

Chapter Nine

1. Mark Mathew Braunstein, *Radical Vegetarianism* (Los Angeles, CA: Panjandrum Books, 1981), p. 89.

2. Manly P. Hall, quoted in http://koti.mbnet.fi/amoira/fatales1.htm.

3. S. Radhakrishnan, *The Bhagavadgita* (London, UK: Allen and Unwin, 1948), p. 49.

4. Linda Johnsen, *The Complete Idiot's Guide to Hinduism* (Indianapolis, IN: Alpha Books, 2002), p. 93.

5. The best books on the subject are: Wendy Doniger O'Flaherty, *Karma and Rebirth in Classical Indian Traditions* (Berkeley, CA: University of California

Press, 1980); Ronald W. Neufeldt, *Karma & Rebirth: Post Classical Developments* (Albany, NY: State University of New York Press, 1986); and Bruce R. Reichenbach, *The Law of Karma: A Philosophical Study* (Honolulu, HI: University of Hawaii Press, 1990).

6. See A. C. Bhaktivedanta Swami Prabhupada, *Bhagavad-Gita As It Is*, (Los Angeles, CA: Bhaktivedanta Book Trust, 1974, reprint), p. 413, purport.

7. For more on these three Hindu views of reincarnation, see Steven J. Rosen, *The Reincarnation Controversy: Uncovering the Truth in the World Religions* (Badger, CA: Torchlight Press, 1997).

Chapter Ten

1. For more on this, see Steven J. Rosen, *Holy Cow: The Hare Krishna Contribution to Vegetarianism and Animal Rights* (New York: Lantern Books, 2004).

2. Rajiv Choudhury, *Hindu Anthropology* (Delhi, India: Randolf Publishing, 2005), p. 8.

3. For elaborate evidence, see D. N. Jha, *The Myth of the Holy Cow* (New Delhi, India: Verso, 2002).

4. For more on comparative religion and vegetarianism, see Steven J. Rosen, *Diet for Transcendence: Vegetarianism and the World Religions* (Badger, CA: Torchlight Publishing, 1997).

5. David Frawley, "The Milky Way," in *Clarion Call Magazine* 3(4) (Fall 1990).

6. Quoted in *The Extended Circle: A Dictionary of Humane Thought*, Ed., Jon Wynne-Tyson (Fontwell, Sussex: Centaur Press, 1985), pp. 91–92.

7. Lewis G. Regenstein, *Replenish the Earth* (New York: The Crossroad Publishing Company, 1991), p. 225.

8. Jeremy Rifkin, *Beyond Beef: The Rise and Fall of the Cattle Culture* (New York: Dutton, 1992), p. 17.

9. Narasimha Dasa, "A Neglected Source of Wealth," in *Back to Godhead Magazine* 25(3) (May/June 1991), an entire issue dedicated to "The Case for Ox Power."

10. Jeremy Rifkin, *op. cit.*, pp. 37–38.

11. See Satguru Shivaya Subramuniyaswami, *Dancing With Siva: Hinduism's Contemporary Catechism* (Concord, CA: Himalayan Academy, 1993), p. 201.

12. Quoted in *The Higher Taste: A Guide to Gourmet Vegetarian Cooking and a Karma-Free Diet* (Los Angeles, CA, Bhaktivedanta Book Trust, 1983), pp. 51–52.

Chapter Eleven

1. See Theodore Roszak, *Where the Wasteland Ends* (Garden City, NY: Doubleday & Co., 1972), chapter 4, "The Sin of Idolatry."

2. Diana Eck, *Darshan: Seeing the Divine Image in India* (Chambersburg, PA: Anima Books, 1981), p. 27.

3. A. C. Bhaktivedanta Swami Prabhupada, *Bhagavad-Gita As It Is* (Los Angeles, CA: The Bhaktivedanta Book Trust, 1989, reprint), chapter 12, text 5, pp. 616–617, purport.

4. A. C. Bhaktivedanta Swami Prabhupada, trans., *Sri Chaitanya-Caritamrta, Madhya-Lila* 2 (Los Angeles, CA: The Bhaktivedanta Book Trust, 1984, reprint), pp. 158–159.

5. An excellent article on deity worship in the Hindu tradition is William H. Deadwyler III, "The Devotee and the Deity: Living a Personalistic Theology," in Joanne Punzo Waghorne and Norman Cutler, Eds., *Gods of Flesh, Gods of Stone: The Embodiment of Divinity in India* (New York: Columbia University Press, 1985), pp. 69–87.

6. Eck, op. cit., p. 34.

7. Ibid.

8. Ibid.

9. Bharatan Kumarappa, *The Hindu Conception of the Deity as Culminating in Ramanuja* (London, UK: Luzac and Company, 1934), pp. 316–317.

Chapter Twelve

1. Bal Gopal Anand, *The Life of Indian Religious Traditions* (Calcutta, India: Munshi & Sons, 1995), p. 6.

2. "Festivals," in John Bowker, Ed., *Oxford's Concise Dictionary of World Religions* (Oxford, UK: Oxford University Press, 2000), p. 193.

3. "Hinduism," in the *Encyclopædia Britannica*. See Encyclopædia Britannica Premium Service, 2005, http://www.britannica.com/eb/article?tocId=59796.

4. For more on Krishna's birth celebration, see Steven J. Rosen, *Introduction to the World's Major Religions* (vol. 6), *Hinduism* (Westport, CT: Greenwood Press, 2006), pp. 102–104.

5. "Festivals," in John Bowker, Ed., op. cit.

6. Much of this information is from the "Hindu Calendar" found on the Wikipedia, or the free encyclopedia, online. See http://en.wikipedia.org/wiki/Hindu_calendar. See also "Calendars Through the Ages" at http://webexhibits.org/calendars/calendar-indian.html.

7. Ibid.

Chapter Thirteen

1. This is elaborated upon in Guy L. Beck, *Sonic Theology: Hinduism and Sacred Sound* (Columbia, SC: University of South Carolina Press, 1993).

2. For a comprehensive look at sound as a spiritual tool in various world cultures, see Joachim-Ernst Berendt, *Nada Brahma: The World is Sound* (Rochester, VT: Destiny Books, 1987).

3. See Rajendra Chakravarti, *The Teaching of Sri Chaitanya* (Delhi, India: Partan Books, 2004), pp. 64–65.

4. Quoted in Sundarananda Sonni, *Vedic Mantras, from OM to AUM* (Madras, India: Bellora Publishing, 1989), p. 7.

5. See Swami B. V. Tripurari, trans., *Gopala-Tapani Upanisad* (Philo, CA: Audarya, 2004).

6. Ibid.

7. See A. C. Bhaktivedanta Swami Prabhupada, trans., *Chaitanya-Caritamrta, Adi-Lila* 7, verse 128, purport (Los Angeles, CA: The Bhaktivedanta Book Trust, 1991, reprint).

8. This important verse is found in the *Padma Purana, Uttara-Khanda* 92. 21–22.

9. For more on this subject, see Norvin Hein, "Chaitanya's Ecstasies and the Theology of the Name," in Bardwell. L. Smith, Ed., *Hinduism: New Essays in the History of Religions* (Leiden, Netherlands: E. J. Brill, 1976), pp. 16–32.

10. For more on the science of the holy name, see Srila A. C. Bhaktivedanta Swami Prabhupada, *Sri Namamrta: The Nectar of the Holy Name* (Los Angeles, CA: The Bhaktivedanta Book Trust, 1982).

11. Norvin Hein, op. cit.

12. Edward C. Dimock, Jr., *The Place of the Hidden Moon* (Chicago, IL: University of Chicago Press, 1966), p. 25.

13. A. K. Majumdar, *Chaitanya: His Life and Doctrine* (Bombay, India: Bharatiya Vidya Bhavan, 1969), p. 1.

14. S. K. De, *Early History of the Vaisnava Faith and Movement in Bengal* (Calcutta, India: General Printers & Publishers, 1942), p. i.

15. See, for example, my own work on the subject: "Who is Shri Chaitanya Mahaprabhu?" in Edwin F. Bryant and Maria L. Ekstrand, *The Hare Krishna Movement: The Postcharismatic Fate of a Religious Transplant* (New York: Columbia University Press, 2004), pp. 63–72. I have noted most of the prominent works on Chaitanya in the text of the above article, addressing both academic and insider perspectives.

16. John Moffitt, *Journey to Gorakhpur: An Encounter with Christ Beyond Christianity* (New York: Holt, Rinehart, and Winston, 1972), pp. 129, 135–136.

17. Bhakitivinoda Thakur, "Nityananda Suryodoy," *in Sajjana-Toshani* (1885), pp. 4–5.

18. Personal communication with the author on June 6 and Aughust 7, 2005.

19. Robert Gass, *Chanting: Discovering Spirit in Sound* (New York: Broadway Books, 2000).

Bibliography

Abhedananda, Swami. 1967. "The Great Saviours of the World" in *Complete Works of Swami Abhedananda*. Vol. 5. Calcutta, India: Ramakrishna Vedanta Math.

Adidevanada, Swami. 1965. "Theistic Samkhya in the Bhagavata." *Prabhudha Bharata*, 70: 393–396.

Agarwala, G. C. 1979. *Age of Bharata War*. Delhi, India: Motilal Banarsidass.

Anand, Subhash, 1982. "The Universality and Supremacy of Bhakti-Yoga." *Purana*, 24(1): 101–127.

Archer, W. G. n.d. *The Loves of Krishna*. New York: Grove.

Athavale, V. B. 1947. "A Summary of the Research Work Done with Regard to the Chronology and Geography of the Events in the Life History of Shri Krsna and the Pandava Brothers." *Poona Orientalist*, 12: 1–4, 34–39.

Banerjee, P . 1951. "Shrımad Bhagavata—the Place of its Origin." *Indian Historical Quarterly*, 27(2): 138–143.

Bhandarkar, R. G. 1913. *Vaisnavism, Saivism and Minor Religious Systems*. Delhi, India: Strassburg.

Bhattacharya, V. 1932. "The Besnagar Inscription of Heliodorus." *Indian Historical Quarterly*, 4(8).

Brockington, John. 1998. *The Sanskrit Epics*. Leiden, Netherlands: Brill.

Bryant, Edwin F. 2001. *The Quest for the Origins of Vedic Culture: The Indo-Aryan Migration Debate*. New York: Oxford University Press.

———. 2004. *Krishna: The Beautiful Legend of God*. London, UK: Penguin.

Buitenen, Van J. A. B. 1988. "On the Archaism of the Bhagavata Purana." *Studies in Indian Literature and Philosophy*. Ed., L. Rocher. Delhi, India: Motilal Banarsidass.

Chakravarti, S. C. 1969. *Philosophical Foundation of Bengal Vaishnavism*. Calcutta, India: Academic Publishers.

Chanda, R. P. 1920. *Archeology and the Vaishnava Tradition* (Memoirs of the Archeological Survey of India, No. 5). New Delhi, India: Archeological Survey of India.

Chandra, A. N. 1978. *The Date of the Kuruksetra War*. Calcutta, India: Ratna Prakashan.

Chari, S. M. S. 1997. *Philosophy and Theistic Mysticism of the Alvars*. Delhi, India: Motilal Banarsidass.

Dahlquist, Allan. 1962. *Megasthenes and Indian Religion*. Delhi, India: Motilal Banarasidass.

Danielou Alain. 1994. *Gods of Love and Ecstasy: The Traditions of Shiva and Dionysus*. Vermont, New England: Inner Traditions International Ltd.

Das, Bhagavan. 1962. *Krishna*. Bombay, India: Bharatiya Vidya Bhavan.

Das, Shukavak. 1999. *Hindu Encounter with Modernity*. Los Angeles, CA: Sri Publications.

De, S. K. 1942. "The Vedic and the Epic Krsna." *Indian Historical Quarterly*, 18: 297–301.

———. 1961, reprint. *Early History of the Vaishnava Faith and Movement in Bengal*. Calcutta, India: Firma KLM Pvt. Ltd.

Dikshitar, V. R. Ramachandra. 1931. "The Age of the Vishnu Purana." *Indian Historical Quarterly*, 7(2): 370–372.

Doniger, Wendy, Ed. 1993. *Purana Perennis*. Albany, NY: SUNY Press.

Flood, Gavin. 1996. *An Introduction to Hinduism*. New York: Cambridge University Press.

———. Ed. 2003. *The Blackwell Companion to Hinduism*. Oxford, UK: Blackwell Publishing.

Gonda, J. 1969, reprint. *Aspects of Early Vishnuism*. Delhi, India: Motilalal.

Growse, F. S. 1882. *Mathura: A District Memoir*. New Delhi, India: Asian Educational Services, reprint, 1979.

Haberman, David. 1988. *Acting as a Way of Salvation*. New York: Oxford University Press.

———. 1994. *Journey Through the Twelve Forests*. New York: Oxford University Press.

Hardy, Friedhelm. 1983. *Viraha Bhakti*. Delhi, India: Oxford University Press.

Hawley, John Stratton. 1979. "Krishna's Cosmic Victories." *Journal of the American Academy of Religion*, 10(9): 210–221.

Hawley, John Stratton, and Wulff, Donna Marie, Eds. 1996. *Devi: Goddesses of India*. Berkeley & Los Angeles, CA: University of California Press.

Hazra, R. C., 1937. "The Date of the Vishnu Purana." *Annals of the Bhandarkar Oriental Research Institute*, 18: 265–275.

———. 1938. "The Bhagavata Purana." *New Indian Antiquary*, 1(8): 522–528.

———. 1952. "The Mahabhagavata Purana." *Indian Historical Quarterly*, 28: 17–28.

Hiltebeitel, Alf. 1979. "Krsna and the Mahabharata." *Annals of the Bhandarkar Oriental Institute*, 65–107.

Hospital, Clifford George. 1973. "The Marvellous Acts of God: A Study in the Bhagavata Purana." Ph.D Thesis, Harvard University, MT.

———. 1978. "The Enemy Transformed: Opponents of the Lord in the Bhagavata Purana." *Journal of the American Academy of Religion*, 46: 200–215.

———. 1980. "Lila in the Bhagavata Purana." *Purana*, 22(1): 4–22.

Hudson, Dennis. 1994. "Vraja among the Tamils: A Study of the Bhagavatas in Early South India." *The Journal of Vaishnava Studies*, 3(1) (Winter): 113–140.

———. 1995. "The Srimad Bhagavata Purana in Stone." *The Journal of Vaishnava Studies*, 3(3) (Summer): 137–182.

———. 1996. "Arjuna's Sin: Thoughts on Bhagavad-Gita in its Epic Context." *The Journal of Vaishnava Studies*, 4(3) (Summer): 65–84.

Huyler, Steven P. 1999. *Meeting God: Elements of Hindu Devotion*. New Haven, CT: Yale University Press.

Jackson, A. M. 1908. "The Child Krishna." *Journal of the Royal Asiatic Society*, 533–534.

Jaiswal, Suvira. 1967. *The Origin and Development of Vaishnavism*. Delhi, India: Munshiram Manoharlal.

Johnsen, Linda. 2002. *The Complete Idiot's Guide to Hinduism*. Indianapolis, MN: Alpha Books.

Kane, P.V, 1971. *History of Sanskrit Literature*. Delhi, India: Motilal Banarsidass.

Kinsley, David. 1972. "Without Krsna There Is No Song." *History of Religions*, 12(2): 149–180.

———. 1986. *Hindu Goddesses*. Los Angeles, CA, University of California Press.

Klostermaier, Klaus. 1969. *In the Paradise of Krishna: Hindu and Christian Seekers*. Philadelphia, PA: Westminster.

———. 1994. 2nd edition. *A Survey of Hinduism*. Albany, NY: State University of New York Press.

Kripal, Jeffrey J. 1995. *Kali's Child*. Chicago, IL: The University of Chicago Press.

Krishnaswami, Aiyangar, S. 1920. *Early History of Vaishnavism in South India*. London, UK: Oxford University Press.

Kurtz, Stanley N. 1992. *All the Mothers Are One: Hindu India and the Cultural Reshaping of Psychoanalysis*. New York: Columbia University Press.

Lorenzen, David N. Ed., 1995. *Bhakti Religion in North India*. Albany, NY: SUNY Press.

Majumdar, A. K., 1961. "The Bhagavata Purana and its Influence in the Sixteenth Century." *Journal of the Bihar Research Society*, 47: 381–393.

Majumdar, Bimanbehari. 1969. *Krsna in History and Legend*. Calcutta, India: University of Calcutta.

Masson, J. L. 1974. "The Childhood of Krsna: Some Psychoanalytic Observations." *Journal of the American Oriental Society*, 94(4): 454–459.

Matchett, Freda. 2001. *Krsna: Lord or Avatara? The Relationship between Krsna and Visnu*. London, UK: Curzon.

Michaels, Axel. 2004. *Hinduism: Past and Present*. Princeton, NJ & Oxford, UK: Princeton University Press.

Miller, Barbara Stoller. 1977. *Love Song of the Dark Lord: Jayadeva's Gita Govinda*. New York: Columbia University Press.

Mittal, Sushil and Thursby, Gene, Eds. 2004. *The Hindu World*. New York & UK: Routledge.

Moffitt, John. 1972. *Journey to Gorakhpur: An Encounter with Christ Beyond Christianity*. New York: Holt, Rinehart, and Winston.

Narayanan, Vasudha. 1994. *The Vernacular Veda*. Columbia, SC: University of South Carolina Press.

O'Flaherty, Wendy Doniger. 1981. *Siva, the Erotic Ascetic*. New York: Oxford University Press.

Orr, Leslie. 1995. "The Vaisnava Community at Srirangam: The Testimony of the Early Medieval Inscriptions." *The Journal of Vaishnava Studies*, 3(3) (Summer): 109–136.

Powell, Barbara. 1996. *Windows into the Infinite: A Guide to the Hindu Scriptures*. Fremont, CA: Asian Humanities Press.

Prabhupada, A. C. Bhaktivedanta Swami. 1977. *The Science of Self-Realization*. Los Angeles, CA: The Bhaktivedanta Book Trust.

———. 2003, reprint. *Krsna: The Supreme Personality of Godhead*. Los Angeles, CA: The Bhaktivedanta Book Trust.

Preciado-Solis, Benjamin. 1984. *The Krsna Cycle in the Puranas*. Delhi, India: Motilal.

Ray, H. C., 1924. "Allusions to Vasudeva Krsna Devakiputra in the Vedic Literature." *Journal and Proceedings of the Asiatic Society of Bengal*, New Series, XIX: 371–373.

Resnick, Howard. 1996. "The Supremacy of Vishnu/Krishna in the Mahabharata." *The Journal of Vaishnava Studies*, 4(3) (Summer): 5–21.

———. 1996. "The 'Daivika-Catustayam' of the Vaikhanasa-Mantra-Prasna': A Translation." Unpublished Ph.D Thesis, Harvard University, Cambridge, MA.

Rocher, L. 1986. *The Puranas*. Wiesbaden, Germany: Otto Harrassowitz.

Rosen, Steven J. 1989. *Archeology and the Vaishnava Tradition: The Pre-Christian Roots of Krishna Worship*. Calcutta, India: Firma KLM Pvt. Ltd.

———. 1992. *Vaishnavism: Contemporary Scholars Discuss the Gaudiya Tradition*, Ed., Foreword by Edward C. Dimock. New York: FOLK Books, reprint, 1994. Delhi, India: Motilal Banarsidass.

———. 1997. *The Reincarnation Controversy: Uncovering the Truth in the World Religions*. Badger, CA: Torchlight Publishing.

———. 2000. *Gita on the Green: The Mystical Tradition Behind Bagger Vance*. New York & London: Continuum International.

———. 2004. *Holy Cow: The Hare Krishna Contribution to Vegetarianism and Animal Rights*. New York: Lantern Books.

Rukmani, T. S. 1970. *A Critical Study of the Bhagavata Purana*. Varanasi, India: Chowkhamba.

Sanyal, Nisikanta. 1933. *Sree Krishna Chaitanya*. Madras, India: Gaudiya Math.

Saraswati, Siddhanta. 1975, reprint. *Shri Chaitanya's Teachings*, Parts I & II. Madras, India: Sree Gaudiya Math.

Sarma, B. N. K. 1932. "The Date of the Bhagavata Purana." *Annals of the Bhandarkar Oriental Research Institute*, 13: 182–218.

Sax, William S. 1995. Ed. *The Gods at Play*. New York: Oxford University Press.

Schweig, Graham M. 2005. *Dance of Divine Love: The Rasa-Lila of Krishna*. Princeton, NJ: Princeton University Press.

Sen, D. C. 1917. *Chaitanya and His Companions*. Calcutta, India: University of Calcutta Press.

———. 1922. *Chaitanya and His Age*. Calcutta, India: University of Calcutta Press.

Sharma, Arvind. 1986. *The Hindu Gita*. La Salle, IL: Open Court.

Sharpe, Eric J. 1985. *The Universal Gita*. La Salle, IL: Open Court.

Sheridan, Daniel. 1983. "The Bhagavata Purana: Samkhya at the Service of Non-Dualism." *Purana*, 25(2): 206–224.

———. 1986. *The Advaitic Theism of the Bhagavata Purana*. Delhi, India: Motilal Banarsidass.

Sheth, Noel. 1984. *The Divinity of Krishna*. Delhi, India: Munshiram Manoharlal.

Singer, Milton, 1966. Ed. *Krishna: Myths, Rites, and Attitudes*. Chicago, IL: Chicago University Press.

Smith, David. 1996. *The Dance of Siva: Religion, Art and Poetry in South India*. Cambridge Studies in Religious Traditions, vol 7. Cambridge: Cambridge University Press.

Subramuniyaswami, Satguru Sivaya. 1993. *Dancing With Siva: Hinduism's Contemporary Catechism*. Concord, CA: Himalayan Academy.

Thakur, Bhaktivinode. 1986 (reprint). *The Bhagavat: Its Philosophy, Its Ethics & Its Theology*. Nadia, India: Shri Gaudiya Vedanta Samiti.

Vaudeville, Charlotte, 1962. "Evolution of Love-Symbolism in Bhagavatism." *Journal of the American Oriental Society*, 82(1): 31–40.

———. 1980. "The Govardhan Myth in Northern India." *Indo-Iranian Journal*, 22: 1–45.

White, Charles. 1970. "Krsna as Divine Child." *History of Religions*, 10:2.

Wolpert, Stanley. 1991. *India*. Berkley, CA: University of California Press.

Woodham, Carl E. 2000. *Bhagavad Gita: The Song Divine*. Badger, CA: Torchlight Publishing.

Index

About the Author

Steven J. Rosen is editor-in-chief of the *Journal of Vaishnava Studies*, an academic quarterly esteemed by scholars around the world. He is also Associate Editor of *Back to Godhead*, the magazine of the Hare Krishna Movement. His recent books include *The Hidden Glory of India* (2001) and *Holy War: Violence and the Bhagavad Gita* (2002). In addition, Greenwood Press has recently released his reference book on Hinduism as part of their "Introduction to the World's Major Religions" series.